The Autistic Atheist

By
Emily Cooper

COPYRIGHT

DEDICATION

This book is dedicated to all the late diagnosed Autistics who grew up feeling out of place and unsupported. Those who have fought tooth and nail to be recognized. It is dedicated to those who have struggled with religion. To those who have been rejected by their communities for daring to question and daring to understand. It is dedicated to those who were told that they could not do something to persevere. To all of those reading this book: science is a tool we use to understand the universe; it is through science that we have come to know anything only through investigation and questioning can anything really be known. Challenge yourself and endeavour to go beyond the confines of convention.

ACKNOWLEDGEMENTS

I would like to thank all the researchers I listed for their hard work, I would not have done this without your foundation. I would like to thank Matthew Farkas-Dyck for inspiring the work. I would like to thank the publisher for helping me to make a great piece. And I would like to thank my friends and family for supporting me in my endeavours.

Contents

The Autistic Atheist

Prologue

The Concept of an Afterlife

The concept of life after death, although an interesting one, is currently unfounded, and somewhat untestable by modern science. As far as we know: life is a series of self-replicating and continuous chemical reactions that are fuelled by the constant input of energy through time. It gives me chills up my spine and a strange feeling in my gut whenever I see or hear people say something like, "I know they are smiling down on me," or "I can't wait to see you again." Is that what you want for yourself? To float on forever somewhere beyond space and time looking down upon us in the living? Do you just want whatever you desire anytime? What if I just want to cease to exist? What do you mean there is a literal place where people are being constantly tortured? Why would such a place exist? What sick revenge fantasy thought of this? Not even the worst people should be here. No sane mind would create such a place, for anyone.

What is even more perplexing to me is when, for the most part, intelligent and well-educated people who would on all other accounts reject such ideals say things like this. What kind of mental gymnastics do you perform within yourself to hold these two conflicting representations? What does it serve you to think that your loved ones are "watching you from some sort of celestial balcony?" Where in physical space do these people reside? And if not in physical space, then where? What cost does letting go of these ideals and accepting what nature presents to you have? Perhaps it is comforting to think that your loved ones are still here with you. For me, knowing that the person and life ceases upon death only to continuously fuel the lives of other organisms is beautiful. I accept it because that is all I can know for now. Perhaps for some people imagining an afterlife where people go to live-on is a little like imagining what it is like to hear colours or to see into the 5th dimension.

Introduction

Introducing the Hypothesis

This book is an integration of the psychology of Autism, how it applies to religion and how I as an Autistic person experience religion.

Why Couldn't I see What Others Could

Eight years old, I remember very clearly asking my father, "were Adam and Eve monkeys?" my father looked at me with a dumbfounded look on his face and said nothing. For his part, my father was not a particularly educated person, and worked low-skilled jobs most of his life. His lack of knowledge was rooted more in a lack of education and understanding rather than an adherence to a particular faith. He did not really have the luxury of questioning things, or pursuing a higher education. He had to work from a very young age, and that is what he did.

I remember the day I realized that I was an Atheist like it was yesterday. Although I would not come to know the word for almost two more years. I was sitting in my parent's basement reading a book about evolution and dinosaurs. I was fascinated by biology and life from a really young age. I started thinking about the Bible, and the Adam and Eve story. It came to me, if evolution were true, and dinosaurs never existed alongside humans, then the Adam and Eve story could not possibly be true. There is no God! Simplistic; I was ten, this was towards the end of grade four. And this self-proclamation led me on a lifelong path of science, discovery, and skepticism. A couple of years later I remember reading the definition for "Atheist" and connecting the two. Since then I have identified as an Atheist. But I never really bought any story from any religion. As I got older concepts of a God just confused me, and I always felt like the simplest answer was *no*. Not that there strictly is no God, but that God does not hold up as an explanation for the universe; nor does there need to be a force which people call God for the universe to exist. Science does not make it impossible to believe in God; it makes it possible to not believe one is necessary. But I always wondered why was it so easy for me to come to that conclusion and for others not to? Why didn't I have a nervous breakdown? Why was religion so foreign to me and so easy for other people? And why do perfectly intelligent people perform all these mental gymnastics and create these cognitive loopholes in their brains to allow God to coexist with everything that does not require and in most cases refutes one? Then the answer started coming to me piece by piece. I just cannot fathom the hyper-agency required. That, combined with the fact that I was never strongly indoctrinated, meant that I had to figure out the world in a different way.

My approach to Atheism is often very different from other Atheists that I know. I had no aha-moment and there was no struggle to leave my faith. I never contemplated that idea that I would surely be dooming myself to hellfire if I thought this way. I did not have some kind of mental breakdown when I came to realize the utter lack of evidence for divine creation. I had no wrestling with science to try to intertwine my faith with the facts, and I never played any mental gymnastics to reconcile the overwhelming mountain of evidence considering the teaching of some religiously grounded texts that arose from the Stone Age. There was no question of where to find morality if I had no faith. My parents did not kick me out of my house or ground me for my lack of belief, they were disappointed, but they merely accepted it and went on their merry way. In short, I was not raised to worship any God and I was not raised to think that there was someone (or something) constantly lurking over my shoulder, watching me, and judging me. I was raised to embrace the wonders of what could be readily observed.

Science came easy to me. I was thrilled at the goal of gaining more and more knowledge, and of exploring the world around me. One of the first books I could not get my head out of was a giant encyclopedia on dinosaurs. In the back was a database of some of the more well-known dinosaurs that were known back then with reconstructions of what they looked like right next to their names. I thought it was amazing that these magnificent creatures once ruled the earth. From dinosaurs I moved onto evolution and then onto the origins of man (this eventually led me to a degree in anthropology). Humans simply being just another animal was no mystery and no battle to me; it just made sense that we were part of the great tree of life.

Ever since I can remember, religion seemed to baffle me. I was an enigma, while others would pray for things to get better, and look to God as if they knew *him* (it); I always wondered what a god really was and how I was supposed to quantify *his* presence. The vague definitions of 'the creator of the universe', 'one who resides outside of time and space in the concocted realm of uncertainty where anything was possible,' 'an immaterial being that somehow created everything that we see before us,' never seemed to resonate with me. "How could something exist outside of time and space?" I wondered. "How could something that was not composed of matter, light, energy, or any particle known to science even exist at all?" The final question, likely one that baffled me most, "if those who believe in God require that a God is necessary for the creation of the universe and all life on earth, then why do they plead so desperately that this God is not in need of a creator itself?" I could not come to reason with this huge fallacy that these people had created to satisfy their need for a creator.

This did not mean that I never experienced hardship, nor that I hopelessly wished for a better life in times of desperation. It does not mean that I never thought that there might be a creator shrouded in the deep unknowns of the cosmos. It did not mean that I never questioned the purpose of my life, nor that I did not ever wonder if there was more to this universe than the material. I often remember wishing upon stars as a kid, or praying at my bedside, or crying myself to sleep just wishing someone would listen. I would often feel inadequate asking for such things, for no matter how hard I asked, or how hard I tried to make myself believe in something, it all felt like a game to me.

As I got older and learned more about the universe, I had a harder and harder time grasping the relationship people claimed to have with the one they called God. I more and more searched for my answers in science and came to trust the logic in its explanations. Many people chalked it up to my lack of religious upbringing, my parent's emotional distance, or my stubbornness; or that I simply chose not to believe so that I could continue to do bad things without consequence.

Adolescence is a time of self-discovery; a time for making decisions that will likely carry with you into much of your adult life. It is often a time to decide what kinds of careers you would like to pursue, the beliefs we wish to follow and generally what our values are. Many people who identify as non-heterosexual come to this realization during their teenage years; others begin to question the religious beliefs they were raised with while others simply re-affirm them. Amidst trying to decide all these huge life decisions that teenagers often feel required to make, I was busy figuring out that I was Autistic. I often likened it to realizing that you are gay, because I determined for myself that I did not think the same way others did, and I had to adapt to a world where I was a minority.

I could never tell what people were thinking, how they felt, or how to interact with them. I was very aloof, and in my own world. I was unaware of the conversations that went on between other children in the school yard. Although I played on occasion, the games tag, red-rover and tether-ball made little sense to me. I would rather run around on the jungle gym and jump from the high-bars pretending I could fly. I grew up with strange rituals that no one could explain. In the time-lapse between pulling the lever to divert the water to the shower and water coming out of the shower I would wait with my hands open and clap when I could hear the water just about to burst from the head.

Autism was a no-brainer to me. From the moment I read what it was on the internet, I knew it was me and I felt happy in that moment. That I had an answer for all my problems and why it felt like I simply just never got life right. I knew then that I was Autistic and that I had a differently wired brain, but I also knew that that was going to make my life harder. To me this was exciting, but to everyone else around me I was still an alien, a weirdo. To them I was still rude, inconsiderate, and lacking in empathy. I knew enough that if I flew under their radar and drew as little attention to myself, I would be better off. This is why, even though I knew it from long before, it took me almost a decade to receive a professional diagnosis. Nine-and-a-half years later, just before my 25th birthday, I was diagnosed with Autism Spectrum Disorder (ASD). I had no mental breakdown, I did not question if I was mad, I was not even surprised, nor was I happy; I just felt complete and mildly relieved. All I wanted was for someone with credentials in Autism to agree with how I felt, and I got that. The only regret that I have in this process is that it did not come sooner. I knew I had this, but some part of me kept telling me that it would go away, that I would get better, that I would grow out of it, or that I could just stop acting this way. This was often reinforced by my ability to go for months to even a year without any noticeable problems or slip ups, only to crash and eventually have it blow up in my face. Sadly, it took many years of it constantly blowing up in my face to finally say that I had enough.

When people see me; they do not usually see Autism. They usually see a very bright and inquisitive person who is always learning and who is quick on her feet when it comes to thinking through problems. They see someone who is always ready for a challenge but often flounders without support. They see someone who is incredibly stubborn to her beliefs, and quick to argue. But people just see a lot of these as being obstructive and closed minded. They never seem to consider that many of these aspects are simply the product of a different brain.

Autism will always be a part of me; it will always be who I am, and I am not sad about that anymore. I may have more bad days than other people and I may struggle to do well in life by the standards of others. But Autism is responsible for my experiences and has shaped the way I view the world; I would not change that for anything!

Introducing the Hypothesis

In recent years, an intriguing correlation has emerged between Autism, Atheism, and a proclivity towards scientific thinking. A study Caldwell-Harris and colleagues (2011) showed that Autistics are more likely to identify as Atheists, or as some non-religious construction, rather than subscribing to Big God religions (Caldwell-Harris et al. 2011). The article also showed that, on the mean, Atheists and Agnostics scored much higher on measurements of Autistic traits than people who subscribed to mainstream religions (Caldwell-Harris et al. 2011). Why would an Autistic person be more likely to identify with Atheism and why might non-Autistic people be more likely to be religious?

Most people in the fields of sciences and mathematics are less likely to be religious. This number decreases significantly with Ph. Ds and the higher up you go. This is particularly the case in the domains of physics and biology. In addition, scientists tend to possess more Autistic traits and tendencies than the general public (or are over-represented by people on the Autism Spectrum) and score higher on the Autism Quotient test than average (Caldwell-Harris et al. 2011). Put this together and you have a correlation between Autistic traits, non-belief, and scientific mindedness.

This book delves into the intricate interplay of Autism, Atheism, and Scientific mindedness. Central to this exploration is the notion that the Autistic brain exhibits a predisposition towards rational, non-supernatural thinking, while the Neurotypical brain tends to gravitate towards religious belief systems. Drawing upon seminal works by researchers like Baron-Cohen, I will dissect the cognitive differences between Autistic and non-Autistic individuals, shedding light on how these variances influence beliefs about the natural world and the existence of a higher power. This discussion will delve into the evolutionary underpinnings of belief systems, and their role in shaping human cognition. We will examine the neurology behind religious thinking, and contrast it with the cognitive processes associated with scientific inquiry. Through this lens, we hope to elucidate why certain individuals are more inclined towards Atheism and scientific rationalism, while others are drawn to religious faith.

This argument implies that those who do not fall under the category of Autism Spectrum Disorders are much more likely to hold religious beliefs, and that their brains are more highly wired towards belief in a God (or gods). The extreme case of this would be in the extreme empathizing brain, or what I will refer to as *Allism*. I will argue that the Allistic brain is more prone to holding beliefs centered on religion, and that are not grounded in reality but in intuition. I shall argue this by examining the parts of the brain that are involved in religious thinking, the role religion plays in society, and how religion evolved.

It is imperative to emphasize that this inquiry is not intended to homogenize the experiences of individuals on the Autism Spectrum, nor to disparage those who hold religious beliefs. Rather, a naturalistic way of thinking is more in line with characteristics of the Autistic brain over agency-based thinking. Thus, Atheism would seem like the more intuitive conclusion for the Autistic person to make, over the existence of a God.

We will examine what Autism is; the evolution of the human brain; the role of belief in human evolution; the potential evolution of Autism and neurodiversity; why people think the way that they do; and how our experiences shape our beliefs (and vice-versa). What I hope to do is to shed light on another side of humanity so that people begin to see Autism less as a disorder or a disability and more as part of natural human variation.

Asperger wrote of many of his patients' blatant disregard for authority (Asperger 1944; Silberman 2015). Asperger remarked that the innate gifts of these children were as central to the condition he was describing as their social difficulties (Silberman 2015; Asperger 1944). Asperger had become convinced that the children he had studied had the potential to become innovators in their fields of interest precisely because they were constitutionally unable to take things on faith (Silberman 2015; Asperger 1944). Asperger was also one of the first people to recognize the unique gifts of Autistic people in the realm of science (Silberman 2015; Asperger 1944). However, I hope to provide a more complete synthesis on why this may be, and bring in some of my own introspection where appropriate. This topic has been discussed before in academic circles with evidence from Caldwell-Harris et al. (2011), and Norenzayan et al (2012). These findings only scratch the surface as to how an Autistic person may experience religion or how Autism influences a person's ability to believe in or accept the concept of God or gods.

What is Autism?

Dr. Baron-Cohen and colleagues (1986) described Autistic children as having a deficit in understanding the social world, while having an intact (and in many cases superior) understanding of the physical world. It is this cognitive deficit that gives rise to the impairments in social abilities (Baron-Cohen et al. 1986) seen in Autism.

According to the most recent edition of the Diagnostic Statistical Manual (DSM-V): Autism Spectrum Disorder is a pervasive neuro-developmental condition characterized by deficits in reciprocal interaction and communication, and repetitive and restrictive behaviours and interests (2013). These characteristics often result in difficulty in social communication. These characteristics must be present in early childhood, and they must limit or impair the everyday functioning of an individual (2013). These deficits cannot be explained by cognitive or intellectual deficits. This point is key for two reasons: as Autism is not an indicator of intellectual deficits or of a lower IQ (2013); secondly, non-Autistic children with intellectual disabilities do not lack the aforementioned abilities and are often highly sociable (Baron-Cohen et al. 1985). Autistic people are often known to have highly specialized interests, a high attention to detail, yet poor social skills, and lack the ability to maintain eye contact. Many Autistic people will react atypically to sensory stimuli; they may be under or over sensitive to everyday stimulation. They may also have poor emotional and self-regulation abilities. Autism is often referred to as a spectrum as an Autistic person may have a range of strengths, capabilities, deficits, and difficulties that are unique to the person. Their abilities and difficulties can vary throughout life, and from situation to situation. Autistic traits exist to varying degrees in most individuals. While most people think of Autism as a purely social phenomenon it is also important to consider the wider range of traits when defining Autism. The traits that make up Autism influence how a person on the Autism Spectrum views and interacts with the world.

When considering the definition outlined in the DSM V, we must remember that the DSM serves as a description of what Autism is, and how to diagnose it in a person; it however, does not explain why the person is this way in a penultimate sense, nor the reason these traits occur in certain people over others. The question becomes: what causes these traits in an Autistic person? To answer this, we draw from the Theory of Mind, and from the concept of the systematizing and the empathizing brain. Both subjects were introduced in the works of Doctor Simon Baron-Cohen.

The key aspects of Autism are deficits in social communication and reciprocal social interactions. This stems from an inability to represent the thoughts and feelings of others in one's own head. They possess a reduced ability to predict how people will react to certain actions; and to share in the feelings and experiences of others.

Structure of the Book

The first chapter of this book will focus on what Autism is, and its relation to the Theory of Mind. What is the Theory of Mind, how does it develop in both Autistic and non-Autistic individuals? What role does the Theory of Mind play in the understanding of beliefs, and executive functioning? I will look at the role imitation plays in the development of the Theory of Mind in non-Autistic children, and its effect on child development. I will explore the parts of the brain responsible for Theory of Mind; and how the Autistic brain differs from that of the non-Autistic brain.

The second chapter investigates different kinds of thinking. We compare systemizing to empathizing, and their strengths and weaknesses in different situations. Systemizing is good for recognizing patterns, and understanding how the physical world works. Empathizing is good at understanding how people work. The behaviour of individuals does not always follow a strict set of rules that one can use in making predictions. We will demonstrate the similarity between systemizing and the Scientific Method. How does brain structure and lateralization affect systemizing and empathizing? Autistic people experience atypical brain lateralization, and neuro-connectivity. How does this affect thinking in Autism? We will lastly consider *Allism* as a counter to Autism.

In Chapter three we will discuss what religion is, and its connection to the Theory of Mind. What does religion communicate? We will look at religion as a product of the brain; the role of brain lateralization in religion; and how it uses ordinary human behaviour and human propensities. How does religion help us deal with difficult situations? How do people recognize agency? What does the ability to recognize agency have to do with Religion? How does a reduced mentalizing capacity interfere with the ability to hold certain beliefs? Is the propensity for religion something that is innate?

In chapter four we will look at religion's role in society and how it evolved. What are the origins of religion? We will discuss the theory of human self domestication and religion's role in this process. How does religion aid in human cooperation? What is religion's role in the diffusion of information? How does information get passed down both laterally and from generation to generation? We will discuss religion's role in the creation and maintenance of civilizations, and the rise of Atheism in the present.

The fifth chapter will look at the evolution of Autism. Does Autism exist outside of humans? Autistic people possess attenuated features of self domestication. If humans are domesticated, what are feral humans? How did Autism evolve, and what is the role of diversity in a population? Why is Autism in conflict with religious thinking?

The sixth chapter will look at Autism, mental illness, and disability. We will discuss religion's connection with mental illness; the connection of Autism to other mental conditions; and how to better help Autistic people live happier fuller lives. This chapter will be a little more personal discussing some of my own experiences with the condition.

Bringing these topics together we see that Autistic people lack (or have a weakened) intuitive sense of Theory of Mind, and possess a strong sense of intuitive physics. This is comparing an intuitive understanding of how the minds of people other than ourselves work to an intuitive sense of how physical laws and processes function. Their gravitation towards intuitive physics over intuitive psychology stems from a highly systemizing mind that puts emphasis on organizing information over empathizing with people. Systemizing forms the basis of the scientific method. Humanity has evolved to assume and recognize agency over the absence of agency as a means of survival. Autistic people are less focused on assigning agency, and are less likely to assign agency to unknown phenomena. They less frequently assign agency and are less able to recognize the presence of agency in their environment. This lack of assumption of agency combined with a propensity for systemization led to a tendency to seek out naturalistic explanations behind phenomena. This would have led them away from the concluding that there is a God and organized religion. Religion played a role in the process of human domestication, selecting for prosociality and reduced aggression. The Autistic phenotype contains attenuated characteristics of domestication and is resistant to the domestication process. A desire to systemize and seek out naturalistic answers for certain phenomena would be selected for in certain situations, and in different environments throughout human evolutionary history. Autism is an important part of the human experience and of human variation.

Chapter 1

Autism and the Theory of Mind

The Theory of Mind refers to the ability to represent the mental states of others in our own minds. It allows us to predict how people around us are feeling, and how they will behave in certain situations. The Theory of Mind is also what is used to attribute intent of actions to others. Without a Theory of Mind, it can often be difficult to predict the actions of those around us (Baron-Cohen et al. 1986; Baron-Cohen 1995). This lack of a Theory of Mind is what often inhibits Autistic children from developing social relations with other children (Baron-Cohen et al. 1986; Baron-Cohen 1995). The ability to recognize and attribute beliefs and feelings different from our own to other people is often referred to as mentalizing (Norenzayan et al. 2012), and as common-sense psychology (Meltzoff 1985). This is contrasted from simple perspective taking which only requires us to see things or events from the point of view of someone else (David et al. 2008). Mentalization requires perspective taking but perspective taking does not necessarily require mentalization.

What is the Theory of Mind?

Deficits in Theory of Mind are visible in Autistic children often from a very young age (Baron-Cohen et al. 1985). Theory of mind refers to the ability to represent the mental states of others in one's own mind. This mediates interactions between individuals, allowing us to empathize with others. The Theory of Mind also allows us to attribute beliefs that are different from our own to others, recognize that other people can hold beliefs different from our own, and possess knowledge which we do not have. It is this inability to attribute mental states to other people that many professionals in the field of Autism believe restricts the ability of an Autistic person to empathize with other people. It has created the idea that Autistic children either lack empathy or have difficulty empathizing with others.

A classic Theory of Mind task is for a small child to be presented with a crayon box that in fact contains something other than crayons (i.e.:

sticks). The child is asked, "What do you think is in the box?" After it is revealed that the box contains something other than crayons the child is then asked, "What do you think someone else who had been presented with this box would think is inside?" If the child answers, "crayons," then they can account for another person's false belief due to limited knowledge of the situation; rather, if the child answers with what was in fact in the box, then it shows that the child is unable to correctly represent the false beliefs of someone else (Gopnik and Astington 1988). Very early work on Theory of Mind led to the conclusion that children begin to develop a Theory of Mind between the ages of 3 and 5 (Wimmer and Perner 1983; Baron-Cohen 1985). This test showed that young children had a hard time representing their previous state of mind as well as representing the false beliefs of another person. The young children were reluctant to apply different (and conflicting) representations to the same object and did not understand that there could be different ways to represent the same situation. Gopnik and Astington (1988) proposed that the young children had difficulty recognizing that another person may perceive the world differently from how they do. Therefore, they have trouble representing others' representations of the world in their own heads. The 3-year-olds in the experiment had difficulty representing change and simply appeared to behave as if their present representation of an object was always how they saw it (Gopnik and Astington 1988). The three-year-old were unable to connect their present selves with their past selves. After the age of 5, the children were able to answer correctly to the above problem; Gopnik and Astington (1988) concluded that the 5-year-olds were able to understand that two people could have different representations of the same object. It is the ability to fathom different representations of the same object which allows a child to hold different representations of different minds in their own mind (Gopnik and Astington 1988).

A study conducted by Wimmer and Perner (1983) aimed to investigate whether young children could understand and represent the mental states of others, particularly in scenarios involving false beliefs and deception. They used a simple narrative involving a character named Maxi and a piece of chocolate to test this ability in children of different age groups. In the first scenario, the children were introduced to the character Maxi. Maxi left a piece of chocolate in the cupboard (represented by a blue box) and then went outside to play. While Maxi was out, his mother moved the chocolate to a different cupboard (this time represented by a green box). Maxi returns from playing hungry and looks for the chocolate. After watching this skit, the children were asked where they thought Maxi would look for the chocolate. Most of the 3–4-year-olds in the group incorrectly answered that Maxi would look for the chocolate in the green box; while the 6–9-year-olds correctly pointed at the blue box for where Maxi would look for the chocolate. From this, Wimmer and Perner concluded that the younger children were unable to ascribe wrong belief to the character (1983). To determine if the small children could construct a deceitful utterance, the experiment introduced another character who was looking for the chocolate. After Maxi came back from the park the character in question asked Maxi if he knew where the chocolate was. It is explained that Maxi does not want the other character to know where the chocolate is. The children are asked to determine where Maxi would point in order to "deceive" the character in question (Wimmer and Perner 1983). Again, the younger children showed difficulty in constructing deceitful utterances by consistently pointing at the blue box rather than the green, which would have been an accurate representation of Maxi's knowledge and his intent to deceive the other character (Wimmer and Perner 1983). These tasks required the children to construct two different models of the hypothetical world (Wimmer and Perner 1983), and to empathize with the characters in question (Davis 1994). In both cases the younger children showed great difficulty in representing the mental states and the intents of others (Wimmer and Perner 1983). By age six, the children showed no difficulty representing the two different models (Wimmer and Perner 1983).

In 1985, Baron-Cohen and colleagues adapted the first test from Wimmer and Perner (1983) to test the hypothesis that Autistic children lack a Theory of Mind. If the children could pass the test, then Baron-Cohen would conclude that they possessed a Theory of Mind. He proposed a hypothetical situation illustrated by puppets to both Autistic and non-Autistic children. The children watched a short skit with puppets named Sally and Suzy. Sally placed a marble in a box and left the room. Without Sally knowing, Suzy moved the marble and placed it in her pocket. The children were then asked where they thought Sally would look for her marble when she came back. The Autistic children most often did not guess that Sally would look for the marble in the box where she had left it. From this, Baron-Cohen and colleagues concluded that the Autistic children were unable to represent the false belief of Sally. They were unable to represent the belief of a person different from themselves. The non-Autistic children on the other hand correctly guessed that Sally would look for the ball in the box where she had last left it. From which Baron-Cohen concluded that these children were able to properly represent the mental states of the doll in question. Baron-Cohen and colleagues also included a group of Down Syndrome children with moderate intellectual disabilities; the Down Syndrome children also answered the question correctly. The fact that the children with intellectual deficits answered correctly over the Autistic children with IQ scores in the average range indicated that the ability to represent false beliefs was independent of IQ (Baron-Cohen et al. 1985).

The Autistic children were able to correctly determine where a person would look for a missing ball if they were asked: "If you left a ball in a room and someone had moved it without your knowledge where would you look for the ball?" The Autistic children answered that they would look in the last place they had left it (Baron-Cohen et al. 1985; 1986). This shows that the deficit is not one in intellect or in logical processing but in the ability to transfer between the mental states of others and oneself (Baron-Cohen et al. 1986).

From studies like this, Baron-Cohen and colleagues have concluded that Autistic children have a deficit in the understanding of the social world (1985; 1986), while their understanding of the physical world remains intact. This points to specific cognitive deficits which would give rise to impairments in social abilities. A very classic way to put this is that the Theory of Mind allows us to immediately put ourselves in someone else's shoes and without that ability, it is difficult for many people on the Autism Spectrum to empathize with other people.

The ability to empathize with others is often an automatic response which involves our brain simply reacting to other people's actions and constructing an appropriate emotional response (Baron-Cohen et al. 1986; Baron-Cohen 1995; Davis 1994). In a follow-up study to the famous doll sketch, the same group of children (with some exception) were subjected to another series of tasks which was meant to gauge their understanding of both the physical and the social world. The children were asked to place pictures of a sequence of events in order of their occurrence. The order would imply either the intentions of others acting on someone, or a sequence of events which involved characters interacting with purely physical objects (Baron-Cohen et al. 1986).

In the case of the "intentional arrangement" task, the Autistic children did significantly poorer than both the "typical" set, and the Down Syndrome set. They were consequently less able to attribute intentions to the characters in a pictorial sequence (Baron-Cohen et al. 1986). The Autistic children in the study were unable to arrange the pictures in the correct order (or at least what the testers saw to be the correct order) more often than any of the other tests (Baron-Cohen et al. 1986). The Autistic children in the study also used fewer intention words to describe the sequence than the other children for both the main and secondary characters in the story. In contrast, the non-Autistic children were more often able to describe events and actions in terms of underlying desires rather than physical behaviours (Lillard and Flavell 1990). From this, Baron-Cohen and colleagues concluded that even though the Autistic children in the study were of similar intellect and mental age as the non-Autistic children (and in some cases higher), they still possessed a deficit when it came to assigning intentions to others and hence completing the sequences that involved intent and belief over the ones that did not (Baron-Cohen et al. 1986). It is from studies like these which many researchers of Autism have concluded that Autistic children possess a deficit in the understanding of the social world (Baron-Cohen et al. 1985; 1986). Baron-Cohen (1995) referred to this perceived lack of Theory of Mind in Autistic children as "Mind Blindness."

In a 1995 study, Frye and colleagues suggested that the ability to understand different mental states of other people is a consequence of a change in a child's ability to reason about the minds of others, which eventually becomes automatic. The Theory of Mind emerges from a child's ability to understand embedded rules, and to resolve conflicts of judgment (Frye et al. 1995). In addition to understanding Theory of Mind, embedded rules are also required to understand causal reasoning and sorting tasks with many rules (Frye et al. 1995). In this study, young children were asked to sort cards into categories and to predict the path a marble would take down a slide (1995). The three-year-old in this study were less able to sort cards by more than two categories and more frequently incorrectly predicted the path of the marble when it took a diagonal path as opposed to a direct path

(Frye et al 1995). The probability of passing these two tests was correlated with the probability of passing the theory mind/false belief test (1995). The young children could reason using simple conditionals (if x then y; if not x then not y) but were unable to reason using more complex rules (Frye et al. 1995). The difficulty associated with shifting across dimensions (the ball moving across rather than directly down) correlated with the difficulty of young children to shift across different perspectives of people other than themselves (Frye et al. 1995). The embedded rules that come with the Theory of Mind are: beliefs can be false, and that people are able to hold different perspectives on beliefs from me (Frye et al. 1995). The use of embedded reasoning permits the switching of the brain between conflicting representations (Frye et al. 1995). Frye and colleagues concluded that the three year-olds in the test were unable to reason with embedded rules, and hence were not able to switch between conditions to make a conflicting judgment (1995). The ability to reason using embedded rules may in fact be related to executive functioning and executive functioning may consequently play a role in one's ability to represent the different mental states of others within their own brains. This may also imply that someone may be able to acquire a conscious Theory of Mind in time by understanding sets of embedded rules involved in the intentions of others (Frye et al. 1995; Frye and Nguyen 1999). The ability to hold these rules within one's head and apply them to multiple situations stems from one's executive functioning abilities (Frye et al. 1995; Frye and Nguyen 1999).

The Theory of Mind and Executive Functioning

Executive Functioning refers to a set of abilities including working memory, problem solving, impulse control, situational flexibility, anticipation, and future planning (Piaget 1954; Ozonoff 1991; Welsch et al. 1991). These abilities combine to allow a person to adapt to varying situations and to navigate a changing world effectively (Ozonoff 1991; Sabbagh et al. 2006). This set of abilities is governed by the prefrontal cortex (Diamond 1988; Welsch et al. 1991). Many Autistic children possess poor executive functioning abilities (Ozonoff 1991; Frye et al. 1995, Frye and Nguyen 1999). They possess rigid and inflexible behaviours and tend to not anticipate the consequences of their behaviour, which is often attributed to a lack of forethought (Steel et al. 1984). The development of Theory of Mind may be connected to this executive dysfunction (Frye and Nguyen 1999; Sabbagh et al. 2006). Executive functioning is what allows us to pull from working memory and to hold multiple competing views about the world within our own heads at once (Ozonoff 1991). Using executive functioning, the child is better able to hold the view that Maxi thinks that the chocolate is in location *A* while still knowing that the chocolate is in fact in location *B*. Executive functioning abilities also develop at a similar time to the Theory of Mind in the typically developing brain. The brain undergoes rapid development in the area of systematic processing at the age of 5-6 which allows for better management of working memory and other executive functioning tasks (White 1970).

Tests which show that Autistic children have poor executive functioning compared to their typically developing counterparts would be the tower of Hanoi and the Wisconsin Card-Sorting task (Ozonoff 1991). The tower of Hanoi refers to a task in which 4 concentric disks with a hole in the center are placed on top of one another on a peg and the person must move all the disks to another of three pegs by moving one disk at a time and by only placing a smaller disk on top of a larger disk (Ozonoff 1991). To complete the tasks requires forethought and to manage multiple moves at the same time. The age-paired Autistic children completed the task in consistently more moves than the typically developing children when paired on intelligence and perceived mental age (Ozonoff, 1991). In Ozonff's card sorting test (1991), the children were asked to correctly determine a card-sorting pattern by placing cards that contained shapes of different colours and numbers either left or right. Once the child identified the predetermined pattern correctly and correctly sorted the cards ten times the researcher would change the pattern and the children were expected to determine the pattern again by continuing to sort cards. In the test, the Autistic children continued to sort cards by the old pattern for longer than the non-Autistic children, despite negative feedback (Heaton 1981; Ozonff 1991). This preservative tendency indicated inflexibility in the task (Ozonoff 1991).

Executive functioning plays a crucial role in the Representative Theory of Mind (RTM) (Benson and Sabbagh 2009). This aspect of Theory of Mind deals with representing mental states separate from one's own. It is this ability that allows us to generate predictions about others thoughts and how those thoughts influence one's behaviour (Dennet 1978). Executive functioning does not correlate with one's ability to understand the intentions and desires of others (Benson and Sabbagh 2009); it is instead an intermediate (Moses and Tahiroglu 2010). Skills in executive functioning predict RTM but not vice-versa (Benson and Sabbagh 2009).

Flynn (2007) showed that executive functioning performance predicted performance in false belief tasks. Executive functioning in this context allowed the child in question to resist the natural tendency to reference what they know to be true and provide an alternative correct response (Carlson and Moses 2001; Benson and Sabbagh 2009). Executive functioning allows children to inhibit the automatic assumption that beliefs match reality (Carlson and Moses 2001). However, this explanation would assume that the Autistic child does in fact understand false belief but is simply unable to answer correctly due to poor central coherence and an inability to suppress their bias of connecting beliefs with realities. Executive functioning also allows the child in question to hold within their brain and to consider multiple separate and conflicting representations of the world (Carlson and Moses 2001). This would aid in representational Theory of Mind reasoning but not in other aspects concerning TOM (Benson and Sabbagh 2009).

Bringing us back to the crayon-box-theory-of-mind-scenario: due to executive dysfunction in the Autistic child (or in the very young child), who has not quite developed the attention skills, may automatically answer with the items that were revealed to be in the crayon box because that is the most immediate thing on their mind, and corresponds to their most up to date form of reality. In this case, executive functioning mediates the Theory of Mind by giving the connection that allows for the recall and the reflection to give the correct answer. However, if TOM was based solely on executive functioning abilities, then one would expect the Autistic children to perform better in the picture sequencing tasks (Baron-Cohen et al. 1986) as those tasks required a similar level of executive functioning abilities as the physical and behavioural sequences (Ozonff 1991; Carlson and Moses 2001). The performance on these tasks suggests that although executive function may be necessary for certain aspects of Theory of Mind, it is not at the core of mentalization.

These behaviours are controlled by the pre-frontal cortex (Fuster 1985); people who possess pre-frontal damage often possess poor executive functioning abilities (Fuster 1985; Welsch 1991; Ozonoff 1991). Prefrontal impairment is also linked to social isolation, decreased affirmative behaviour, impaired social communication, and a lack of appreciation for social rules; these are also traits that many Autistic children possess (Ozonoff 1991). Executive functioning abilities help modulate Theory of Mind abilities in representing the beliefs and perspectives of other people (Ozonoff 1991). There is a considerable amount of neuro-overlap of executive function and Theory of Mind such that they become intrinsically intertwined (Sabbough et al. 2006; Benson and Sabbough 2009). Thus, Theory of Mind deficits encountered in Autism may be a result of poor executive functioning and poor communication between different parts of the brain which would normally allow children to hold multiple representations of the same outcome within their mind (Ozonoff 1991; Sabbough et al. 2006; Benson and Sabbough 2009).

As executive functioning continues to develop, the child is better able to process and represent the beliefs of others as products of the world around them to form predictions regarding other humans and correctly act on these predictions (Carlson et al. 2002). The key is to act on these predictions; for someone may be able to conceive that another person's belief is indeed false once they recognize it; once determined, they must now represent that construction in their brain separately from their own representation and use that alternate representation to determine the thoughts of an individual other than themselves. Therefore, someone with poor executive functioning abilities may intellectually recognize that the person has beliefs which are separate from their own or may be able to construct the feelings of another person based on their behaviours and beliefs but may not readily process how to act on these representations (Russel 1996; Sroufe et al. 1999; Carlson 2001).

The Theory of Mind and Early Development

The dominant view used to be that children under the age of three did not possess a Theory of Mind. However, Onishi and Baillargeon (2005) observed that young infants (15 months of age) may recognize that people's knowledge of the world differs from their own. When the infants observed a false belief story acted out with puppets where a man placed a person in a barrel, walks away, and later returns to throw the barrel off the cliff (2005). What the man did not know was that the person who was in the barrel had been replaced with a weight of similar mass (2005). The infants smiled as the man tossed the barrel off the cliff. When the verbal component was removed from false belief tasks, children as young as three were able to pass it, or were shown to have some comprehension of false beliefs than originally thought (2005). Similarly, Southgate et al. (2007) showed a skit like the Sally-Anne Skit to two-years-old and followed their gaze rather than asked them any questions. They found that the children looked longer at where the character imagined the marble to be upon re-entering the room, rather than where it was after it was moved. From these experiments, the authors concluded that the infants (on some very rudimentary level) realized that people's actions should depend on what their experiences are (Onishi and Baillargen 2005; Southgate et al. 2007). Children were shown to demonstrate sensitivity to false belief very early on in direct measures in online and interactive tasks. Leslie (1987; Leslie et al. 2004) describes that in false belief experiments young children looked longer at where the object used to be when the character returned rather than where it was. The authors remarked that the eyes gave the correct answer and the mouth the wrong one (Leslie 1987; Clements and Perner 1994; Ruffman et al. 2001). From here, we can infer that children younger than three possess some understanding that other people's beliefs can be (A) different from their own, and (B) false (Leslie 1987; Clements and Perner 1994; Ruffman et al. 2001). The studies demonstrated that young children possess nomic knowledge about motivational and informative states causing behaviour. However, in these experiments, there was nothing that forced the infants to consider the real states of affairs as different from their own, such as being asked questions (Roessler and Perner 2013). Thus, executive functioning was not required as a liaison between multiple representations of the world (Ozonoff 1991; Roessler and Perner 2013). In the case of direct and declarative tasks which required the children to connect their representations of the world with that of reality, they simply defaulted to teleological predictions of what a person would do based on their own knowledge of how the actor *should* act to reach the prescribed goal (Roessler and Perner 2013). Roessler and Perner devised that young children are teleologists; they make predictions of one's behaviour based on the assumption that people will follow the most rational course to achieve their goal (2013). In this sense, suggesting that mistaken Max should look for the chocolate where it is rather than where he remembered it makes perfect sense even if their representation is inconsistent (Roessler and Perner 2013). This does not negate work done by Gopnik and Astington; It more serves to show the process of the theory of mind's development and its connection to other cognitive abilities that must be present. How does the ability to mentalize develop within the mind of a small child and how is this development different in the Autistic child?

Imitation: The Theory of Mind Mechanism

A primary task of cognitive development is to build a connection to others. A key component in the development of the Theory of Mind and mentalization is imitation (Meltzoff and Moore 1992; Meltzoff 2002). Infants possess an innate propensity for imitation (Meltzoff and Moore 1992; Meltzoff 2002). From a very young age, children begin to imitate the expressions and actions of people around them (Meltzoff and Moore 1992; Meltzoff 2002). The act of mutual imitation allows infants to recognize other people as like themselves, separate from inanimate objects, and even other living things (Meltzoff and Moore 1992). Entities which can be imitated, and who can imitate me are like me (Meltzoff and Moore 1992). Early imitation allows the child to recognize that their thoughts and expressions can be projected onto others, and what these actions may look like through the lens of the observer (Meltzoff 2002). This process allows the infant to connect to those who imitate it, and those that it is imitating as "like me" (Meltzoff 1985; 2002). Infants take pleasure in mutual imitation games as they allow them to determine what around them is "like me" and what is "not like me," (Meltzoff 1985; 2002).

When the movements of the infant are imitated by the actor, the infant is able subconsciously map external behaviours, and connect them to internal bodily functions. From there, they can map externally perceived bodily movements onto intentions (Meltzoff and Gopnik 1993). "When I do this, they do this; thus, that is what this looks like." This process also allows the young children to recognize how their own expressions and gestures appear to others around them. Knowledge of the body = knowledge of the mind (Meltzoff and Gopnik 1993). Meltzoff and Moore (1992) observed that infants 12-21 days of age can imitate mouth movements. The infants in the observations responded by imitating facial movements and not simply to the presence of a face; the imitations were inexact as they had never seen their own faces (1992). The fact that the children attempted to match the expressions of the adult in the imitation games indicated that the children's intentions were to match the target rather than reflexively respond to facial movements (1992). Meltzoff (1991) showed that newborns were capable of imitating gestures as well. "The capacity to imitate is part of a child's innate endowment," (Meltzoff 1991). As we would examine and tinker with objects to better understand how they work; imitation is a form of tinkering with the minds of others' to better understand how both theirs' and our own minds operate (Meltzoff 1991). Imitation also allows the infants; to engage with the world around them by duplicating how others manipulate objects (Leslie 1987; 1991; Leslie and Frith 1988). Leslie (1987) observed the infants imitating their parents' manipulation of objects when the parent was the original imitator. The children were more responsive when the parent imitated their actions rather than simply moving the object within the infant's view, indicating that there was a higher connection to the act of imitation (1987). When the infant's actions are imitated, the infant learns that the other person in the room is paying attention to them and is "like me," (Meltzoff 1985; 2002). The recognition of self-other equivalences is the starting point for social cognition.

In 1995 Meltzoff went beyond simply testing if young children can imitate others, to determine if they could infer the goals of someone else by completing an incomplete task shown to them. Meltzoff formulated a set of experiments to determine if 18-month-olds could infer someone's goals by watching their behaviours (1995). Meltzoff (1995) formulated five experiments. In the control state 18-month-olds watched adults perform 5 sets of complete tasks and they innately imitated the adults; in the experimental setting however, a different set of same-aged children were shown the same five tasks, but instead, the adults were shown to attempt and fail at the tasks. Without prompting, rather than simply mimicking the actions presented to them, the infants completed the task instead. For example, if the adult was shown attempting to take apart a toy dumbbell by the ends and their hands slipping off, the children pulled apart the toy dumbbell instead (1995). Meltzoff analyzed the results of the test and concluded that there was no significance in success rates between the control and the experimental group for all five tasks (1995). This indicated that the children were able to infer—or project—the goal of completion onto the initial agent (Meltzoff 1995). Furthermore, the children did not complete a similar task when the same motion was shown to them performed by an inanimate device as opposed to a human (1995). The children also maintained their gaze longer with the human demonstrator compared to the mechanized demonstrator (Meltzoff 1995). Tests like this show that young children recognize other people as agents with goals and desires like their own and are separate from inanimate objects; it also shows that they are able to represent the minds of others within their own mind (1995).

These mutual imitation games provided infants with a rudimentary window to connecting with others, thus, showing them that the person imitating them thinks in a similar way as they do and is capable of similar actions and cognition. Thus, imitation provides a tutorial for common-sense psychology (Meltzoff 1991; Meltzoff and Gopnik 1993). The thoughts of others are like mine; but can also be different. Imitation sets a primer for later reasoning: if I imitate X then I am like $X;$ then the same thing that happened to X should happen to me. Imitation lays the groundwork through which children recognize humans as separate from inanimate objects and as thinking beings with desires and goals like their own (Meltzoff 1991; Meltzoff and Gopnik 1993). Through imitation, the child can begin to develop representations of others' desires as like yet separate from their own.

The quintessential reaction of meeting a baby is a person (typically a woman) gets really close, down to their level, starts speaking in a really high-pitched voice and makes gestures at them for them to imitate. As an adult, I have always found this exchange of gestures strange and alien. When I see a baby, I have no desire to engage in such actions. I don't get much enjoyment from staring at a human infant or engaging in the imitation games that others thrive in. I think this speaks to the absence of the Theory of Mind mechanism within me. These people are priming the infant for future interactions where imitation and Theory of Mind are critical; and I am simply a stranger who wants nothing to do with this interaction.

Imitation and Autism

If imitation, which allows young children and infants to develop a connection between themselves and the minds of others, exists as the bridge towards mentalization; then how is this bridge altered in Autism?

From their work on imitation, Meltzoff and Gopnik (1983) concluded that children who lack the *aboriginal* capacity for perceiving self-other equivalences in such imitation games might enjoy them less, and will thus be less successful at making predictions concerning other people's behaviour through imitation. "They seemed to lack the extended attention to faces and voices that is noticed in typically developing children," (Hobson et al. 1990; 1991). Hobson and colleagues (1990; 1991) referred to Autism as a disturbance in the core mechanism for detection of commonality in body movements between the self and others. There was no mention of Autistic children in Meltzoff's work (Meltzoff et al. 1991; Meltzoff and Gopnik 1993; Meltzoff 1995), as the children in these studies were mostly too young to have received a professional diagnosis by the standards of the time. However, Leo Kanner's first observation of Autism recounts:

He paid no attention to those around him. When taken into a room he completely disregarded the people and went for objects, preferably those that spun (1943).

Kanner describes that the boy (in recollections from his parents) "never responded to people in the usual ways, even as an infant." From these recollections, Kanner assumed that the condition was inborn (1943). Kanner also describes the child, rather than withdrawing from the social world, as being born outside of it (1943; Silberman 2015). Similar stories of the failure of Autistic children to engage with people in a social context are described by both founders of the condition (Asperger 1944; Kanner 1943; Silberman 2015), and by Baron-Cohen (1995). These accounts give us a window into how Autistic children may have responded to imitation games. One can assume that these children would have paid little attention to the adults and would not have readily imitated their behaviours. Thus, the children would not make the rudimentary "like me" connections until much later in life.

Earlier in the chapter, we saw that Autistic children tended to describe events happening between two or more characters in a purely physical sense; while non-Autistic children tended to lean more towards attributing intent, and emotion to characters when describing the same events (Baron-Cohen et al. 1986; Lillard and Flavell 1990). Silberman (2015) also echoes this very concept from a much earlier time in both Asperger's and Kanner's early descriptions. Perhaps to the Autistic infant: a person imitating them is not different from anyone else in the room.

If mutual imitation exchanges are the tutorial for common-sense psychology, then the absence of or diminution of this may lead to deficits in social understanding and communicative functioning. Imitation and empathetic inclination is the substrate of early empathetic reactions (Lipps 1906); thus—even with empathetic inclination—without imitation, one does not have the foundation for empathetic reactions. Where does this disconnection come from? Perhaps Autistic children are born without the inclination to imitate those around them (this would be a rational conclusion given the stories from both Asperger and Kanner). Without this mechanism they cannot create the connections needed for social interaction in a typical manner. This is shown in the subtle ways in which Autistic children interact with the world, most notably through eye-contact.

Lack of eye-contact is a key component of the Autism Spectrum, so much so that it is a defining characteristic that parents are advised to watch-out for when they are wondering if their child is in fact Autistic (Fernandez-Duque and Baird 2005). The lack of eye contact in Autistic children can be observed from a very young age; young babies who are observed to not follow basic hand movements of adults with their eyes, and who do not smile when a familial adult interacts with them tended to develop more Autistic traits as they grew up (Fernandez-Duque and Baird 2005). A child who does not make eye contact with the actor is less likely to engage in imitation games, and is therefore less likely to acquire the "like me" common-sense psychology associated with them. I am not simply suggesting that the Autistic child is unable to imitate simply because they fail to make eye contact with the actor (that would place us in a chicken-and-egg fallacy); the lack of eye contact Autistic children—even as infants—present provides us a window into the differences in the Autistic brain. Roessler and Perner (2013) remark that Autistic children may find the types of interactions described in the prior section between themselves and others as less predictable, and are thus less likely to engage. The Autistic child may fail to engage in mutual imitation out of an innate wiring that does not draw them to others in the same way that typically developing children are drawn (Roessler and Perner 2013). In Autism, the connections between imitation and the discovery that people have agency separate from their own and beyond that of mere objects—or even to some extent other animals—appears to be decoupled (Meltzoff and Gopnik 1993). If the Autistic child is unable to make these connections through the observations of imitation, then they are unable to become active participants in these imitation games. Without active participation they fail to develop the common-sense psychology necessary for early Theory of Mind development. Other authors go so far as to suggest that the ability to see others as person's rather than objects and extensions of the self is damaged in the Autistic brain (Rogers and Pennington 1991; Hobson 1990; 1991). Due to a developmental disconnect, young Autistic children fail to engage in imitation games and do not make the eye-contact necessary to engage with the actors (Rogers and Pennington 1991; Hobson 1990; 1991; Meltzoff and Gopnik 1993). They fail to develop the "like-me" primer in common-sense psychology that is essential in representing the thoughts of others. Imitation is what allows the young child to engage with the world and acts as the foundation for the Theory of Mind mechanism. Without this innate connection with others, the Autistic child lacks the foundations for which the Theory of Mind develops out of. This combined with the deficits in executive functioning observed in Autistic people makes it increasingly harder to imagine the intentions and beliefs of other people in addition to being able to hold multiple representations and move among them freely within their own brain. Without this foundation, the Autistic child must consciously learn how to tap into the Theory of Mind, rather than subconsciously absorb Theory of Mind cues from the world around them (Leslie 1987; 1991; Leslie and Frith 1988). If young Autistic children simply fail to engage in imitation because of an inability to take pleasure in such games, then they simply may not "see the point" in reciprocating. Perhaps the ability to create these connections, and to find enjoyment in imitation is an innate process which the Autistic brain lacks.

Of course, when I look at the simple false belief tasks as an adult, I understand why Sally or Mistaken Max may choose the wrong location; thus, as an adult, I have some grasp of the Theory of Mind that I clearly would not have had as a small child. I use my intelligence to circumvent any Theory of Mind deficit I may have. The Theory of Mind may take longer to develop in Autistic children for the foundation of folk psychology that lies in imitation is lacking. Alternatively, it could be concluded that my *grasp of the Theory of Mind* is a learned response, and that my unconscious Theory of Mind is still far behind that of the normal adult (Senju et al. 2009). To attain what most people naturally produce; my brain often must go far beyond what other brains need to do. It may be that my brain lacks the seemingly innate ability to mentalize, an ability that the general public places a great deal of emphasis on in everyday functioning...

And now to delve into neurology. Neurology is the inner workings which psychology is born out of. We will look at what parts of the brain are responsible for the Theory of Mind, for executive functioning, and what may be different in the Autistic brain.

Organization of the Human Brain and Cognitive Processes

The human brain, and subsequently the nervous system, is vital for feeling, movement, and consciousness. Different brain regions perform different functions and communicate with one another to create a dynamic experience of the outside world. The brain can be divided into three parts, the cerebrum, the cerebellum, and the brain stem (Carter 2019). The part of the brain that we are most concerned with for our analysis is the cerebrum, which is responsible for higher cognitive processes such as Theory of Mind. The cerebrum is the largest part of the human brain and is the most anterior. The cerebrum is composed of folded cortical tissue. Each fold increases the surface area for cognitive function, and the amount of contact the tissue has with itself (Carter 2019). The inward folds are referred to as sulci while the corresponding outward folds are called gyri (singular: sulcus and gyrus); each sulcus comes with a corresponding gyrus (Carter 2019). The cerebrum has two sections (right and left), which are often referred to as brain hemispheres (though the brain is not a sphere). The human brain can be further divided into lobes based both upon location and the overarching functions that are performed; the lobes are the same in both the left and right hemispheres (Carter 2019). The junctions are where different lobes communicate and integrate their functions in order to create a coherent picture of the world and perform required tasks. In addition, the outer part of the brain is known as the cortex (Carter 2019).

The frontal lobe is most anterior and is responsible for emotional expression, problem-solving, language, judgment, reasoning, sexual behavior, and empathy (Fuster et al. 2002). It is the center of communication and motor function. The frontal lobe integrates the senses into our experience of the world. Within the frontal lobe lies the prefrontal cortex (Fuster et al. 2002), which is the central processing area for all this information, and the subsequent behaviors that rely on it. The prefrontal cortex is where higher-level cognitive processes such as working memory, executive functions, inhibitory control, and the ability to multitask take place (Curtis and D'Esposito 2003; Duncan and Owen 2000; Miyake et al. 2000). The prefrontal cortex is also the center for motor memory, and task completion (Shadmehr and Holcomb 1997). The prefrontal cortex is exceptionally well connected to other brain structures (Fuster et al. 2002); it is this connectivity that allows neurons within the prefrontal cortex to access the memories we have accumulated in other parts of the brain that remind us how to communicate and interact appropriately in social or public situations as well as for simpler tasks such as mathematical computations and motor tasks. The frontal lobe collects information from other parts of the brain and uses this information to make decisions regarding the outside world (Sira et al. 2014). From an evolutionary perspective, the frontal lobe (particularly the prefrontal cortex) has become larger proportionate to the rest of the brain over time (Fuster et al. 2002). This is to be expected, as it is the center for higher level cognition and information processing (Fuster et al. 2002).

The Parietal lobe is responsible for integrating visual, auditory, and somatosensory information together for the purpose of guiding behaviour (Gonzalez and Flindall, 2015). The Parietal lobe codes for motor action, and provides representations of these motor actions with specific sensory information (Fogassi et al. 2005). The Parietal lobe is responsible for our senses, and allows us to integrate our perception of the world with our working memory (Gonzalez and Flindall 2015). The Parietal lobe is also responsible for helping us to understand these actions when someone else is performing them (Fogassi et al. 2005). In an experiment with rhesus macaque monkeys (Fogassi et al. 2005), the same neurons within the Parietal lobe activated when the monkey grasped a piece of food to eat it as when it watched another monkey perform the same task. These specific neurons which fire both when the subject is performing a task as when they are simply watching the person perform a same or similar task are called mirror neurons. This is the place where contagious yawning/laughter comes from; they allow us to interact with how others around us are feeling and respond in kind (Acharya and Shukla 2012). The highest concentration of these neurons lies within the Parietal lobe (Acharya and Shukla 2012). The activation of mirror neurons, allowing us to read the intentions of others, occurs in the Inferior Parietal Lobule (IPL) (Acharya and Shukla 2012). It is the mirror neurons located in the Parietal lobe that allow observing individuals to understand the observed neural act (Gallese et al. 1996; Rizzolatti et al. 2001). The activation of the mirror neurons to non-self stimuli also provides the basis for the distinction of ourselves from others; they allow us to differentiate how we would react compared to how others would react when performing the same tasks; these different activation sequences allow us to for prediction regarding the behaviours of others (Ruby and Decety 2004). The activation of mirror neurons also supports imitation as the mechanism for Theory of Mind development in small children. By becoming more familiar with the differences in activation between the self and the other when another person is performing the same task, they learn to differentiate the self from the other and learn to take on others' perspectives (Fogassi et al. 2005; Acharya and Shukla 2012). This is the mechanism for understanding the minds of others (Inferior Parietal Mechanism; Fogassi et al. 2005).

The Temporal lobe is located beneath both the Parietal and Frontal lobes and in front of the occipital lobe (Carter 2019). The Temporal lobe is consequently located directly behind the ears (Carter 2019). The Temporal lobe receives, and processes sound (Carter 2019). It is responsible for selective hearing and selective attention (Carter 2019). Neurons receive sensory information from the ears, such as sound and speech, and process this information to allow us to understand it. The Temporal lobe is the center for short-term memory, episodic memory recall, selective attention, and long-term memory (Scoville and Milner 1957; Corsi 1972; Simons and Spiers 2003; Ghetti et al. 2010). The Temporal lobe is also home to the hippocampus, which is the center for short-term memory (Scoville and Milner 1957; Milner 1954). The role of the Temporal lobe in these actions has been demonstrated in cases where patients with damage to these areas were unable to consciously remember events and/or were unable to recall instructions or lists of items that were given to them after a certain amount of time or after switching tasks (Scoville and Milner 1957). The hippocampus in particular is responsible for mediating memory and item recollection based on the context of the situation at hand (Baddeley 2001; Holdstock et al. 2002; Yonelinas et al. 2002; Davachi et al. 2003; Ghetti et al. 2010). The hippocampus allows us to recall certain memories depending on the situation and to integrate new memories with past experiences based on their similarities (Carter 2019). The Temporal lobe is the area of the brain which allows us to access information based on the situations and allows us to recall different information based on the task at hand when changing tasks (Baddeley 2001; Holdstock et al. 2002; Yonelinas et al. 2002; Davachi et al. 2003; Ghetti et al. 2010). Patients who have lost function of their Temporal lobe or parts of the Temporal lobe due to lesions or removal (be it partial or full) have a hard time recalling events and integrating new information into memory as well as within the context of preexisting episodic memory (Scoville and Milner 1957; Milner 1954). The Temporal lobe is lastly home to the Wernicke's Area, which sits on the superior-Temporal gyrus (Petersen et al. 1989; 1999). This area is responsible for sentence comprehension and syntax (Petersen et al. 1989; 1999).

Finally, the occipital lobe is responsible for processing visual information and for image recognition (Carter 2019). It receives visual information from the eyes and processes it to correctly understand what our eyes are seeing in the real world (Carter 2019). The occipital lobe is also what allows us to correctly assess the size, distance, and depth of objects compared to others (Carter 2019). It is the center for visual memory, and image recall (Grill-Spector et al. 1998; 2001). Neurons within the occipital lobe activate during object recognition, and allow us to differentiate between objects in the real world and mere representations of objects (Grill-Spector et al. 2001). The occipital lobe can represent the shapes of objects independent of their constituents which define them (Grill-Spector et al. 2001). It is the occipital lobe which allows us to process specific images and objects which exist in the real world and fit them together to create a consistent and cohesive image of the world outside of our minds (Grill-Spector et al. 2001).

The four main regions of the human brain work together to receive information, process it, and allow our bodies to understand and participate in the world around us. The occipital lobe is responsible for processing visual information, and visual recognition; the Temporal lobe is responsible for processing auditory information, for integrating various information into short-term, and long term memory and subsequently calling upon that information for the task at hand; the Parietal lobe is responsible for connecting our own bodily movements and interpretations of the world with the movements, and behaviours of others in order to understand how others see the world, and to predict their behaviours consequently; and finally, the frontal lobe is responsible for collecting all this information together in order to generate higher level thinking. The frontal lobe allows us to interact with the world, and with others in a variety of situations.

The two hemispheres of the brain are held together by a bundle of nerve fibres called the corpus-callosum; which connects the right and the left hemispheres together and transmits neural messages between them (Sperry et al. 1969; Berlucchi 1965; 1972; Kreuter et al. 1972; Diamond 1976). In cases where the corpus-callosum was removed patients experienced disassociation between the right and left hemispheres, and difficulty transferring learned information (Gazzaniga 2005). The evolution of the corpus-callosum may have aided in the differentiation of brain hemispheres (Gazzaniga 2000). By providing a medium for communication, and the exchange of information it would have allowed the right and left-brain hemispheres to take on different cognitive functions, thus saving cortical space (Gazzaniga 2000) and reducing interference (Magat and Brown 2009).

The mirror neurons in the Parietal lobe mediate interaction by allowing us to relate to the behaviours of others while the role of the Temporal lobe is memory recall based on task (Baddeley et al. 2001; Holdstock et al. 2002; Yonelinas et al. 2002; Davachi et al. 2003). The Temporal lobe allows us to call upon certain memories based on the task at hand, and thus is responsible for selective attention and attentional shifting (Baddeley et al. 2001; Holdstock et al. 2002; Yonelinas et al. 2002; Davachi et al. 2003). The act of mentalizing refers to the ability to shift one's perspective from within themselves to another person, and to be able to rely on past experiences of both themselves and those of other people to subsequently make sense of and predict behaviours given situational information. The primary contributors to the Theory of Mind are both the Parietal and the Temporal lobes (Saxe and Kanwisher 2003), particularly where these two structures meet. Next, we will look at this region and its role in processing false-belief and Theory of Mind tasks.

Theory of Mind and the Brain: The Temporal-Parietal Junction

The Temporal-Parietal junction (TPJ) refers to the region of cortical space at the intersection of the Parietal and Temporal lobes as well as the surrounding neural tissue (Carter 2019). Much of the studies involving the pinpointing of the TPJ in mentalizing and perspective taking involve Functional Magnetic Resonance Imaging (FMRI) of specific Regions of Interest (ROIs) where areas of the brain are shown to be activated or recruited during the performance of a given task that involves some level of mentalization and/or perspective taking compared to a control task (Saxe and Kanwisher 2003).

Saxe and Kanwisher (2003) set up an experiment in which they could compare activation during reasoning about true and false beliefs to determine the role of the TPJ in false belief reasoning. In this study, adults were shown four different stories: one concerning false beliefs, the next mechanical influences, human actions, and finally nonhuman descriptions. They predicted that the TPJ would respond significantly more to false belief stories than to stories about human actions, less to nonhuman descriptions, and even less to mechanical sequences (2003). They found increased responses in the TPJ in response to false beliefs stimuli and to stories regarding human actions, specifically in the medial regions of the TPJ (2003). The left TPJ responded more strongly to verbal descriptions of objects and to verbal stories, while the right responded more to general nonverbal stimuli such as photographs (2003). They secondly compared the response of the TPJ using false belief and false representation stimuli. There was an increased response from the TPJ to stimuli that involved reasoning regarding false belief over false representations (2003). The TPJ did not show an increased response to the mere presence of a person in the corresponding stimuli; the requirement was for the subject to reason about another person's beliefs (Saxe and Kanwisher 2003).

David and Colleagues (2008) wanted to determine the differences in activation between perspective taking and mentalizing using Functional and Structural MRI scans. They did this by presenting participants in the experiment with a virtual character; on either side of the character was an object of the same category (fruits, shapes, etc...). The virtual character expressed a preference for one of the two objects using facial expression in which the participants in the study were supposed to infer the character's preferences from. The participants had to indicate which object was elevated from both their perspective as well as the character's perspective (perspective taking), in addition to being able to indicate which object they preferred and the one the character preferred using facial expressions (mentalizing) (2008). During third person mentalizing, regions within both the Temporal and Parietal lobes were activated in determining the preferences of the character while mostly the frontal lobe was active when participants were asked to describe their own preferences (2008). The difference in activation between third person perspective taking and third person mentalizing was the activation of the Superior Temporal Sulcus (STS: the cortical fold connecting the Parietal with the Temporal lobe), which was activated only during mentalizing (2008). The posterior STS is involved in the perception of social cues and in the detection of animated entities, which are important in the understanding of behaviours and in a person's mental states (David et al. 2008). Patients with lesions to the posterior STS were unable to infer the virtual character's preferences but were able to perform perspective taking tasks (Cohen et al. 2008). The act of perspective taking involved the activation of the TPJ (Aichhorn et al. 2009); but for mentalization, the recruitment of neighbouring cortical regions was required. Both regions of the TPJ, as well as neighbouring regions, demonstrated stronger signalling when subjects were asked to reason about others' mental states compared to their own (Cohen et al. 2008; Aichhorn et al. 2009).

Saxe and Wexler (2005) demonstrated activation of the right TPJ (RTPJ) during the attribution of mental states to others. Using MRI analyses, they were able to show increased activation of the RTPJ when participants had to read passages concerning the mental states of characters over simply the social and cultural backgrounds of them. In addition, the MRI response was even higher when the mental state of the character in question was different from what could have been expected when reading about the character's background (Saxe and Wexler 2005). A different mental state than what is predicted may indicate a failure of the brain to correctly predict a character's behaviour in a given situation; the surprise causes increased activation of the area in question in compensation. The activation of the RTPJ during mental state attribution shows that this area of the brain plays a key role in mentalizing; the over-activation when the mental states were incongruent with the information given shows that this part of the brain is attempting to make sense of the disconnect. The response of the RTPJ reflects the process of constructing a coherent model of the mind of someone else (Saxe and Wexler 2005). The left TPJ (LTPJ) on the other hand responded strongly when the socio-economic backgrounds of the characters described in the scenarios were different from their own, compared to when backgrounds were familiar (Saxe and Wexler 2005). The implications of Saxe and Wexler (2005) are that the left side of the Temporal Parietal junction takes in information concerning another person's background relative to one's own, while the right uses this information to predict the mental states of the person in question. Bzdok et al, (2013) further shows how the two different components within the Right TPJ work together to create a cohesive picture of another person's perception of the world and how to predict their behaviours. The anterior part of the RTPJ taking in visual and auditory information and discriminating different sounds and speech patterns while the posterior RTPJ processes this information in episodic memory (Binder et al. 2009) to create social judgements and moral decisions based on it and in reflection of the behaviour of others (Bzdok et al. 2012a; 2012b). The anterior RTPJ is also responsible for sustained attention which would allow for continued processing of information (Bzdok et al. 2013). Thus, showing that not only the different sides of the brain process information differently but also how anterior and posterior compartments work together to create a fuller picture of human behaviour. The fact that the TPJ is recruited specifically in the processing of Theory of Mind stimuli to predict behaviour indicates that it is where the processing of other people's beliefs and the prediction of behaviours take place. The mirror neurons activate when we see someone performing a task and they activate as if we were performing the tasks ourselves; while the Temporal lobe holds our attention for us to predict the behaviours at hand. As discussed earlier, the Temporal lobe is also the center for short term memory, and is responsible for processing those memories into long term storage. As these processes continue, they become better able to predict behaviours and pull from information both concerning the present task as well as past experiences (Bzdok et al. 2013). The more predictable stimuli become, the more the process becomes detached from the current sensory environment for new information, and becomes more reliant on past experiences and intuition in predicting social situations (Bzdok et al. 2013). Information concerning mentalization is taken in and communicated laterally, while information is processed and reacted upon longitudinally.

In addition to the recruitment of the Temporal and Parietal regions in Theory of Mind tasks, Frith and Frith (1999; 2006) have shown recruitment of the frontal and Temporal cortices (the outer layer of these corresponding regions) adjacent to the Parietal cortex during mentalization tasks (Frith and Frith 1999; 2006; Gallagher and Frith 2003). Brunet et al. (2003) and Aichhorn and colleagues (2006), demonstrated the activation of the superior Temporal sulcus (the fold of cortical tissue on the superior surface of the Temporal lobe which connects to the inferior part of the Parietal lobe) during perspective taking. To successfully recognize the perspective of someone else, one must suppress their own perspective (Ruby and Decety 2004). This is where executive functioning comes in: executive functioning allows us to put the perspective of another person over our own in a given situation. Even if the TPJ is the center of activation in TOM tasks, unless the perspective of someone else is put to the forefront of our mental processing, we cannot consider the mental states of others, and thus third person perspective taking requires the differentiation and the regulation of the self perspective (Ruby and Decety 2004). Thus, the neurons in the TPJ and surrounding regions must relay the information to the frontal cortex where it can be prioritized over the self and then back so that one can predict the mental states of others (Ruby and Decety 2004).

Since the TPJ is where Theory of Mind processing takes place, then the question is: How does the functioning and general responses of the Autistic brain compare to that of the non Autistic brain? If the TPJ in the Autistic brain responds differently to Theory of Mind stimuli, then how does the rest of the brain process this information? For the next section, we will investigate whether different parts of the brain are activated during Theory of Mind tasks in Autistic people, and whether the activation of the TPJ during perspective taking tasks is different. This should show us why predicting the mental states of others—especially in cases when a person's perception of the world is incorrect—is more difficult and not intuitive for Autistic people.

The Autistic Brain

The next step is to define what makes the Autistic brain *Autistic*. To do this, we will look at how various aspects of the Autistic brain differ from that of the non-Autistic brain. We will focus on general connectivity between sections of the brain, as well as activation of brain regions during specific tasks or exposure to specific stimuli. From there, we will be better able to see how these differences contribute to Autism-specific deficits and to how an Autistic person may see the world differently.

Studies of the Autistic brain show that specific sections within the Corpus Callosum are smaller (Casanova et al. 2002; Just et al. 2004; 2007). The Corpus Callosum is the main hub for inter-hemispheric connections. Therefore, the deficits noticed in Autism should stem (at least in part) from a lack of inter-hemispheric brain connectivity. Executive functioning is a product of different regions within the brain being able to communicate with one-another to perform more complex tasks, and solve complex problems that bridge different thought processes (Ozonoff et al. 1991; 1994; Just et al. 2007; 2004; Itahashi et al. 2014). Thus, we should be able to link differences in connectivity to Autism-specific deficits.

When we discuss different types of connectivity, the two main ones that are often differentiated are structural and functional connectivity. Structural connectivity refers to the physical connections made between neurons and the pathways within the brain that connect one region of the brain to other sections (Rudie et al, 2013; Itahashi et al, 2014). Structural connectivity can be far reaching as, in from the posterior end of the brain to the anterior part of the brain or the left hemisphere to the right hemisphere; or it can be localized, from one part to another adjacent part of the brain (Rudie et al, 2013; Itahashi et al, 2014). The analogy would be taking a plane across the Atlantic Ocean vs taking a bus to the next city over. Conversely, functional connectivity refers to the ability of these connections to relay information from one place to another (Rudie et al, 2013; Park and Friston 2013). The physical connection may be there, but that does not tell us about how good it is at getting the information from point A to point B. Much of the literature points to the Autistic brain having more regional structural connections, but being less well globally connected and possessing fewer functional connections overall (Rudie et al. 2013).

Focusing on functional connectivity, Ingelstrom et al. (2016) found reduced functional connectivity between the TPJ region and the Cerebellum, which are both involved in social function and cognition (Kelly et al. 2014; Ingelstrom et al. 2015). Ingelstrom et al. (2016) found out using fMRI imaging that the organization of the TPJ in Autistic participants was not significantly different from that of the control group; however, the connectivity between the TPJ and other regions was what was greatly reduced. This is echoed in work done by Just and colleagues (2004; 2007). Just et al. carried out two fMRI studies that tested the functional connectivity of Autistic people during the performance of language-based (2004) and executive functioning (2007) tasks. They found that Autistic people had lower overall functional connectivity compared to the control group (2004; 2007). This was particularly the case for the Autistic group when it came to sentence comprehension tasks (Just et al. 2004). The Autistic group tended to focus on individual words of the sentence rather than the syntax of the entire sentence. This may be why Autistic people have trouble with understanding figurative language (DSM-V 2013). In both cases, the Autistic participants showed lower inter-hemispheric connectivity, as well decreased connectivity between the frontal and Parietal regions (Just et al. 2004; 2007). This may explain the deficits in executive functioning that are observed in Autism. The hallmark of executive functioning is that it requires the communication of often multiple brain regions to comprehend a complex task (Just et al. 2007; Ingerstorm et al. 2016). Mentioned earlier, the Corpus Callosum of the Autistic brain is smaller which may account for some of the decreased interhemispheric connectivity. With a smaller Corpus Callosum, information may take more time to travel between hemispheres, it may need to find another path, or it may not get there at all and other parts of the brain within the corresponding hemisphere may need to compensate. In addition to the decreased long-range connectivity, Rudie et al. (2013) showed that there were more localized connections between adjacent regions in Autism. There is also reduced functional connectivity in networks connected to the Theory of Mind. The brain is making up for that lack of long range connections with many more short range connections between areas. Both the TPJ and the cerebellum are involved in social and cognitive functions that may be disturbed in ASD. This includes things like TOM, episodic memory, emotional processing, and empathy. The authors found decreased connectivity between the right TPJ, and the social regions of the cerebellum in Autistic subjects compared to non-Autistics (Ingelstrom et al. 2016).

Muller (2007) suggests that brain abnormalities in ASD can best be understood as a network disorder. This disorder is characterized by brain overgrowth in childhood followed by a rapid period of decline in brain size from adolescence to middle-age as a result of connection pruning (Courchesne et al. 2011). Itahashi and colleagues (2014) used neuroimaging to determine an increase in "randomness" in the connectivity of Autistic brains. This increased randomness was found to be a result of fewer long-range connections and an increase in the number of short-range connections between adjacent regions within the brain (Itahashi et al. 2014). There is less predictability of functional connectivity based on the structural pathways within the brain (Itahashi et al. 2014). Like getting on a bus, and not knowing your destination; or travelling to a bunch of other unexpected places that may lead to distortion of information before getting to your destination. There was also less activation in the anterior cingulate cortex, due to this reduced functional connectivity (Itahashi et al. 2014). This brain region is associated with emotional processing, conflict monitoring and behavioural regulation (Botvinick et al. 2004; Solomon et al; 2009; Etkin et al. 2011). They also noted altered functional connectivity in the motor-network, which is responsible for motor tasks (Itahashi et al. 2014). Lastly, Itahashi et al. (2014) found dysfunction in the mirror neuron network; as we recall, the mirror neuron network can be thought of as the imitation hub, and thus the center for the origin of Theory of Mind thinking. The mirror neuron network, as we recall, is also located in the Parietal lobe. A disruption in connectivity between the Parietal regions and the Frontal regions, combined with dysfunction in the hub of TOM may indicate that any Theory of Mind information that is received by the Parietal lobe is not making it to the Frontal lobe, and is thus not being processed fully or is simply taking a longer time to process. The disruption in functional connectivity in these specific area's likely accounts for the social and perceptual impairments of Autism, particularly the difficulties in inhibition of behaviours, and social deficits in Theory of Mind (Boddart et al. 2004; Hadjikhani et al. 2006). The decrease in functional connectivity between hemispheres, as well as between distant parts of the brain compared to adjacent regions characterizes Autism as a neurobiological disorder of integrative circuitry, and processing; which results in a deficit of integrating information at the neural and cognitive levels (Just et al. 2004).

In addition to the decreased connectivity between Theory of Mind regions and the Frontal areas of the brain, fMRI studies from David et al. (2008) indicated decreased activation in the right TPJ during both exposure to Theory of Mind stimuli and the completion of Theory of Mind tasks— perspective taking and mentalizing. Subjects were shown virtual characters in proximity to various objects and were asked to infer both preference (mentalizing) and proximity of the object to the character in space (perspective taking) separately. They were able to isolate a particular area of the superior Temporal sulcus that became activated exclusively during mentalizing, but not during perspective taking. This area became activated specifically when subjects made inferences about the character's preferences; but had decreased activation in the Autistic group compared to controls.

Taking a closer look at connectivity, connections between individual brain cells tended to be disrupted by abnormalities in brain white matter formation and decreased white matter integrity (Barnea-Goraly et al. 2004; Bloemen et al. 2010). White matter connectivity differences in Autism consisted of disruptions in connectivity in the Fronto-Temporo-Occipital regions (Ameis et al. 2011). Disruptions in connectivity were related to the processing of novel stimuli, visual learning, and the decoding of emotional aspects of verbal information (Schmahmann et al. 2007). There was a greater axonal density and increased connective tissue (Ameis et al. 2011); this combined with increased diffusivity led to decreased white matter organization and less-focused movement of information between regions. These differences in white matter tracts may have led to delayed or disrupted transport of information between brain regions and impaired processing of information in regions related to emotional processing in Autism (Ameis et al. 2011). Reduced functional connectivity in frontal regions may lead to differences in the ability to connect and interpret different types of stimuli in daily life (Schmahman et al. 2007; Ameis et al 2011).

The Autistic brain lastly appears to follow a different developmental trajectory compared to the non-Autistic pattern. This trajectory is characterized by accelerated brain growth in early childhood followed by a period of accelerated decline in brain size from adolescence to middle age (Courchesne et al. 2011). This leads to the brains of Autistic children being larger on average (60-70th percentile relative to population norms) compared to age-matched children (Minshew and Williams 2007). Increased brain size is typically associated with decreased interhemispheric connectivity—a previously described characteristic of the Autistic brain—as information simply needs to travel further (Hashimoto and Sakai 2002; Sakia et al. 2002). A study conducted by Courchesne and colleagues in 2011 showed that (of a sample size of 6 Autistic children and 7 non-Autistic children postmortem) Autistic children had larger brains and a much higher neuron count in the prefrontal cortex. Although their brain sizes were larger on average, they were smaller considering the increased neuron count in the prefrontal cortex (2011). Although the sample size was small, this may be a result of overall smaller under-development of neurons or fewer neurons in other places that were not accounted for in the study. Prenatal apoptosis (programmed cell death) is what leads to the specialization of cells and neural pathways later in life. The lack of pruning in the Autistic brain early in life may account for particular deficits in the Autistic phenotype (Kanold 2009; Kostovic and Judas 2010). Neural apoptosis or pruning normally leads to the connections considered necessary for lateral and inter-hemispheric functional connectivity later in life, which is necessary for executive functioning and communication between different regions within the brain (Kanold 2009; Kostovic and Judas 2010). In short, this difference in growth trajectory may account for the differences in connectivity patterns observed in Autism, as well as for why Autistic traits tend to decrease with age in most cases. The onset of brain overgrowth may be part of the neuro-developmental trajectory leading to the expression of the Autistic neurotype (Minshew and Williams 2007).

The Autistic brain differs in connectivity as well as how the brain processes Theory of Mind stimuli. The decrease in functional connectivity, primarily between the Parietal regions and the Frontal regions, as well as inter-hemispheric connections implies that there is a distinct deficit in processing of information that would require multiple brain regions: particularly social tasks. In addition, the decreased response of areas in the brain that are classically related to representing the beliefs of others within their own head space gives us a clear link to the perceived social difficulties that are expressed in Autistic individuals. Autism is a neurobiological condition of both rewiring, and of decreased activation in key regions of the brain. From this, we are better able to see how people may be more or less affected by Autism, or how people who are on the Autism Spectrum may have varying degrees of difficulty at different times. The decreased functional connectivity may be in slightly different regions from one person to the next. The people may be able to perform complex tasks, if they require regions of the brain that are adjacent to one another or there may be a pathway that is created in the Autistic person that is not present in non-Autistic people due to increased randomness. Finally, the difference in brain size and neuron count shows that there is a different layout of the brain that focuses more strongly on parts of the prefrontal cortex over other areas and a greater emphasis on intra-hemisphere connectivity, leading to the de-emphasis on Temporal and Parietal regions. The concentration in these areas is what ultimately accounts for the differences in cognitive strengths observed. The Autistic configuration can result in traits that are often seen as both deficits and strengths. Perhaps we ought to move towards looking at Autism as a cognitive difference rather than simply a "disorder."

Summary

Theory of Mind refers to the ability to represent the thoughts and experiences of others as our own. Autistic people often have difficulty with this task. Early studies of the Theory of Mind involve young children answering questions regarding the false beliefs of characters (Wimmer and Perner 1983; Baron-Cohen et al. 1985; 1986). The Autistic children in these studies consistently failed to give the correct answer compared to non-Autistic children and to children with Down Syndrome; this indicated that the Theory of Mind deficit that Autistic children possessed was not correlated with a difference in intelligence.

Theory of Mind was originally thought to only emerge after the age of three in typically developing children. This was based on studies that required a high level of verbal comprehension (Wimmer and Perner 1983; Baron-Cohen et al. 1985; 1986; Onishi and Baillargeon 2005). When the verbal component of the test was removed, Theory of Mind capabilities could be tested for in children as young as 15 months, and the precursors to Theory of Mind in as young as neonatal infants. The Theory of Mind likely originates from the innate ability of infants to imitate expressions of their caregivers and the caregivers imitating it back in a kind of *imitation game.* Accounts from caregivers and from clinicians tell us that Autistic infants engage less in this behaviour and may be less inclined to enjoy it from a young age. If Autistic children as less inclined to engage in imitation games, there is less opportunity to develop the "like me" response (Meltzoff 1985; 2002), and thus to an Autistic child an adult making a face at them expecting a response may be no different from anything else moving in front of them. Thus, the Autistic children lack the innate social cognition of Theory of Mind.

Further studies showed that Autistic children also tended to possess deficits in executive functioning. Executive Functioning refers to a set of abilities such as working memory, problem solving, impulse control, situational flexibility, anticipation, and future planning. These abilities combine to allow a person to adapt to varying situations and to navigate a changing world effectively. In addition to the social deficits, Autistic children often possess rigid and inflexible behavioural routines. Executive functioning allows us to pull from working memory and to hold multiple competing views about the world within our own heads: this process is the hallmark of Theory of Mind. Executive functioning is a core aspect of Theory of Mind that deals with the representation of mental states separate from one's own within our minds. Executive functioning allows children to hold conflicting views within their minds and thus, provides the mechanism to resist the natural tendency of young children to reference what they know to be true when the person-in-question's beliefs conflict with reality. Executive functioning is what allows the child to inhibit the automatic assumption that beliefs must match reality (Carlson and Moses 2001). This aids in representational Theory of Mind reasoning but not in other aspects concerning Theory of Mind. Within the brain, executive functioning takes place in the Prefrontal cortex (the outer frontal part of the brain). People who possess Prefrontal damage often possess poor executive functioning abilities. Prefrontal impairment is also linked to social isolation, decreased affirmative behaviour, impaired social communication, and a lack of appreciation for social rules; these are also traits that many Autistic children possess (Baron-Cohen et al. 1985; 1986; Carlson and Moses 2001). These characteristics show that the Theory of Mind is connected to executive functioning. Thus, Theory of Mind deficits encountered in Autism may be a result of poor executive functioning and poor communication between different parts of the brain which would normally allow children to hold multiple representations of the same outcome within their minds. It is important to differentiate that Autistic people do not outright lack a Theory of Mind, but that they may lack certain innate building blocks that lead to the expression of the intuitive rather than a conscious Theory of Mind.

Moving onto the brain as an organ composed of multiple parts, the Temporal-Parietal Junction is thought to be the center for Theory of Mind processing; particularly, the part of the Parietal lobe which contains mirror neurons. The mirror neurons are what help us to generate the same feeling when we see someone performing a task or a behaviour which the person in question has already performed, thus, connecting our experiences with the person outside of ourselves. If information within that region is not activated as strongly or under different circumstances, then the person in question may perceive the feelings of others differently and thus, may have difficulty generating the empathy required to make those "like me" connections. But the difference does not only lie in the ability to activate in response to key information but for that information to travel to different parts of the brain, be processed by different areas and ultimately be made sense of in a meaningful way. Within the brain of the Autistic person lies increased structural connectivity but decreased functional connectivity; this means that the connections are present, but the information is not going to the places one would normally expect it to go or it is not going there as fast as it needs to process the information in a reasonable time frame. Like trying to connect a circuit with a material that conducts electricity poorly or not at all; the connection is structurally there, but may not be functionally useful. For Theory of Mind information to be processed, it must be received by the mirror neurons in the Prefrontal cortex and then information is later relayed to other parts of the brain. Autism is the outcome of these connections either not being present (lack of functional connections) or the connections linking to other places; this leads to different outcomes in information processing. As a result, the brain may simply be putting a stronger weight on certain kinds of information; information which can be processed and retained using short-length adjacent connections rather than long-range inter-hemispheric connections that may be harder for the brain to create. In addition, increased randomness may lead to information that the non-Autistic may think of as irrelevant remaining present in the brain for a longer time or may create short term meaningful connections that do not last.

The Autistic brain develops along a different trajectory; but different does not mean less—Albert Einstein's brain was 15% larger than average and he did not speak until three years of age. Throughout research into this topic many of the studies used words like "healthy individual" to describe non-Autistic people in comparison to Autistic people (Vissers et al 2011), or framing Autism as a pathology when the brain simply developed a little differently. Ameis et al. (2010) refer to effects of Autism an insult on the neurotypical brain. Living in a world where most people are not Autistic does lead to many characteristics of the Autistic brain being seen as deficits, perhaps we should look more at some of the strengths of the Autistic brain rather than viewing it only from the non-Autistic lens. Venturing further, takes us deeper into the work of Simon Baron-Cohen and the concept of different kinds of minds.

Chapter 2

The Systemizing Brain

In the previous chapter, we addressed the concept of the Theory of Mind and why Autistic people seem to possess social deficits. This addressed one of the main diagnostic characteristics of Autism Spectrum Disorders: deficits in reciprocal interaction and communication. However, it does not fully address the other prominent aspects of the Autism Spectrum, particularly repetitive and restrictive behaviours, and interests. In addition, it does not address the strong gifts that Autistic people at times seem to have in relation to the physical world, in the presumed absence of their relationship to the social world. Where there are deficits, there are great strengths. Autism is often a balancing act that is played by a group of people who are wired for a different world. What does this world look like? How are these people's brains wired differently? And can this difference properly explain both the strengths and the weaknesses of Autism? To explore the balance of deficits and gifts which Autism brings, we need to explore further the kind of brain that Autism produces, as well as the kind of brain that we consider *normal*. Autism may be thought of as one extreme, but are there others? Is Autism more a difference than a disability?

To begin, we will first look at different ways of thinking and relating to the world around us. We shall look at Simon Baron-Cohen's work on systemizing and empathizing as different ways of thinking and coming to conclusions. By contrasting these two approaches we will see how brains can be wired for either systemizing or empathizing. Systemizing and empathizing are both situation dependent and different problems may require a different school of thought. From there, we may be able to better understand the kinds of environments in which being Autistic may be beneficial rather than a deficit, as well as where the brain of the average person may not fare as well. Is Autism the expression of one extreme brain type (Baron-Cohen 2006; 2009)? If so, then what does the other side of the extreme look like? We shall start by defining two key terms.

Empathizing vs. Systemizing

In the previous chapter, we spoke about what it means to empathize with others, and how the brain empathizes to connect with other people as agents who are similar to ourselves and who experience the same emotions as we do. To begin here we start by defining the ability to systematize as a contrast to the ability to empathize, and compare these two different cognitive processes as ways of viewing everyday problems, and of seeing the world.

Systemizing refers to observing how change in the input of a system changes the output of the system in a physical, lawful, cause and effect manner (Baron-Cohen et al. 2002; Baron-Cohen 2008). By observing these effects, one is able to deduce how things in lawful systems will change given a set of rules. These laws are adhered to a high percentage of the time. Systemizing is our most powerful tool for predicting change in the physical world (Baron-Cohen 2006). Systemizing refers to the detection of laws through the observation of patterns in the physical world; it allows us to search for structure in data, formulate laws governing change, and to organize objects based on their properties. An excellent example of a system would be a computer, which takes input from the user and produces output on the screen in a predictable manner.

One systemizes by collecting observations on physical phenomena around them to establish a pattern. It is through this observation which structures in the natural world are revealed to us (Baron-Cohen 2002). Think of Linnaeus and his classification system (Linnaeus 1735). By observing the physical traits of organisms, he was able to create an interconnected nested hierarchy that is still used to this day in the classification of species. The cognitive style of systemizing searches for truth, and to identify lawful and consistent patterns within data. Baron-Cohen (2002) identifies six main types of systems: technical systems, natural systems, abstract systems (mathematical), social systems, organisable systems, and motoric systems.

There are five main phases of systemizing (Baron-Cohen 2008):

1. Analysis: observing the input and output of a system

2. Operation: performing an operation on the input, which changes the output, and the change is noted

3. Repetition: repeating the same operation to test for patterns

4. Law Derivation: determining a law from the pattern of input and output.

5. Confirmation: if the law holds true for all instances, then the law is retained and integrated into general knowledge.

Using these phases, we can see how systemizing is a powerful tool for observing changes in the physical world and integrating these observations into knowledge. Systemizing is what allows us to draw new conclusions and create new knowledge regarding law-governed systems (Baron-Cohen 2008). In fact, systemizing very much mirrors the scientific method, which is used throughout the natural sciences to test hypotheses (Staddon 2017).

The Scientific method:

1. Ask questions about observations and gather information (very similar to phase 1)

2. Form a hypothesis – a tentative description of what's been observed and make predictions based on that hypothesis (phases 2-4)

3. Test hypotheses and predictions in an experiment that can be reproduced (Phase 3)

4. Analyze data and draw conclusions. Accept or reject hypothesis or modify existing hypothesis if necessary (Phases 3-5)

5. Reproduce the experiment until there are no discrepancies between observations and the theory. No reproducibility, no science (Phase 5).

By directly comparing the scientific method to systemizing, we can see why someone with a disposition towards systemizing may be more drawn to the fields of sciences. In fact, science students are more systemizing driven compared to those in the humanities and social sciences (Focquaert et al. 2007).

Systemizing is a powerful tool when there is a low degree of variance in the behaviour of the system in question (Baron-Cohen 2002; 2008). However, the higher the degree of variance in a system, the less useful a process like systemizing becomes (Baron-Cohen 2002; 2008). This is because, with a higher level of variance, repetition becomes less likely, and it becomes harder to determine a law based on the relationship between input and output. The problem with systemizing as a tool for understanding the world arises when the changes in the system in question start to be governed by a mind or an agent (Baron-Cohen 2002; 2008). Systemizing non-agentive systems is easy because the change is simple and governed by a set of laws. No one is deciding to change the laws halfway through, or on a whim. To properly understand systems with high degrees of variability or systems in which the change is governed by a mind, empathizing is often required.

Empathizing refers to the drive or ability to identify another person's emotions and thoughts, and respond to them with an appropriate emotion (Baron-Cohen 2008). Empathizing is our way of decoding social information and judging a person's mental state (Hall 1978). Empathizing allows us to predict change in agentive systems because it allows us to connect with the emotions and internal state of the agent in question and better predict the outcomes based on how they feel (Baron-Cohen 2008). Empathizing involves connecting one's mental states with that of our own to predict an appropriate outcome using the Theory of Mind (Baron-Cohen 2008). We can predict the outcomes by predicting changes in mental states. Empathizing allows us to determine intent and therefore purpose where systemizing cannot (Chakrobarti and Baron-Cohen 2006). Empathizing is what also stops people from doing things that would hurt another person's feelings, and/or from inflicting physical pain onto another person. Empathizing is what allows us to tune into someone else's world and develop moral laws about the universe. When considering the two different strategies it is easy to see where we would choose one over the other (Baron-Cohen 2008). Systemizing involves empathizing with physical non-agentive systems, while empathizing involves systemizing agentive systems. Empathy often requires the ability to let go of our own perspectives and attribute separate mental states to other people based on the signals, which they give off, and their previous knowledge (Leslie, 1987; Dennet 1987). Using empathizing as a different cognitive style, it is easy to see how people who are strong empathizers would be drawn to professions such as social work, childcare, or others where connecting with and assisting people is an asset, as opposed to understanding the physical world (Focquaert et al 2007). Our ability to empathize is what allows us to connect with other people and create relationships; similarly, our ability to systemize is what allows us to connect with and make predictions regarding an apathetic physical world (Baron-Cohen 2008).

Systemizing and empathizing are useful skills in the modern world for different situations. With most skills, people vary in their abilities to empathize and to systemize. In addition, like most skills, one may be able to become better at them through practice. Like any other skill or talent, some people are going to be naturally better talented in something and no matter how much we practice, we may never reach their level. Some people may have a natural disposition towards systemizing over empathizing, vice-versa, and some people may be relatively good at both.

Empathizing and systemizing are usually measured using a metric called the Empathizing Quotient (EQ) and the Systemizing Quotient (SQ) respectively (Baron-Cohen et al. 2003; Baron-Cohen and Wheelwright 2004). The Systemizing Quotient (Baron-Cohen et al. 2003) measures a person's tendency towards systemizing by asking questions like: do you enjoy games that involve a high degree of strategy? Or are you intrigued by the rules and patterns that govern numbers in math? These questions are meant to assess someone's affinity for figuring out the rules that govern systems. This contrasts with the EQ (Baron-Cohen and Wheelwright 2004), which asks questions like: Can you easily tell if someone wants to enter into a conversation? Or do you find it easy to put yourself in another person's shoes? These are clearly questions that assess a person's ability to read the emotions of others, and respond in ways that are comforting and engaging. Many of the questions in both the EQ and the SQ overlap, and it is the answer to the question that tells the tester one's affinity for either side. An example of an overlapping question would be: do you find it hard to know what to do in social situations? Lastly, both tests contain filler questions to distract a person from thinking solely about empathizing or systematizing, and thus rigging the results. One who knows a lot about systemizing and what people who have an affinity for systemizing like may be able to infer the correct answers to questions that gauge systemizing without being a strong systemizer themselves and vice-versa. The higher one scores on either test, the more they lean towards either empathizing or systemizing. In most cases, there is a moderately strong and significant anti-correlation between the SQ and the EQ (Goldenfeld et al. 2005; Wheelwright et al. 2006). Therefore, we can place systemizing and empathizing on a continuum with strong systemizers on one end and strong empathizers on the other based on their scores in these two tests and on their general affinity towards either of these two cognitive styles (Baron-Cohen 2002; 2003). We have essentially created three brain types: the systemizing brain, the empathizing brain, and the balanced brain (Baron-Cohen 2002; 2003). People who score higher on the EQ tend to be more agreeable and more extroverted than those with a tendency towards systemizing (Nettle 2006; 2007). EQ scores are also correlated with larger numbers of social relationships and connections (Nettle 2006; 2007). In contrast, systemizing often translates to strengths in mental rotation, pattern recognition, map navigation, and other skills that require spatial awareness and visualizing where objects are in space (Hegarthy and Waller 2004). When testing large groups of people on systemizing and empathizing using these questionnaires, the average leans towards empathizing over systemizing (Goldenfeld et al. 2005). This means that humans as a species (as far as healthy and averagely intelligent adults go) currently lean more towards empathizing as a cognitive style over systemizing (at least in 2005 and among that current sample size). For an average group of people, I would be inclined to believe that this would hold true as a population rule; however, I would imagine that this would vary greatly depending on the education level and the professions of the people tested. The ability to empathize and read people's emotions was likely selected for at higher rates in our evolutionary past over systemizing.

The first time I took the EQ test, I got a 4 out of a potential 80 with average scores being between 40 and 50 (Goldenfeld et al. 2005; different sources may use slightly different scoring techniques, but still give averages leaning slightly towards empathizing http://myframeworks.org/testmyeq/). This by no means that I am a monster, but that I simply lack the innate framework for tuning into the emotions of others. When reading people, I often follow my own path and thus, cannot not predict their actions well. It can often be hard for me to determine consistent rules in the ever-changing system of the human mind. Often the same operation yields multiple results on different people and at different times.

A key strength often associated with systemizing is mental rotation abilities (Kozhevnikov and Hegarty 2001; Hegarty and Waller 2004). This involves the ability to imagine the movement of objects separate from oneself in space (Kozhevnikov and Hegarty 2001; Hegarty and Waller 2004). Mental rotation abilities are often useful in navigating and in recognizing the relationships between inanimate objects in space. A strong association has been found between tests that depend on object based spatial transformations and those that depend on transformations of a person's spatial perception of said transformations—egocentric spatial transformations (Hegarty and Waller 2004). Preliminary evidence suggests that object rotation and self-rotation depend on different neural structures (Hegarty and Waller 2004). While object rotation relies heavily on visualizing objects in space, egocentric rotation involves a change in one's perspective of the object while keeping both the object and others around it stationary in relation to one another (Hegarty and Waller 2004). The latter is very reminiscent of perspective taking as the ability to see an object from different points of view. Egocentric rotation relies on the ability to look outside of one's self, whereas mental rotation relies on the ability to imagine changes in an object within one's own mind irrespective of other perspectives. Since these two tasks involve somewhat different skills, it makes sense that they are neurologically dis-sociable (Hegarty and Waller 2004). People who are strong in mental rotation are often weak in egocentric rotation. It is easier for them to imagine relationships between different objects in space than to imagine their own relationship to other objects in a particular environment. When rotating objects, our position is static, when imagining different perspectives, the objects are often static, and it is our viewpoint that changes. The duality of these acts bears a striking resemblance to perspective taking and Theory of Mind (Hegarty and Waller 2004). It serves to hypothesize that they are similarly derived. We would predict that people who are strong in egocentric transformations would perform better in Theory of Mind and other perspective taking tasks, over people who possess stronger abilities in spatial object rotation. Mental rotation and systemizing contrasts well with Theory of Mind concepts which is a skill associated with empathizing.

As seen in chapter 1, the Frontal lobe of the brain is responsible for problem solving, spatial judgment and reasoning. The Prefrontal cortex is the central hub for information processing. This area is responsible for most of the information processing that occurs in the brain. It stands to reason that the frontal lobe is the area of the brain primarily responsible for systemizing.

Brain Lateralization

In addition to being divided into different regions that perform different functions, the brain can also be divided into two separate brain halves laterally (also referred to as hemispheres). These two halves possess different functions, control different thought processes and movements, and communicate with each other via trans-neural connections. The lateralization of the vertebrate brain is very widespread among species and speaks to a very early evolutionary origin (Vallortigara et al. 1999; Bisazza et al. 1998), although convergent evolution may also play a role (Bradshaw and Rogers 1993). Although brain lateralization is widespread, the direction of this lateralization and dominance may vary among different biological families (Vallortigara et al. 1999). When faced with complex computational problems, it is often more efficient to segregate them into smaller subproblems that differ in typical ways, allowing the brain to complete smaller tasks, leading up to the solving of the larger problem; this is likely how regional specialization and lateralization within the brain arose (Vallortigara et al. 1999). Research concerning birds provides strong insight into these processes.

Vallortigara and colleagues' (1999) work with chicks indicates differential specialization of the two sides of the brain. Using only the left eye, chicks showed marked navigation and topographic orientation advantages over the exclusive use of the right eye (Vallortigara et al. 1999). Hens and other chicks tended to be viewed more with the right eye, suggesting an affinity for familial interactions and gregarious behaviours over novel stimuli (McKenzie et al. 1998). By isolating the eyes, it is easy to see the differential specialization of the left eye towards spatial orientation and the processing of novel stimuli, compared to the left eye (Vallortigara et al. 1999; McKenzie et al. 1998). Since optical fibres cross over to opposite sides of the brain, the right eye is controlled and relays information primarily to the left hemisphere and vice-versa (Vallortigara et al. 1999; McKenzie et al. 1998; Carter 2019). During development, the chick embryo is usually oriented within the egg such that the right eye is facing up towards the air-pocket while the left eye faces downward towards the body (Vallortigara et al. 1999; Rogers 1995). This leads to the right eye taking in more light earlier on in development compared to the left (Vallortigara et al. 1999). In the chicks, asymmetry was triggered by differential light exposure before hatching and became apparent after birth (Vallortigara et al. 1999; Deng and Rogers 1998). Chicks from eggs reared in the dark during their final days of development do not express as strongly a differential affinity for ocular stimuli (Rogers and Bolden 1991). In this condition, overall hemispheric differentiation was less greatly specialized, this indicates a developmental trigger for brain lateralization (Rogers and Bolden 1991). The developmental orientation of the embryo is likely influenced by both genetics and environmental factors *in ovo*. Vallortigara et al. (1999) show an example of how development reinforces the evolution of lateralization in a positive feedback loop which continues to influence lateralization in the vertebrate brain (Rogers and Bolden 1991). Using this as an evolutionary proxy, one can infer a rudimentary Chordate with laterally positioned eyes, viewing different parts of the field separately, evolving an inclination to different forms of stimuli over time being continuously reinforced. A strong argument can be made that brain asymmetry was already present in a common reptilian ancestor shared by birds and mammals. Even when frontally placed eyes began to evolve, it was almost impossible to revert. But what does lateralization mean for different styles of thinking? What do these two brain halves do particularly, and how do they compliment each other in the human brain?

In the human brain, functional asymmetry is well-established (Whitelson and Pallie 1973). Decisions and tasks concerning language are typically controlled by the left hemisphere (to remember we can think "left for language"), while the right hemisphere is activated during the completion of visuospatial and mental rotation tasks ("rotation for right") (Brocca 1861; Annett 1999; Homae et al. 2003; Klass et al. 2003; Proust-Lima et al. 2008). In particular, the Brocca's area in the left hemisphere along with the left Temporal-Parietal gyrus and the left Frontal gyrus were activated more strongly during language processing tasks (Klass et al. 2003). This is contrasted with the right Parietal lobe and the right Inferior frontal gyrus receiving greater blood flow (indicating activation and usage) during visuospatial tasks (Klass et al. 2003). The visuospatial tasks seemed to activate a larger area of the brain from the anterior to the posterior; whereas, the language tasks locally activated the left side of the brain (Klass et al. 2003). Activations in the left side of the brain were more centralized to posterior regions and were more concentrated (Klass et al. 2003). This asymmetry in activation is mirrored by differences in morphology; with the left hemisphere being larger in the posterior region and the right larger in the frontal regions (Bradshaw 1989). Since the visuospatial and the language tasks were presented using the same medium in Klass' work, we are better able to see the left-right divide and how the two halves work separately at the same time to process information and complete different tasks (2003). Other indicators of left-right duality can be seen in how the human brain responds to certain stimuli. The left ear is more sensitive to music and to sounds while the right ear is more sensitive to speech and verbal stimuli (Blackstock 1978). Since the ears are associated with the contra-lateral part of the brain (much like the eyes), the right side of the brain would be more sensitive to music and the left to the verbal stimuli. When listening to music, the brain is responding to rhythm, tempo, and meter, all of which can be determined through deconstructing what is heard and systemizing. On the other hand, understanding a person's speech is a facet of the Brocca's region as well as the ability to connect with a person socially, and would therefore be associated more strongly with empathizing (Brocca 1861; Annett 1999; Klass et al. 2003). The left side of the brain predominantly processes social input and the association of social rewards with input (Hobson et al 2018). One key visuospatial task that is primarily controlled by the right side of the brain is mental rotation.

Mental Rotation is a strong indicator of systemizing abilities. One must be able to imagine the object in multi-dimensional space and perform operations on it to arrive at the favourable output—or lack thereof. Can the object in question be manipulated into the target outcome by rotation or any other operation (Shepard and Cooper 1982)? Mental rotation allows us to perceive where we are in space as well as objects in relation to our mental image of them (Zacks 2008). We can likewise closely attribute language and the reading of facial expressions to empathizing as we use these tools to communicate with and connect with other people (Brocca 1861; Ogden 1997; Annett 1999; Vallortigara 1999). The mathematical simplicity of mental rotation lends itself well to systemizing and is used as a proxy to indicate a preference for systemizing by the right-side of the brain (Zacks 2008). During visuospatial tasks such as mental rotation, it is the right-brain which becomes activated over the left hemisphere (Heilman et al. 1983), particularly the right inferior Parietal lobule and the Temporal-Parietal Junction. These regions play key roles in judging angular distance and imaging in the brain (Zacks 2008). Cerebral blood flow to these regions is in fact proportional to the number of rotations (or steps) required to achieve the goal (Ratcliff 1979; Harris et al. 2000; Zacks 2008). The right-brain being more closely associated with spatial awareness and visiospatial perception is also illustrated well in observations of lesions to the right hemisphere (Karnath et al. 2001, 2004, Karnath 2009). Patients with lesions on the right side of the brains typically experience a condition called "spatial neglect" where they are unable to see certain things, or their sense of direction and ability to manipulate objects in space is impaired (Karnath et al. 2004). Particularly, people with damage to the right Temporal-Parietal regions of the brain possess deficits in spatial processing much more often than people with damage to these areas in the left side of their brains (Karnath 2009; Karnath et al. 2004; Suchan and Karnath et al 2011). Conversely, people who experienced lesions to these structures in the left side of the brain typically experience deficits in language processing (Annett 1999; Suchan and Karnath et al 2011; Becker and Karnath 2007). In cases where people do experience disorders in spatial processing and awareness due to damage to the left side of the brain, the deficits are not as severe and are likely an evolutionary relic of when our ancestors used our brains more bilaterally to navigate the world than a pure switch of brain roles (Suchan and Karnath et al. 2011). Vallortigara (1999) further describes that as human ancestors became less and less arboreal, the right side of the brain became more specialized towards tool-use, problem solving, and exploring novel stimuli in a changing environment, while the left side of the brain became more specialized towards language and connecting with other individuals. The regions of the brain highlighted in this section were the Temporal, Parietal and Occipital lobes, as well as the Frontal cortex. From the previous chapter we recognize the Temporal-Parietal regions being parts of the brain that are subject to impairments in Autism Spectrum Disorders.

The left-hemisphere becoming more activated during tasks which involve language and socialization while the right-hemisphere becoming more active during the completion of visuospatial tasks such as mental rotation and navigation, illustrates well the left-right duality as well as the systemizing-empathizing divide within the brain. Many of these regions (particularly the Temporal and Parietal regions) become bilaterally activated during either task, it is simply that one side becomes more active and therefore dominates over the other side for a given task. The disproportionate activation of each hemisphere during different tasks illustrates well the specialization of each side of the brain.

The right hemisphere and the left hemisphere create two different perceptions of the world which they both attend to differently depending on what is readily required (McGilchrist 2009). We draw on these different hemispheres to complete different tasks to survive and thrive in the environment. The two brain halves work in tandem with one another, focusing on two different aspects of the exterior world. The right brain is more focused on the novel while the left on the familiar. Only when the novel becomes more familiar can the left brain attend to it. This specialization allows for individuals to attend to what is necessary, to feed while paying attention to predators (Van Zomeren and Brouwer 1994; McGilchrist 2019). There are many tasks that would require varying degrees of both systemizing and empathizing, and would therefore require the access of information from both sides of the brain to solve problems. It is the combination of these two cognitive styles that allow us to navigate the world and form strong connections with the people around us. When I introduced the concepts of systemizing and empathizing, I described them as a spectrum from one end to the other. Some people would be strong systemizers, others would be strong empathizers, and most people would fall somewhere along the middle (but lean slightly towards empathizing). From here, it would seem logical that people who are stronger systemizers would use more of the right side of their brain over the left side of their brain. Furthermore, being exposed to different environmental and evolutionary factors, it would serve to reason that males and females would have different skill sets when it comes to empathizing and systemizing. Do men and women differ in their abilities to systemize and empathize? How does this affect their mental strengths and weaknesses? How do these strengths and weaknesses complement each other in both our evolutionary history as well as in current society? Finally, how does the duality of systemizing and empathizing play a role in Autism?

Gender Differences

Throughout evolution, males and females have been exposed to different evolutionary pressures, which in response are going to affect the different survival and adaptation strategies that each of our brains devise. This is most obvious in things such as overall body strength, but how might this play out when it comes to different dominant cognitive styles? Males tend to have a stronger affinity for systemizing while females for empathizing. When comparing the sexes: from a young age, girls on average show a strong tendency towards empathizing rather than systemizing (Baron-Cohen et al. 2005). There is a stronger tendency towards turn taking, fairness, and emotional themes in girl play compared to that of boys (Chakrabarti and Baron-Cohen 2006; Baron-Cohen and Hammer 1997). Young girls tend to be ahead of boys in TOM and are more sensitive to facial expressions (Baron-Cohen et al. 2003). Young girls score higher in social faux-pas tests than do boys (Baron-Cohen et al. 1999). Conversely, boys show a strong tendency towards systemizing rather than empathizing (Baron-Cohen et al. 2003). Young boys tend to outperform young girls in mental rotation tests (Grimshaw et al. 1995; Knickmeyer et al. 2005), embedded figures tests (Jolliffe and Baron-Cohen 1997), and in map-learning tests (Baron-Cohen 2005); which are all reliant on the ability to analyze systems. Relating this back to SQ and EQ scores, males tend to have higher SQ scores compared to population averages, while females score higher in empathizing (Baron-Cohen et al. 2003).

Many may wish to argue that sex differences are culturally enforced onto children from a young age, and that much of these differences can be accounted for by differences in socialization. Interestingly: young male vervet monkeys prefer to play with trucks while females play with dolls (Hines 2002; 2010). Female infants as young as one-day-old spend more time looking at social stimuli over mechanical or non-social stimuli compared to one-day-old male infants (Connellan et al. 2000); a similar trend is observed at twelve months of age (Lutchmaya et al. 2002). Psychological, and neurological sex differences exist, and these differences are set in motion by hormones which have been evolutionarily engineered (Haussman et al. 2017). These hormones influence neural connections both in the prenatal brain as well as throughout life (Gong et al. 2009; 2011; Bless et al. 2015; Hausmannn 2017). It may be worthwhile to consider how our current culture reinforces many of the differences that are seen between males and females, but to say that it is exclusively culture is simply ignorant; you must have a previously existing basis for culture to act upon.

A study by Connellan and Colleagues (2000) concluded that the female infants only showed a slight preference for focusing on the face of the scientist over looking at the mobile—only 56% of female infants in the study spent more time looking at the face over the mobile. The study concluded that the female infants either showed no significant preference or a slight preference for the face with a few outliers showing a strong preference for the face. The male infants, on the other hand, showed consistent preference for the mobile (2000). This may imply that the brains of female human infants (perhaps even extrapolating to other primates) are more elastic than that of males in this area.

When observing the differences in functional connectivity, females tend to exhibit greater overall latitudinal connectivity between hemispheres (Harshman et al. 1976; Kertesz et al. 1987; Kimura 1999). Women tend to have a larger, more bulbous Corpus Callosum by mass, which facilitates communication between hemispheres better than men (Kertesz et al. 1987; Kimura, 1999; Leonard et al. 2008). Men, on the other hand, tend to possess greater functional connectivity within each hemisphere and between intra-hemispheric regions (Tomasi and Volkov 2012). The amount of connective tissue in the brain is positively correlated with the SQ scores in males and with the EQ in females (Chou et al. 2011). In males, connective tissue is typically concentrated in the medial prefrontal cortex and spread longitudinally within hemispheres, rather than concentrated laterally and within the Corpus Callosum facilitating interhemispheric processes. More connective tissue spread longitudinally leads to faster and more connections from one end of the brain to the frontal regions, which are responsible for analytical thinking and problem solving, rather than the social parts of the brain (Chou et al. 2011; Lai et al. 2012). These interhemispheric connections also tend to be shorter (Tomasi and Volkov 2012). In females, fewer nodes possess numerous connections compared to males (Tomasi and Volkov 2012). Fewer points with many connections tend to increase the processing efficiency during latitudinal cognitive processes (Tomasi and Volkov 2012). This increased efficiency and latitudinal connectivity may reflect why women tend to excel in areas that require the synchronization of multiple areas of the brain from different hemispheres such as language and verbal processing (Nettle 2007; Gong et al. 2009). In comparison, the lower latitudinal connectivity in males may reflect specialization and optimization of cognitive functions towards certain areas such as spatial reasoning (McEwen 2001) in men.

Fetal testosterone levels are related to the development of behaviour and cognition and may be involved in shaping sex differences in the brain (Kimura 1999; Hines 2004). Auyeng and colleagues (2006) conducted a study measuring fetal testosterone levels in expectant mothers via amniocentesis. The study showed a positive association between prenatal testosterone levels and SQ scores of the children at 6-9 years of age. Fetal testosterone levels were a stronger indicator of systemizing tendencies than the child's sex alone (Auyeung et al. 2006). Fetal testosterone levels are linked to narrow interests, the Systemizing Quotient, and the hidden figures test (Lutchmaya et al. 2002). The amount of time that a child maintains eye contact is inversely correlated with the amount of fetal testosterone (Lutchmaya et al. 2002). Girls with Congenital Adrenal Hyperplasia (a genetic condition which causes increased androgen production beginning prenatally (New 1988)) exhibit male-typical interests and possess enhanced spatial orientation skills (Hampson et al. 1998; Hines et al. 2003). Studies indicated that these were not due to parental influences (Nordenstrom et al. 2002; Pasterski et al. 2005). Increased levels of progesterone and estradiol during development tended to cause increased inter-hemispheric connectivity and decreased lateralization of thought processes (Hausmannn and Gunturkun 2000; Hausmannn et at. 2002). These relations are most clearly laid out at times throughout adult female hormonal cycles when progesterone levels are high compared to other instances (Smith et al. 1987a; b; Arnold 2009; Hausmann and Gunturkun 2000). Furthermore, the presence of testosterone caused decreased interhemispheric connectivity and a tendency towards right-brain dominance in development (Bayer and Hausmann 2010; Beking et al. 2018). Exposure to Estrogen increases left to right hemispheric connectivity (Filippova 1996) and increases left-hemisphere activation for language and reading tasks in development (Smith et al. 1987a; b). The role of progesterone and estradiol may explain why women tend to exhibit higher activation of both hemispheres during tasks compared to men (Hausmann 2017). Using these hormones as a primer, we can clearly see why men are more likely to exhibit right-brain dominance and decreased interhemispheric connectivity while women exhibit left-brain dominance along with greater interhemispheric connectivity (although the dominance is to the same degree as seen in men). With these hormones being higher in their corresponding sexes on a population level, sex differences in functional cerebral asymmetry and connectivity are small but reliably significant (Hiscock et al. 2001). These differences would also explain cases where females exhibit male-typical strengths and interests due to increased testosterone in cases of CAH, and why castrated males often are often more nurturing and have stronger verbal skills—traits more in line with females (Hines 2010). The differences in hormonal levels combined with their effects on the human brain may also suggest that the female brain is more plastic than the male brain. The increased connectivity and decreased lateralization allow the brain to pull information and processing strategies from different regions when approaching complex cognitive tasks.

The dichotomy of male and female differences lies not in the absolute gender, but in the hormones and environmental factors that program sex and gender expression. Increased presence of testosterone increases right-brain connectivity and activation, which leads to stronger systemizing abilities; whereas, estrogen activates the left side of the brain. Using sex hormones as proxies, we are better able to see the link between sex, behaviour, cognitive processes, and cognitive strengths. If hormone levels are strong indicators of left-brain and right brain-dominance, do the effects of hormones play a role in Autism? Can Autistic traits be explained using the systemizing-empathizing dichotomy? What does brain lateralization look like in the Autistic brain?

Autism and Atypical Brain Lateralization

Autism is marked by atypical brain growth and an increased abundance of longitudinal structural connectivity over functional connectivity. The Autistic brain tends to contain a greater abundance of short-range connections and a greater abundance of connections overall. An increased prevalence of longitudinal connectivity combined with a smaller Corpus Callosum predicts decreased interhemispheric communication. Thus, we expect to see a decrease in lateralization of the two brain halves, wherein there is greater activation in both sides of the brain and each side working more independently. Further, because short-range connections are more typical of the right-brain, we would expect a strong disposition towards thinking and processing strategies typically associated with the right-brain in response to stimuli. A smaller Corpus Callosum and decreased interhemispheric connectivity is typically observed in males over females. This has led to the view that Autism is a case of exaggerated male-typical features within the brain (Baron-Cohen et al. 2008). Autism's deficits in communication and language have led neuropsychological research to primarily focus on the left hemisphere as the site of neurobiological disruption (Rinehart et al. 2002). However, this is a very normative approach that focuses mainly on the difficulties presented in Autism rather than its strengths. Many of the strengths associated with ASD include skills in spatial processing, attention to detail, intuitive physics, and intuitive mathematics (Shah and Frith 1993; Binnie and Williams 2003; Iuculano and Kadosh 2013; Muth et al. 2014). Both these strengths and difficulties can be attributed to a difference in brain lateralization and connectivity within the brain that begins very early in development and is something innate to Autism.

A greater number of longitudinal connections, more short-range connections, and fewer inter-hemisphere connections characterize the Autistic brain (Beorsma et al. 2013). Fewer inter-hemisphere connections (further magnified by a smaller Corpus Callosum) mean that each side does not communicate with one another as much, and each side must do more work to complete the same task as a brain that would have those inter-hemispheric connections available (Beorsma et al. 2013). This leads to each side doing everything separately to arrive at the same conclusions, requiring more brain power.

Abnormal functional lateralization in the Frontal and Temporal regions of the brain has been consistently observed in Autism (Eyler et al. 2012). Eyler et al. (2012) observed increased activation in the right hemisphere and decreased activation in the left, compared to non-Autistic controls. Since the left hemisphere is typically more responsible for the processing of social information and rewards, this may help to explain some of the socialization difficulties in Autism (Hobson et al 2018). Eyler et al. (2012) observed a greater activation of the right hemisphere in response to language sounds during natural sleep via functional MRI scans. Areas that typically respond to speech stimuli like the left superior Temporal gyrus are less responsive in Autism; while areas that are not normally associated with speech become more active—as in the middle occipital gyrus (Eyler et al. 2012). This shows a marked difference in the way the Autistic brain processes language compared to that of the non-Autistic. Neilson et al. (2014) showed decreased lateralization with hemispheres working more independently compared to the typically developing controls during fMRI scans. The majority of these differences existed in the connections that typically involved left lateralized networks; particularly a decrease in activation of the Broca's and Wernicke's areas in response to language stimuli (Neilson et al. 2014); these areas of the brain are also notably smaller and comprised of less grey matter in Autism compared to typically developing controls (Knaus et al. 2010). Instead, there is increased activation of the right Inferior Frontal gyrus in response to language tasks in Autism (Neilson et al. 2014), which is larger in people with ASD (Herbert et al. 2002; De Fosse et al. 2004). The major white matter tract governing language is larger in the right hemisphere in ASD compared to the control population, wherein it is larger on the left (Kumar et al. 2010). Apart from language deficits in Autism, weakened left-brain responses can be seen in a general neglect for visual-stimuli presented in the right-hemispace compared to the left (Rineheart et al. 2002). Other indications of differences in lateralization include right ear preference for speech processing (Prior and Bradshaw 1979), increased prevalence of left-handedness in the Autistic population (Escalante-Mead et al. 2003), and reversed cortical asymmetry in response to language stimuli (Escalante-Mead et al. 2003). This difference is present from very early; infants and toddlers 12 to 36 months who were either diagnosed with Autism or pegged for early signs showed increased activation of the right side of the brain over the left during exposure to language stimuli during natural sleep in an MRI scanner (Cardinale et al. 2013). Areas of increased rightward activation included the auditory and visual cortices (Cardinale et al. 2013). Studies like these indicate that there is a decreased response from the left side of the brain to language stimuli and an increased response from the right. Different laterality patterns appear to be more pronounced in individuals with impaired language development early in life (Escalante-Mead et al. 2003); these differences decrease with age (Eyler et al. 2012). This decrease in the overall response from the left hemisphere to social and language stimuli may be the catalyst for the difficulties Autistic people experience in the areas of social behaviour and social language comprehension especially in youth and early life. The response of the right side of the brain to language stimuli over the left may indicate a form of compensation due to decreased specialization of the left hemisphere (Eyler et al. 2012; Bishop 2013).

The right-brain is typically responsible for the response to and processing of physical and visuospatial information. It also plays a dominant role in the understanding of rules-based systems. Autistic people are often known to have superior visuospatial skills (Shah and Frith 1993; Lee et al. 2007). Autistic people tend to possess enhanced processing capacity for inner detail rather than a global processing style (Shah and Frith 1993; Happé and Frith 2006). These strengths often lead Autistic adults to pursue careers in the sciences (Greenberg et al. 2018). But where do these strengths come from; the answer seems to lie in how the Autistic brain processes mathematics. Iuculano and Kadosh (2013) set out to study if there was a difference in the way Autistic individuals processed and hence solved mathematical problems. He had them, along with IQ and age-matched controls complete a series of math problems while observing neuro-responses via fMRI scans. The Autistic group tended to score higher in basic numerical and arithmetic skills (2013). When solving simple math-problems, Autistic children used the decomposition method to arrive at answers more quickly compared to controls (Iuculano and Kadosh 2013). Decomposition is a more sophisticated strategy that breaks down equations into easier to solve components as opposed to counting or going through slow arithmetic steps. From an adult perspective a six-year-old recognizing that $4 + 2$ is the same as $4 + 1 + 1 = 6$ might not seem like a big deal or it might seem like an unnecessary step, and that it makes things longer. This kind of thinking helps prime children for more complex math problems later. Rather than trying to work out 99×5 on paper, we can easily see that it is $500 - 5 = 495$; 43×3 is equivalent to $(40 \times 3) + (3 \times 3) = 129$, as opposed to performing long-form multiplication. This is the skill that becomes more easily apparent to children who understand decomposition early (2013). In addition to the different approaches, there was a difference in activation patterns in the subregions of the prefrontal cortex that correspond to mathematical problem solving (Iuculano and Kadosh 2013). The fMRI scan showed increased blood-oxygen level demand (BOLD) in the prefrontal, posterior-Parietal, and the ventral-Temporal cortices (Iuculano and Kadosh 2013). The scans particularly showed a greater engagement of the posterior parts of the brain which is also supported by: Baron-Cohen and Belmonte (2005), Samson et al. (2012), and Souilers et al. (2009). During the solving of math problems there was a greater overall activation of brain regions and increased activation in both hemispheres compared to controls (Iuculano and Kadosh 2013). Areas of interest included the hippocampus and the occipital regions associated with visual processing. These are areas associated with visual processing and memory recall. We also see similar patterns of brain activation in mathematically gifted children and adolescents during mathematical and fluid reasoning tasks (O'Boyle et al. 2005; Desco et al. 2010). Studies like this show that a larger portion of the brain is engaged during mathematical reasoning tasks in Autistic youth. By accessing a larger part of the brain and by using both the left and right side to recall information and complete these kinds of tasks—studies like this may show us—the Autistic brain may be better equipped at processing different kinds of information compared to the non-Autistic brain. This may seem irrelevant in a highly computerized world with calculators constantly at our fingertips, the key is, it shows an increased understanding of number theory and mathematical sense from a young age.

With the Autistic brain processing spatial and physical information about the world using the left side of the brain more, areas of the brain that are associated with the processing of language would be utilized for other tasks. This would allow for more intuitive and faster processing of information, like how the left hemisphere processes language (Annett 1999; Klass et al. 2003). With the left and right hemispheres working bilaterally to solve these kinds of problems, the brain uses a larger area to solve these problems faster and in different (novel) ways. Conversely when it comes to language and social problems, the Autistic brain seems to rely more heavily on the right-hemisphere, leading to social problems (2003). The Autistic brain may be trying to over-analyze and breakdown language and social information into a set of rules that are easily recalled. Unfortunately, we cannot always extract simple rules that we can readily recall out of the social world like we can from science, math and the physical world. Autistic people tend to score higher on the SQ and much lower on the EQ compared to the wider population (Baron-Cohen et al. 2003; Wheelright et al 2006; Greenberg et al. 2018). Furthermore, tests such as the SQ are often used as indicators of Autism and Autistic traits (Baron-Cohen et al. 2001;

Wheelwright et al. 2006). This is where Baron-Cohen's concept of the systemizing brain and Autism comes in (Baron-Cohen 2008; Baron-Cohen et al. 2006; 2008; 2009; 2010). A higher proportion of mathematicians are on the Autism Spectrum (Greenberg et al, 2018). People on the Autism Spectrum are often more inclined to pursue careers in sciences, technology, engineering, and mathematics (STEM) over the general population—whether they are successful in these careers may be up to other factors beyond raw talent and interests in these areas (2018).

Understanding the Autistic brain and how it learns and processes information can inform experts in how to better help Autistic people. Breaking down language and social information into easily remembered and applied rules can help Autistic people gain social skills and form relationships with their peers (Ozonff and Miller 1995; Golan and Baron-Cohen 2006). By being able to better predict people's thoughts and emotions in certain situations, Autistic people may be able to learn Theory of Mind skills (Golan and Baron-Cohen 2006). Rather than right-brain or left-brain dominance, it may be easier to describe the Autistic brain as two right brains, or dancing with two right feet! If Autism represents a strong tendency towards right-brain thinking styles, leading to difficulties in communication and empathizing, then what would someone on the opposite side of the extreme look like?

Before I move on, I want to make it clear that I do not mean to infer that ALL Autistic people are very strong in mathematics and the sciences, nor that they are all innately classically intelligent despite their social difficulties. I am merely speaking to trends and differences in ways of navigating the world. People come in all shapes and sizes and often require different kinds of support systems to achieve their goals. Autistic people may also be strong in areas of music and art, areas that are often not associated with the classical sciences but still involve an understanding of rules-based predictable systems. Furthermore, I am not advocating that all girls are bad at science and math, and that all boys are competition driven apathetic bullies; these are population level tendencies that are fuelled by evolution and culture. Each individual should be free to explore whatever interests and goals they are inclined to and should be provided with the resources to do so in educational settings and elsewhere. I was particularly strong at math and sciences as a child and found an interest in it as a career in later years, but only because I had the right supports.

Autistic people representing the far end of the systemizing brain may account for the skewed gender ratios observed in Autism Spectrum Disorders (Whiteley et al. 2010) that have been observed since the time of Kanner and Asperger (Silberman 2015). On other hand, our perceptions of Autism may have led us to overlooking Autism in females in a self-fulfilling prophecy. It may also be fair to consider how our cultural perceptions of systemizing may influence how we classify men and women into systemizers and empathizers. Women may be more inclined to be systemizers than we think. They may simply express this in different ways that we may not normally think of. The over-diligent mother scheduling every event and business meeting down to the second; she is eager to help her children and to facilitate her coworkers, but also to keep a routine and bring control to chaos. Systemizing could also manifest in the fashionista with the perfectly organized shoe closet. The drive to systemize comes in all shapes and sizes. It may be that hormones and hormone levels at particular times are a key determinant over absolute sex (and hormones correlate with sex, making sex a good proxy rather than the real correlate). As more and more Autistic females come out of the woodwork, our perceptions of Autism will continue to change (Marshall 2014; Hendrickx 2015).

Putting Autism Together

Given the framework that I have laid out, Autism seems to lie at the intersection between a deficit in the Theory of Mind, and tendency towards systemizing as opposed to empathizing. The Autistic brain exhibits right-centric wiring, decreased asymmetry, increased density of short-range connections and a relative insensitivity towards the personal and Theory of Mind-related stimuli--normally processed by the area in the brain known as the Temporal-Parietal Junction. These innate characteristics are what create the baseline Autistic phenotype. It is a system-thinking, analyzing brain living in an intuitive, social, and emotional world that in many ways was not built for it. The average person does not require a scientific mind to complete their job, get groceries, socialize with their friends, or talk to a person on the street. Rather the average person will use systemizing at very specific times and call upon that part of their brain to complete specific tasks. For the Autistic person, their null state is to systemize. This drive to systemize leads to rigidity in thought and an aversion to change, particularly change that disrupts the system in an unpredicted way. The social brain is more able to handle change because emotions and ideas change all the time in very fluid ways that can not as easily be analyzed.

We can see this in the classic playing methods of young Autistic children. Spinning the wheels on a truck, lining up toys in a long row, and their hypersensitivity to change in their world (DSM-V). This is often juxtaposed to the ways we typically see kids playing with toys. Trucks are supposed to be scooted along the floor, not picked up and examined. But it is the examination that shows us that they see the world in a different way. Playing like this helps to reinforce their skill sets within their world.

Autism is more than the tendency to systemize. It is a brain programmed to systemize, rather than to let information fall into place intuitively. People on the Autism Spectrum often have difficulty processing external sensory information (Dunn et al, 2002; Baraneck 2002). This is their brain trying to process the entirety of incoming information and not knowing what parts to filter out. It can often be exhausting to try to integrate all the information and sensation coming at them at any given time (Prince-Hughes ed., 2002). They often become overwhelmed by this chaotic and incoherent world. This often leads to meltdowns, episodes of aggression, and withdrawal in both children and adults (Myles 2003; Myles and Southwick 2005).

Parents may ask, "how can I change my child so that they are more social, more engaged in this world?" "How do I make my kid more normal?" I would say, "you are asking the wrong questions." Rather than force your child into a certain mindset, we can use the strengths of their mindset to help them (Baron-Cohen 2008; Baron-Cohen et al. 2009). The question ought to be, "How can I help my child to better navigate a world that they often seem inadequate in?" The simple answer is to use their strengths to teach them these skills. The difficulties in Autism can often be explained by the incoherence, fragmentation, and uncertainty of the social world coupled with a passion for predictable systems to organize input, and make sense of a world that is in desperate need of structuring (Belmonte 2008). Thus, we need to give them a system in which predicts social interaction comes more easily (input + operation = output). Teach them, "When you say something like that, people may react in this way. If you feel this way when someone is mean to you, chances are someone feels that way when you say something like that to them; even if you did not mean it and you cannot see it. If you would go back and look for the cookie in the wrong place because you did not see someone else move it, then maybe that is why that other child did that too." If we teach them to understand Theory of Mind and more intuitive concepts by using the part of the brain that is more available and more intuitive to Autistic people, they will be better able to learn and adapt to this world. A person who can memorize bus schedules, periodic tables, and understand science in a way to predict how the ball is going to fall, can absolutely be taught to memorize social cues, understand perspectives, and predict the social world around them. They may just need more time to process things in their own way. Giving an Autistic person structure and a method in which they are able to predict things is very beneficial, as if you are giving them the system (Ochs et al 2004) they require. When we apply science to people who are not as "good at science" using metaphor to connect it to something in their personal life, they understand the concepts better. They start to see things differently, they take the time to care about things, and they are better able to learn these concepts. Autistic people may need more brain power to learn something foreign to them in a way that makes sense to them. It is also helpful if we provide people on the Autism Spectrum different ways to communicate that may be better for them. This way they are not constrained by the medium of learning and are better able to focus on the task at hand.

The Extreme Empathizing Brain, Characterizing Allism

William's Syndrome (WMS) refers to a genetic condition that is caused by the deletion of a group of genes, mostly on the lower portion of the seventh chromosome (Korenberg et al. 1996; 2000; Ewart et al.1993). Most people with this condition are missing one copy of 20-30 genes from one of the two chromosomes. This condition carries with it heart and circulatory complications, moderate intellectual disability, unique facial characteristic, and a hypersocial disposition (Karmiloff-Smith et al. 1998). People with this condition are often reported to be overly friendly, and having a heightened vocabulary relative to overall IQ (Bellugi et al. 1994). Words used to describe the personality of people with William's Syndrome are loquacious, empathetic, and charismatic (Bellugi et al. 1994). They tend to have a knack for narrative and often seek to strike up conversations with complete strangers (Jones et al. 2000). They have a reduced fear of strangers, and tend to report people as being more friendly based on faces compared to the wider population (Jones et al. 2000). People with William's Syndrome often show an increased tendency to react empathetic towards others (Tager-Flusberg and Sullivan 2000). They tend to perform well on Theory of Mind Tests compared to Autistic children of the same mental age (Karmiloff-Smith et al. 1995). In addition, people with this condition tend to have poor spatial and number skills (Farran and Jarrold 2003). They perform poorly on tests that people on the Autism Spectrum tend to excel in, like the Block-Design test (Bihrle et al. 1989; Bihrle 1990; Bellugi et al. 1994). Their hypersocial nature in combination with their relatively preserved social abilities compared to overall intelligence is on the surface a direct contrast to the communication abilities of people on the Autism Spectrum (Jones et al. 2000; Brock et al. 2008).

When we delve deeper, people with William's Syndrome do have Theory of Mind deficits. Only 24-29% of 4-9-year-olds with the condition pass standard TOM tests (Tager-Flusberg and Sullivan 2000); however, this may be more a result of delayed cognitive abilities rather than true mentalization deficits. Similar to ASD, children with WMS exhibit issues with joint-attention exercises (Laing et al. 2002). Children on the Autism Spectrum fail joint attention tasks because they are unable to follow the gaze of the person and are instead more focused on objects (Swettenham et al. 1998; Laing et al. 2002). They often do not respond to adult pointing gestures (Mervis and Bertrand 1997). On the other hand, children with William's Syndrome are often too focused on the eyes of the caregiver to realize where they are pointing (Laing et al. 2002). The subjects in question found the objects far less interesting than the faces (Mervis and Bertrand 1997). People with WMS may use social behaviours as a means to deflect from activities that may be difficult for them. This contrasts starkly to experiences I (as well as other children on the spectrum) have had growing up where I would engage in cognitive activities or lone-play rather than engage socially with other children to distract myself from social deficits. When engaging with peers and adults I would often show off my higher-than average math skills, my knowledge of animals or whatever I learned in class that day, rather than engage the other person in a back-and-forth conversation. Conversational speech of Williams Syndrome is often parasitic on other participants (Stojanovik et al. 2001; 2006), meaning that they rely much on what other people have to contribute to a conversation rather than speaking about themselves or their interests (Stojanovik et al. 2001; 2006). This is in contrast to how people on the Autism Spectrum are often described to participate in conversations. People on the Autism Spectrum are often described as dominating dialogue with topics of special interest to the expense and exclusion of other participants (Baron-Cohen 2008; DSM-V 2013).

Differences like these perfectly demonstrate the juxtaposition of Autism Spectrum Disorder and William's Syndrome: An asocial, thing-centric condition; as opposed to a hypersocial, person-centric condition respectively. The two conditions are even more intertwined when you consider that many of the genes that are affected in Autism are on the seventh chromosome either in or near the region that is missing in William's Syndrome (Badner and Gershon 2002). The friendly hypersocial nature of people with William's Syndrome has even led some to speculate that it is a form of hyper-self-domestication (Niego and Benitez-Burraco 2019). This hypothesis is made more convincing by the fact that many of the genes that are hemizygous in WMS also play a role in the domestication process for non-human animals (Niego and Benitez-Burraco 2019). Would this make Autism an example of anti-self-domestication syndrome? It may be better to compare WMS to Kanner's older (perhaps outdated), much narrower, definition of Autism (Silberman 2015). When we look at the wider continuum of Autism where we have people that range from non-verbal and severely affected, to those with high verbal acuity and intelligence, the specific affectation of William's Syndrome does not seem to cut it as its true opposite. To properly categorize such a condition let's return to the current definition of Autism Spectrum Disorder as described in the DSM V.

Etymologically, Autism refers to the self, which comes from the asocial, object-centric, and inward behaviours that Kanner and Asperger first described in their patients (1943; 1944; Silberman 2015). Therefore, when we think of a foil to Autism we would think of people who are hyper-social, people focused, able to hold conversations, and have a strong Theory of Mind. This condition would not necessarily come with cognitive delays; however, these people would likely experience relative challenges in mathematics and spatial problem solving. They may pay more attention to people and would therefore pay less attention to objects being described. They would also likely miss smaller minute details at the cost of seeing the bigger picture. Yes, to Autistic people this may sound like the average person. To make this comparison, we will breakdown and create a foil to each of the criteria in the DSM-V.

Autism Spectrum Disorder 2.99 DSM V (2013)

> A. *Persistent deficits in social communication and social interaction across multiple contexts, as manifested by the following, currently or by history (examples are illustrative, not exhaustive, see text):*
>
> > 1. *Deficits in social-emotional reciprocity, ranging, for example, from abnormal social approach and failure of normal back-and-forth conversation; to reduced sharing of interests, emotions, or affect; to failure to initiate or respond to social interactions.*
> >
> > 2. *Deficits in nonverbal communicative behaviors used for social interaction, ranging, for example, from poorly integrated verbal and nonverbal communication; to abnormalities in eye contact and body language or deficits in understanding and use of gestures; to a total lack of facial expressions and nonverbal communication.*
> >
> > 3. *Deficits in developing, maintaining, and understanding relationships, ranging, for example, from difficulties adjusting behavior to suit   various social contexts; to difficulties in sharing in imaginative play, or in making friends; to the absence of interest in peers.*
>
> A. Over emphasis on social relationships based on trivialities rather than shared interests. A strong need for social interaction which expresses itself as an inability to fully appreciate the minute details of conversations or to continue to delve into a single and unique topic.

1. When it comes to deficits in social approach, we may see an over-emphasis on the interests of others such that conversations are often driven by them, but they participate little in questions posed to them. Those affected may seem completely disinterested in subjects that they do not understand and stray away from engagement in topics that involve a deep understanding of the physical world. They may instead prefer to converse solely about superficial topics that do not require higher levels of thought or consideration of details that would lead up to a big picture. This often leads to the missing of smaller integral details in favour of seeing the larger picture. Often does not pick up on, and lacks a fascination with patterns in nature.

2. Makes strong eye contact such that they have little to no interest in the non-social information of conversations. Individuals often become fixated on the face. Individuals often hold their gaze on the face for longer than one would expect. As a consequence, they would have difficulty in pointing and gaze-following exercises.

3. Deficits in understanding the physical properties of objects or the world. May become fixated in a world of imagination well into adulthood. Expresses difficulties in sharing interests in physical concepts or numbers. Tends to change subjects when discussing things that are outside of their current understanding in favour of easier to grasp topics (the person who says "math is hard," or "I can't possibly figure this out," rather than trying to solve problems.

4. An over emphasis on the general meanings of sentences rather than focusing on the etymology of words and what each word actually means. Relying strictly on context rather than on the literal meaning of words or phrases.

B. *Restricted, repetitive patterns of behaviour, interests, or activities, as manifested by at least two of the following, currently or by history (examples are illustrative, not exhaustive; see text):*

1. *Stereotyped or repetitive motor movements, and use of objects, or speech (e.g.: simple motor stereotypes, lining up toys or flipping objects, echolalia, idiosyncratic phrases).*

2. *Insistence on sameness, inflexible adherence to routines, or ritualized patterns, or nonverbal behavior (e.g., extreme distress at small changes, difficulties with transitions, rigid thinking patterns, greeting rituals, need to take the same route, or eat the same food every day).*

3. *Highly restricted, fixated interests that are abnormal in intensity or focus (e.g, strong attachment to or preoccupation with unusual objects, excessively circumscribed or perseverative interest).*

4. *Hyper or hypo-reactivity to sensory input, or unusual interests in sensory aspects of the environment (e.g., apparent indifference to pain/temperature, adverse response to specific sounds or textures, excessive smelling or touching of objects, visual fascination with lights or movement).*

B. Lack of repetitive patterns of behaviour. Wide range of interests such that it is hard for the individual to focus on one specific area of interest.

1. A lack of interest in pattern-seeking and a confusion when witnessing pattern seeking by others. May view the seeking of patterns as strange or disruptive to social topics of interest.

2. An extreme over-focus on the emotions and problems of others to the point of extreme interest or obsession, rather than having an interest in non-social, nonhuman subjects. An over concern with social rules and social norms.

3. Interests in others interfere with ability to understand the inner-workings of the physical world. Often leading to an over-focus on agency rather than process. A preoccupation with agency in the absence of it. They may create agents to explain phenomena that can be explained by non-agentive physical processes.

Paranoia that someone is constantly watching and/or influencing them.

4. A reliance on authority or popular opinion to form beliefs and perspectives.

5. Under-sensitivity to sensory aspects of the environment, and an over-sensitivity to the emotions and behaviours of other people. An exaggerated requirement to normalize certain behaviours and deem behaviours that fall out of that norm as disturbances that interfere with the ability to operate within set social parameters.

C. Symptoms must be present in the early developmental period (but may not become fully manifested until social demands exceed limited capacities or may be masked by learned strategies in later life).

C. Symptoms may only become present in times of stress or lack of knowledge of overarching situations. Symptoms may be masked by an outwardly social demeanor and a keen ability to pick upon and infer the emotions of others.

D. *Symptoms cause clinically significant impairment in social, occupational, or other important areas of current functioning.*

D. Symptoms cause significant impairment in a person's ability to navigate the world unassisted.

E. *These disturbances are not better explained by intellectual disability (intellectual developmental disorder) or global developmental delay. Intellectual disability and Autism Spectrum Disorder frequently co-occur. To make comorbid diagnoses of Autism Spectrum Disorder and Intellectual Disability, social communication should be below that expected for general developmental level.*

E. Concerns are not better explained by Intellectual Disability or any other developmental disorder or mental illness. Intellectual disabilities may co-occur but do not fully explain all symptoms.

When we compare Autism to a hypothesized extreme of the opposite-side of the Spectrum, we begin to see where everyday individuals fall. It also allows us to better question what we mean by the term "normal." Many individuals within the *Autism Community* (Kim 2013; 2014) have coined the term *Allism* to refer to anyone who is not Autistic. As Autism is a clinical diagnosis with clearly laid out deficits and strengths; we cannot simply say that everyone who falls outside of this categorization is somehow the opposite of us. Autism being a spectrum means that most people in the greater population are going to demonstrate some traits, more some days than others, in different situations. Rather than characterize Allism as anyone who is not Autistic, we should characterize it within the current zeitgeist wherein a small fraction of the population falls on this side of the extreme with the norm being off-center towards an empathizing brain. Within this paradigm, we would expect to see differences in brain development, connectivity, and activation as we do in Autism (Karmiloff-Smith et al. 1998; Brock et al. 2008). Conversely, we can frame it in a hypothetical context wherein Autism would be much more prevalent and an off-center brain towards systemizing would be the norm. The former showcases how certain people would appear disabled within our current societal framework, while the latter hypothesizes how Autistic people view the outside world as strange and inept for them. Pathologizing the normal better helps us to define things that lie in the middle, and to better see a gradient. One can make a case for truly Allistic people who are overly social with deficits in spatial processing, and pattern recognition such that it inhibits their understanding of the physical world. Many Autistic people reject the concept of functioning or support levels (often using terms like "functioning labels) for the same reason.

What About *Severe* Autism?

The concept of the systemizing brain and increased right-ward asymmetry may seem all well and good for the *high functioning,* intellectually gifted Autistic people. *What about those other Autistic people?* Those who cannot speak, those who will never be able to live on their own, those who have difficulty with motor control, and fine motor skills? It may be all well and good that my *low functioning* child has this amazing brain, but what good is it if they type 12 words per minute, and won't sit up straight to communicate with me? Surely *these people* are different.

As a person on the Autism Spectrum and as an advocate, I really do not like terms like *Severe Autism* or *low functioning* to describe anyone. However, how can we apply the model of the systemizing brain to the type of person you may be trying to describe? In the case of motor coordination and verbal speech, many Autistic people who experience these difficulties also have conditions like dyspraxia which affects motor control and coordination (Scandurra 2012). Much of what I have discussed differentiates between what is intuitive and what is deductive to a person. The Theory of Mind may not be as readily intuitive to a child or an adult on the Autism Spectrum, that does not mean they are unable to learn and appreciate it. The brain is a complex organ; when we want to move or complete a task, the brain must send a neurological signal to our extremities to perform said task. The brain must tell my fingers to type out this sentence before I can type it. This is something that most people take for granted because this is part of the autonomic nervous system; it just happens without us thinking about it. But what if you had to consciously tell your brain to make your fingers move a certain way because they do not naturally do that? What if whenever you wanted to say something all the words in your head got jumbled up? The connections in the Autistic brain are different, perhaps so different that certain tasks that we take for granted as intuitive, the brain must work out all the bio-electronic signals it has to create and each individual connection like an old computer? What if, rather than the most direct route to doing something, your brain takes the longer way; processing each step rather than intuitively creating the shortest distance? Your movements would be slower; you may over-obsess about precision rather than just doing what you are told. You may blurt things out, rather than be able to ignore things and read a situation. You may have a thought, but not be able to say it because your brain cannot make the connections between thinking something and the sounds that match the words to communicate what is in your mind. This may also be why some Autistic people (whether they may be completely nonverbal or simply have trouble with verbal speech) prefer to communicate in writing or typing. Within their brain, it may be easier to make the connections to type something out and give their brain time to think rather than to speak.

Often Autistic people are left to process the thoughts going on inside their brains all alone in a world that does not understand them. Being alone with my thoughts have often driven me towards the more classical and surface-level versions of self harm and self destruction. When left with my own ideas swirling around my head, my emotions at times would become painful and I would need to distract myself. At first, I would try other things like reading or watching TV, but I would later do other things like overeat, I eventually would start banging my head, punching my own hand until it hurt, punching walls until my knuckles bled, or something broke, and cutting. Hey, I was a teenager, I couldn't exactly pick up a bottle of Whisky and drown my sorrows in alcohol. Think about it when what we may consider to be a normal functioning adult resorts to alcohol or cigarettes or some other mind-body altering substance in times of grief or pain. The loss of a loved one, the breakup of a marriage, these are all things that will break and at times irreversibly change people. When people are left with their own heavy and painful thoughts, they may resort to dangerous methods to escape and to control these thoughts. They can also reach out and try to talk to someone about their thoughts and feelings; this also tends to help lift the pain away. Suddenly, this person is no longer alone with their own thoughts. Someone else is there to help them through. They also start to see their own thoughts as just that, thoughts. Often understanding your own thoughts from another person's perspective can be helpful in healing, rationalization, and making better use of your time with your thoughts. For Autistic people however, who are often trapped in their own brain and are unable to communicate, either because they physically cannot verbally speak or because they find it insurmountably difficult to process their thoughts in the words that need to be said, it can lead them to dealing with their thoughts, emotions, needs, and desires in strange and unhealthy ways. If being alone with one's thoughts can drive seemingly normal people to self-destruction, one can only try to imagine how a person like the one I described must feel.

This concept of the maze-like mind can also be applied to things like control over bodily functions or a sense of fear. Sometimes Autistic children may wish to do something, but their brain does not properly process the danger in the action they are committing. When I was a child, I absolutely loved to climb trees, or climb up and over on the outside of the playground equipment where you were not supposed to climb. I scared the crap out of my parents a few too many times; my brain simply did not process fear or consequence the same way. Think of the Autistic child darting out into traffic. The processes that our brains take for granted must be programmed into this Autistic brain and that can often result in a body that does not respond to the brain. When Autistic people cannot communicate, this is when meltdowns occur, the brain is overloaded, and it does not know how to get its needs across. By providing your child with alternative methods of communication and a little extra patience, you may be able to help your child express their needs and emotions.

Summary

Empathizing and systemizing refer to different ways of thinking and understanding the world around us. They serve different purposes in daily life; one may be better in some situations than in others and vice-versa. Everyone possesses varying capacities to empathize and systemize, and our brains may be wired differently to better utilize one style over another.

Empathizing refers to the drive or ability to identify another person's emotions and thoughts and respond to them with an appropriate emotion. When we empathize, we are viewing the world through a social lens. We are attempting to decode social information, how it relates to us, as well as how it relates to people around us. Empathizing comes from the Theory of Mind. When we empathize with someone, we recognize that people have feelings both similar yet separate to our own and we acknowledge the agency behind events around us. By recognizing and relating to other's feelings we are better able to connect with people and predict their actions. Empathizing allows us to assign intent to agents through the understanding of one's emotions in relation to past events. We can connect our experiences with those of others and see agency in the things others do and their reactions. Our actions have consequences on people, not everyone has the same experiences as we do. Through empathizing, we see our emotions in others. We laugh when others are happy, we feel sad at funerals, and we can understand other's fears. Empathy helps us to navigate the human world and to help others in their struggles as well as to simply relate to people in everyday life.

Systemizing, on the other hand, refers to understanding changes in the physical world. It refers to analyzing how changing the input of a process changes the outcome, and how we can create predictions based on these changes. Systemizing is the basis of the scientific method. By observing how systems change in the natural world we are able to see how each piece of the puzzle affects others. By learning rules and discovering patterns, we can predict new outcomes and create new knowledge.

It can often be hard to empathize with the physical world because it won't change if you relate to it hard enough. Likewise, there is often a lack of a pattern which we can base our predictions on to understand the emotions of people. People can change their minds on a whim. Agentive systems do not always follow the simple rules that physical ones do. Over-empathizing may lead us to see agency where there is none and over-systemizing may lead us to miss the agents that are pulling the strings. Systemizing may impede our ability to relate to people because we are looking for answers rather than simply talking to and trying to relate to feelings. Both are necessary in understanding the world around us.

People often have differential abilities to systemize or empathize and these two traits are often anti-correlated. We can measure these abilities and give rough scores that assess a person's ability in and preference for either one or the other. Women tend to be empathizers and men systemizers. These generalize on an average and are not meant to paint everyone with the same brush. The general population seems to be more skewed towards empathizing as a likely evolutionary byproduct of living in a social society where people depend on one another greatly for survival. People on the Autism Spectrum tend to score higher in tests that look for systemizing abilities and tendencies over the general public.

When we look at the brain, certain parts seem to become more active over others in situations that require systemizing skills over empathizing skills and vice-versa. Different connections to different parts of the brain are made in different situations. Often, one side of the brain is favoured over the other. The left side is favoured for language and social situations, while the right is favoured for spatial and logical problems. Ultimately both sides work together to help us navigate the world.

The smaller Corpus Callosum within the Autistic brain restricts communication between hemispheres, often leading them to have to work more independently compared to the non-Autistic brain. In addition, activation in the left hemisphere is over-all decreased in the Autistic brain, leaving the right hemisphere to over-compensate. Thus, the right side of the brain is more responsive to language and social stimuli than that of the non-Autistic person. However, the right side of the brain will process this social information the only way it knows how, it will solve it by trying to determine rules that are governed by input and out-put. It will try to identify patterns to make predictions, rather than try to connect with the social information on a more personable level. This can often lead to a cold and dry over simplified approach to social situations that may leave the person in question feeling confused when things do not go as planned or when someone responds to a situation not in the way predicted. In the social world, the same operation on the same data does not always produce the same outcome, and this can be hard on the program.

The increase in shorter-distance connections and structural connectivity means that there are more points over which information travels. Information is integrated over a wider area of the brain and more of the brain is hence used. This allows the brain to pull from different strategies as well as past experiences. Both hemispheres of the Autistic brain are more tuned towards identifying patterns and rules. Increased activation of the right hemisphere combined with the unique connectivity of the Autistic brain produces both deficits and strengths. Many of the strengths associated with ASD include visuospatial skills, attention to detail, intuitive physics, and intuitive mathematics. Autistic people often focus on small details rather than seeing the big picture (Happe and Frith 2006). This allows them to approach problems in ways that others may not see at first, but they may also miss the big picture for the little pieces. Both these strengths and difficulties can be attributed to a difference in brain lateralization and connectivity within the brain that begins very early in development and is something innate to Autism. Autism is a difference in programming, and a difference in thinking style.

By introducing Allism as a foil to Autism, I showed what the wider spectrum of humanity can look like. One person's strength is another person's weakness. Everyone works off of one another to create a functioning society. People with better systemizing skills may be more predisposed to the fields of sciences and understanding the physical world while people with stronger empathizing abilities may take on careers in the social sciences or in working with people. Presenting the other side of the spectrum as a disability normalizes Autism and better shows how people can be disabled in different situations.

By introducing a framework wherein people on the Autism spectrum can find structure and predictability in social systems, they may become better equipped to understand these difficult situations. Autistic people may simply need to be provided the opportunity to create their own rules of cause and affect in a social environment with the help of a committed teacher. Increased short-range connections may mean that things that are intuitive to most people may not be as intuitive to the Autistic brain. Controlled unconscious movements may become more conscious to be completed. Thought processes may take longer and what is easy for us, may be difficult to them. Giving Autistic people more time and offering alternative methods of communication can help them to better interact with the world and communicate their needs.

In this chapter, my goal was to discuss a spectrum between systemizing and empathizing, defining Autism as lying on one side far from the median. Painting a gradient of options that people can fall into. Using this, we are better able to see where people within a given population fall, in comparison to one another. Most people will display at least some Autistic characteristics, and more in some situations than in others. This helps us view Autistic traits as naturally occurring and as a core aspect of the human population. These traits lie on a broader spectrum that begins long before the point at which they could be considered a clinical impairment (Baron-Cohen et al. 2002; Wheelwright et al. 2010). We require both empathizing and systemizing to understand the world and to interact within it; we need these tools to make new discoveries and to better understand people. Autism is something to be understood, supported, and harnessed; not something to be cured. Although rates of Autism may appear to have increased within the last few decades, this is not an epidemic. With our wider understanding of Autism, we are able to better recognize symptoms and diagnose more people correctly. With the introduction of the DSM IV and the DSM V we have broadened the definition of Autism such that we are better able to see Autism in and diagnose it in more people. We have only been able to properly measure the rates of Autism for the last twenty to thirty years, and I suspect rates to stabilize around 2-5 %. The world is changing and humanity changes with it; Autism is not a disease; it is our brains.

This book is called *The Autistic Atheist,* yet I have not discussed religion or its connection to Autism yet. Next, I would like to investigate religion's role in shaping humanity. How can we define religion and the evolution and psychology of religion and religion's role in human evolution? If Autism has always been a part of humanity, then it serves that there must be an evolutionary role or advantage to being Autistic. An advantage to being different in a species that thrives off cohesion and the ability to work together.

Chapter 3

Religion and Autism

This chapter is not concerned with proving or disproving the existence of a God or a universe creator. Nor is its goal to convince someone that the God claim is true or untrue. Whether or not a God exists, the psychology of religion is very interesting and important to the future of humanity. I wish more to look at why and how religions formed over the course of human evolution from the view that religion is a social phenomenon. Whether or not a God exists, God has taken many forms throughout the course of human history and currently all over the world, religion cannot be easily separated from the human experience. The existence of a God or Gods (although it may prove one or more religions, or groups of religions correct over others) would not wholly account for the diversity of religions, origin stories, and God claims in existence throughout human evolution. What is religion? Why is it important when discussing Autism? As laid out in the introduction, there would appear to be a higher percentage of people on the Autism Spectrum who identify as Atheist or do not ascribe to a particular religion. Much of this book builds on the concept of Theory of Mind, how it applies to Autism, and what it means to be human. What does the Theory of Mind have to do with religion?

Religion and Concepts of God

Religious beliefs and behaviours are a hallmark of human life, found in almost all cultures (Bulbulia 2004). However, what exactly is Religion? Webster's dictionary defines religion as: The service and worship of a God or the supernatural (Merriam Webster). This indicates that the two primary factors of a religion are the concept of a God and the act of worship. However, definitions like this do not get at the psychology of why people believe, religion's place in the modern world, where religion comes from, nor the role religion and faith play in our everyday lives (Usman 2006). Religion is so pervasive in human society and the human experience that no one definition would be sufficient either in the legal sense nor in the practical sense (Usman 2006). Similarly, humans tend to have a hard time pinning down the definition of a God and tend to define it in the best way they see fit to their everyday lives (God is energy!). Why does religion exist? Why do human beings resort to the existence of a God as an answer to the unknown, or as a means to control and dictate morality within ourselves and others? Why did Jesus have to die on the cross so that all of humanity could be forgiven for our sins, is that really a symbol of love?

Emile Durkheim described religion as:

> *"A unified system of beliefs and practices relative to sacred things, that is to say, things set apart and forbidden—beliefs and practices which unite into one single moral community called a Church, all those who adhere to them"* (1912).

For Durkheim, what mattered was not a concrete definition of religion, how religions differ, nor how humans conceptualized religion and Gods, but the roles religion played in both primitive and modern societies. In *The Foundational Falsehoods of Creationism,* Ra (2016) describes religion as, "the beliefs and behaviours surrounding the notion that some part of the human experience survives the act of physical death (a soul)." I like this definition, for it brings together the one commonality of all religions, as well as gives us a starting idea from which religions spawn.

Most religions tend to postulate the existence of entities that exist outside of our perceptions, these entities exist typically as thinking and acting minds without physical bodies (Barrett 2004; Atran and Norenzayan 2004a; 2004b; Norenzayan 2013). The primary entities within religions are typically referred to as Gods; however, the term *God* can often be hard to define. Religions also tend to posit other lesser entities which primarily consist of unseen minds without material bodies such as angels, and ghosts (ancestors). Gods typically refer to an agent who created the universe. Among most modern religions, God or gods play an active role in our lives as well as in the forces of nature that shape the world. The three main Abrahamic religions describe God as infinite, limitless, all perfect, all knowing, unchanging, immaterial, perfectly simple, omnipotent, omniscient; neither bound by space time nor physical laws, and eternal—Judaism and Christianity (Kohler 1918; Smith 1955); having no equal, and entirely separate from humanity— Islam (Ziaullah 1984: 19).

Religion comes from the Greek *re-legos*, which means to re-connect (Saler 1987). Religion is a force that binds people together through the common beliefs in a shared reality (Norenzayan 2013). It is this force that allows people with little to no direct kinship or history to know something about one another and cooperate. Through shared common beliefs, people are better able to work together because they share common goals, and (more importantly) they both perceive that they are being watched by an entity who exerts some level of control over their lives and their community. If their goals are similar than by helping them, they help themselves. If the two individuals did not both believe in a super-powerful agent who was watching them, then one person may take advantage of the other; there is no implied obligation of reciprocity (Norenzayan 2013). This perspective addresses the utility of religion as well the notion of supernatural agents watching over us; mutually believed in entity(s) that can affect our lives. Viewing religion from different lenses allows us to take a holistic approach to defining it. Looking at its origins and the role it plays in both the human mind and in human cultures around the world prevents us from being led astray by concepts of specific religions or the validity of certain religious claims. My goal here is to define religion based on its role in the brain and how this pertains to the human experience. We will start by examining the psychology of religion to understand its role in the human mind, from there we can extrapolate into society, culture, and evolution.

Viewing religion from a psychological standpoint, all religions begin with the postulation of the existence of supernatural, counter-intuitive, psychological, intentional, creative entities (Boyer 1994). The existence of these entities is quantified by the completion of acts that defy known laws within the given time or dimension (i.e.: a person rising from the dead or creating material out of *nothing*). The completion of such tasks further warrants their existence because these abilities are seen to be outside of the capabilities of natural processes or human skill. These entities often possess *folk psychological* traits of humans (agency, wants, desires, emotions), but usually do not possess the biological or physical traits of humans (being corporal, requiring energy). These entities typically transcend physical nature and/or the boundaries of time—although that may not have been a criteria throughout human history (Boyer 1994). The existence of these entities is often centred around a desire for meaning and control in a seemingly meaningless and random existence (Boyer 1994; Bering 2002).

Their existence is also often tied to the concept of an afterlife and the idea that some part of the human experience continues to exist beyond that of the physical body (Boyer 1994; Bering 2002). Describing religion like this removes the necessity of Gods or creation from the equation and focuses more on how humans perceive agency in the world around them through both time and space. We may never be able to prove that these entities exist, but their tangible existence is not psychologically significant. Thus, religion is a set of behaviours and values that are centred on a belief in immaterial unseen agents whose stories contribute to a shared history, lifestyle and set of moral systems. The key word *shared* points to religion as an emergent property of humanity. One person is not a religion, these sets of ideas only become a religion as they become integrated into the wider culture and thus, the human condition.

The hypothesis that these agents exist demands the capacity to conceptualize beings that defy typically recognized criteria of existence. While attributing physical phenomena and the existence to the universe leads us to ask why these things happen; it is this questioning that often leads us to the desire to know the mind of God and thus, begin to attribute mental states such as beliefs, knowledge, and desires to it (Boyer 1994). To envision a thinking, creating and agentive God also requires human beings to conceive of a mind and thoughts as separate from the human body (Willard and Norenzayan 2013). We seek to communicate with these entities through encoded symbolic actions or rituals (Boyer 1994; Bering 2001; 2002). We connect with Gods in a similar way in which we would connect with other people around us, through a Theory of Mind.

Religion and the Theory of Mind

It may seem obvious to the nonbeliever that religion is a product of the mind. But is this the same as Descarte's concept that we could reduce everything to being a product of the mind? A central theme of this book has thus far been the relationship between Autism and the Theory of Mind. We first properly defined the Theory of Mind, then we explored it in the context of Autism, we then explored its place in the brain, and then we explored how people use it to relate to one another. We saw how different people approach different kinds of problems based on their tendencies to either systemize or empathize (Baron-Cohen 2010). Whether a person is a strong empathizer or a strong systemizer will impact their perceptions of both physical and social phenomena. The empathizers sought to solve their problems by understanding people. They learned to connect with others to better predict their behaviours. It is this ability to predict behaviours that gives people control over social situations.

Religions tend to revolve around assigning agency to physical and naturalistic phenomena to better understand cause and effect (Guthrie 1993; Barrett 2004; Norenzayan 2013). They consequently attribute agency to phenomena that would otherwise appear agent-less. By doing this, we are essentially attempting to empathize with the physical phenomena that affect our everyday lives to give us a better understanding of why things happen that are out of our control. We use the Theory of Mind to connect with a God to understand why things are happening to us similarly to how we would use our Theory of Mind to connect with the people around us to better understand their thoughts, feelings and consequently their behaviours. Religions also revolve around the idea that you are more inclined to act a certain way if you believe someone or something is watching you, and judging your actions (Norenzayan 2013; 2016; Norenzayan et al. 2016). Further, religions are concerned with the management of people in large, anonymous interdependent groups (Kelly 1995; Norenzayan and Sharif 2008; Klein 2009; Powell 2009; Norenzayan 2013).

The Theory of Mind refers to one's ability to correctly determine the mental states of others. It allows us to attribute agency to others and recognize that their beliefs are separate from our own. Expanding upon that, the Existential Theory of Mind (ETOM) refers to the attribution of mental states to physical phenomena, objects, animals, or things that do not typically possess human thoughts (Bering 2002; 2003). ETOM allows us to attribute agency to events in our lives where agency may not readily be detectable. ETOM is about attributing thoughts and desires to occurrences that seem thoughtless. Human beings do this so often that it is almost subconscious: my computer is not cooperating, my dog is happy, addiction just *wants* to destroy your life, God just *wanted* another angel up in heaven (one of my favourites). If religion is an extension of the Theory of Mind, then parts of the brain that are correlated with Theory of Mind thinking should become active when thinking about Gods. It follows that if religion is an extension of the Theory of Mind, then people with a weak Theory of Mind (or who lack an intuitive Theory of Mind) would necessarily present with challenges when it comes to believing in supernatural phenomena, and connecting with a God.

Religions typically posit that some part of us (or consciousness) exists as separate from us and continues to exist after we die. This piece of us that continues to exist is often referred to as the soul (Ra 2016). The soul is often defined as immaterial and separate from the physical body. The concept that the soul is separate from the human body and continues to exist beyond the body's physical existence is referred to as Dualism (Bloom 2005; Damasio 1994). The concept that the soul is a nonphysical substance that is related to the body but not reliant on it opens us up to the possibility of minds existing without bodies. The ability to think of the soul (or the mind) as separate from the body opens us up to the possibility of the existence of ghosts, spirits, and the existence of other supernatural phenomena (Bloom 2007). Without a concept of dualism, the existence of these entities and the concept of our consciousness extending beyond the physical body becomes hard to comprehend (Povinelli and Bering 2002). On the other hand, the concept of a soul is counter-intuitive (Barrett, 2004). The soul refers to a thinking mind or consciousness existing without a material brain; however, this kind of counter-intuitive concept is attractive to us because it allows us to attribute a mind and thinking agency to certain phenomena (Barrett 2004) that we must account for in our lives. If humans did not have a desire and mechanism to connect and predict the mental states (and thus, behaviours) of other people, there would be no mechanism to connect with disembodied souls (Bering 2006a; 2006b). If one cannot intuitively and correctly infer the mental states of others, how does one expect to be able to infer the mental states of disembodied souls they cannot even see? To explore religion, we begin with the Hyperactive Agency Detection Device—HADD (Guthrie 1993; Barrett 2004).

It is rather easy to imagine a hunter-gatherer hearing a rustle in the bushes or a loud sound from above and thinking that someone or something is out there about to get them. One could assume that the noise or movement is just the wind, and they are in no imminent danger, or they could assume the presence of another person or predator going to get them. Assuming the latter when there is a threat and thus, getting out of the way of danger, will save you your life. Thinking that there is no danger and letting whatever is out there jump out and attack you gets you killed. An extremely dangerous option would be to investigate, and you just walked into the mouth of a predator. Contrarily, thinking that something is there when it is not is not nearly as costly (Barrett 2004). Those who assumed the presence of an agent were more likely to survive and pass on their genes to the next generation (Guthrie 1993; Barrett 2004). This leads one to over attribute the presence of an agent to unseen phenomena—be it a tiger in the forest or a voice in the clouds (Guthrie 1993; Barrett 2004). Sometimes you just must believe something before you know it; by the time you look for evidence you could be dead. These traits get passed down from generation to generation, as well as laterally through cultural transmission. People would communicate the presence of entities to other group members so that they may know to avoid certain dangers (Barrett 2004). Looking at it this way, we see how the assumption of agency is a consequence of ordinary human cognition (Boyer 2003; Barrett 2004). As this thinking becomes more and more intuitive over time, questioning it becomes harder and harder (Atran and Norenzayan 2004a; Barrett 2000; 2004; Bloom 2007; Boyer 2001; 2008; Kelemen 2004). Eventually, these agents started to gain desires, and experiences; they started to take on a mind of their own and separate from the ideas in our heads (Guthrie 1993). Looking for answers in the absence of science leads one to ascribe evil spirits as the cause of death after their band-mate ate a little too much lion liver one night—vitamin A poisoning did not exactly come to mind. It is far easier for a person living in a pre-scientific era to get themselves caught up in a thunderstorm and to think "who is doing this to me?" rather than ponder weather dynamics—pondering weather dynamics gets one stuck in the rain.

When humans posit the presence of an agent, they must then determine the desires and behaviours of said agent to determine why something is happening, and to decide how to act; similarly, when a human encounters another person they must determine the context of this encounter, and how to act accordingly using the Theory of Mind (Bering 2003; 2006a). How does one know how to interact with others? Through our past interactions with them and the concept of how one wishes to be treated. From our past interactions with others, we predict the future interactions and how they are related to relationships (Bering 2003). If another person does something bad to us, we may ponder "What could I have done to upset them?" Likewise, when we get caught in a thunderstorm or come back empty-handed after a long hunt, one may wonder who is out to get us (who is not happy with us). Wondering how one's actions affect natural phenomena causes us to take a more active role in our choices, and thus exploit readily accessible information processing mechanisms (Boyer 2000; 2001; Bering 2006). What is more dangerous than a tiger lurking in the bushes? Another person lurking in the bushes. What is more dangerous than a person lurking in the bushes? A person who's angry at me. What is more dangerous than a person who is angry with me lurking in the bushes? Ten people who are angry at me with spears! Beyond that, a person lurking in the skies.

Since humans are so heavily reliant on others to survive, we have developed a keen sense of human group dynamics, built upon from our primate ancestors (Norenzayan 2013). Humans are constantly simulating strategies to derive information about the minds of others (O'Neill and Chong 2001). These cognitive processes often run offline to a point where we project mental states subconsciously (Boyer 2003, Barrett 2004; Epley et al. 2009). The assumptions that humans must constantly make lay the groundwork for assuming hidden agency in our everyday lives. If humans did not live in large groups where we constantly had to infer the mental states of others, there would be less need to infer the mental states of a God (Bering 2006). Once mental states and desires are attributed to unseen active entities, these entities can then project their desires back down to group members and help to foster group cohesion (Haidt 2007). Watchful deities give group members something to answer to (Norenzayan 2016).

The final moments prior to one's death take us from a person who we have deep intimate connections with to that of an inanimate object (Von Hippel and Trivers 2011). The dead body no longer has thoughts or feelings, or any ability to communicate with us. Where did this person go? Where is the person I once loved and cherished memories with? Will I ever get to spend time with them again? In addition to this person no longer being present, the status of their body has completely changed. Their body is now a liability, it does not move on its own, it drags you down. The rotting corpse attracts predators and diseases (Von Hippel and Trivers 2011). To witness death without a concept of what has occurred must have been traumatic for our ancestors. It forces us to come to the realization that no other species before us has come to; one day I shall die too. When that happens, everything that I am experiencing right now will happen to someone else. The concept of a soul and an afterlife helps to bridge this gap. That person's essence, the things that composed our relationship with them, has left the body and gone somewhere else. We needed a way to better contextualize death as a state transition. The existence of a soul allows us to communicate and maintain a relationship with someone after death. It helps to ease the blow of them leaving this world (Von Hippel and Trivers 2011). A *person* leaving their physical body and going to another place gives one solace that they are no longer in pain, "they are in a better place." Concepts of an afterlife additionally allow us to project our desires for revenge on the wicked, giving us the illusion of control and peace of mind that their deeds will not go unpunished (Barrett 2004). Once we have conceived of a person existing beyond the life of their physical body, it becomes easier to imagine them projecting mental states onto us as we do onto them (Bering 2006).

A study by Bering and Bjorklund (2004) showed that small children readily made psychological attributions to a dead mouse. The natural inclination to attribute mental states to non-living entities lays the foundation for the belief in an afterlife (Bering and Bjorklund 2004; Bering 2006). Multiple people projecting mental states onto the same entity modifies the actions of a group of people, and lays the groundwork for systems of morality. The idea that a mind can exist separate from a body is referred to as dualism, we are essentially treating these mental states as their own entities (Dennett 1987). The existence of a mind with desires that are of consequence to us without a physical body is a counter-intuitive concept (Atran and Norenzayan 2004a). It is only minimally counterintuitive however, because it violates our understanding of the world in a small and specific way that our brains can readily account for using the Theory of Mind (Atran and Norenzayan 2004a). Minimally counterintuitive ideas are remembered because they stick out in our psyche from the mundane (Atran and Norenzayan 2004a). They violate core tenets of an object but not so much as to take us away from what the object is (Atran and Norenzayan 2004a). These concepts are often claimed as true because they stand out from the mundane. It must be true, or you would not have thought of such a thing. As concepts accumulate more and more counter-intuitive traits they start to become harder to hold in our heads and thus, harder to believe (Atran and Norenzayan 2004a). The Minimally Counterintuitive Ideas (MCIs) that pervade time and generations are those with predictive power and those that add to the human experience (Atran and Norenzayan 2004a). A thinking mind without a tangible body has the power to interact with the world and to interact with us. It can manipulate the world and has thus importance to humanity. The same cannot be said for other minimally counterintuitive ideas such as a man who walks on water, or a child who never grows up.

The extrapolation of agency detection posits a mechanism between the Theory of Mind and religious thinking. It follows that people who are more inclined to mentalize compared to others would be more prone to religious thinking. The idea that minds exist without bodies gives further weight to the proposed existence of a God. What is a God but a mind without a body after all? It is our cognitive biases regarding physical processes, natural phenomena, and people that make us more or less likely to accept or reject the God hypothesis. These biases come from an innate tendency to attribute mental states to others, honed in by the Theory of Mind. The ability to think dualistically is a necessary condition for understanding concepts such as ghosts and spirits, or any other disembodied supernatural agent (Bloom 2007). Further, thinking dualistically also requires one to conceive of thoughts and desires existing outside of one's body, and predicting those thoughts and desires as actions. This becomes nearly impossible in the absence of a Theory of Mind. Religion is integrated into so many distinct mental processes that it makes it extremely hard to come out of. This is on top of the social pressures intertwined into religion (Atran and Norenzayan 2004a; Boyer 2003; Barrett 2004). You literally have to rewire your entire way of thinking.

Religion exists very much in the realm of the intuitive. These are responses that require minimal reflection, acting on basic impulses. This likely comes from generations of honing our social intelligence (Boyer 2003; Barrett 2004). As a pre-industrial species, humans would have relied heavily on intuition and group dynamics to survive. We needed to be able to have quick access to easy solutions rather than spend precious time coming to more reflective answers (Atran and Norenzayan 2004a; Barett 2000; 2004; Bloom 2007; Boyer 2001; 2008; Kelemen 2004). The attribution of minds to the mindless is also referred to as anthropomorphism (Willard and Norenzayan 2012). Without this ability, we would not be able to attribute intention to natural phenomena, and we would not ascribe human thoughts to entities who do not think like us (Willard and Norenzayan 2012). This is what also makes the idea of talking animals so inviting.

The studies conducted by Shenhav et al. (2011) and Pennycook et al. (2012) shed light on how intuitive thinking can influence beliefs, including religious beliefs, and how it can lead individuals to incorrect conclusions. They showed that people who are more prone to intuitive thought are more likely to possess a belief in a God and to engage in religious activities. The example that these articles use is a simple math problem. The total cost of a bat and a ball is $1.10, the bat costs one dollar more than the ball, how much is the ball? Both articles give ten cents as the most popular and intuitive answer; however, a simple calculation that requires a sixth grade-level of math would show you that the correct answer is five cents, while the bat would be one dollar and five cents. In these studies, participants who gave an answer of ten cents were more likely to hold belief in a God and possessed stronger beliefs compared to those that gave the correct answer (Shenhav et al 2011; Pennycook et al. 2012). These findings highlight the potential pitfalls of intuitive thinking, and the importance of critical reasoning, even in seemingly straightforward tasks. This relationship held true regardless of cultural background or the religious orientation of family members. Intuitive thinking's influence on religious beliefs transcends individual differences in upbringing and environment (Shenhav et al 2011; Pennycook et al. 2012).

Gervais and Norenzayan's (2012) study contributes to our understanding of the relationship between cognitive processes and religious belief by demonstrating how analytical thinking can influence belief in gods and supernatural entities. Their research utilized cognitive techniques to prime participants to engage in more analytical thinking about certain concepts. Following this priming, individuals were less inclined to strongly proclaim belief in gods or other supernatural/paranormal entities. This suggests that when individuals engage in reflective, analytical thinking, they are more open to considering alternative explanations and less inclined to rely on supernatural explanations for phenomena. Whether or not these people reverted to their baseline religious beliefs after they went home is unknown; but it may be an interesting subject to investigate. After all, Religion is in the situation, not in the person (Norenzayan 2013). Reason truly is the enemy of faith (Martin Luther).

In the case of the ball and bat question, a simple calculation can show us where and why the intuitive answer is the incorrect one. It is very similar to when a person is asked a series of rapid-fire questions that are set up in a way to trick you.

What is the opposite of least? Most. When you are proud of something you... boast. Where the sea meets the land is the... coast. What do you put in a toaster?

When questions like these are rapidly fired at someone, looking for a quick answer, you may be tempted to answer the last question with *"toast"*; however, this is not correct—you put bread in a toaster. When faced with a question that requires further thought, you prime your brain to probe further and consider alternative answers (Shenhav 2011; Gervais and Norenzayan 2012). Questions like these are specifically phrased in ways that lead you astray (Shenhav 2011; Gervais and Norenzayan 2012).

What would happen if the same test was conducted on participants who identified as Atheists? If analytic thinking leads one to reconsider the God belief and other questions concerning the paranormal (Pennycook et al. 2012) then a group of Atheists should overwhelmingly exhibit analytic thinking over intuitive and would guess correctly compare-of? Or would the lack of belief in a God be seen as so intuitive to the seasoned Atheist that it does not impact how they approach such a question? Only if we prompt someone to think critically in the moment, are they forced to question other beliefs they thought were obvious and true (Shenhav 2011; Gervais and Norenzayan 2012). Further, would this kind of test prompt participants to reconsider their closely held beliefs regarding God and religion in the long run or would they simply resume their beliefs after the test?

What does this have to do with Autism? Hyperactive agency detection likely exists on a continuum within different human populations depending on an interplay of social, genetic, and environmental factors. People on the lower end of this continuum may have difficulty in understanding the concepts that religions put forth into the population. They would have a hard time relating to people on the other side of this continuum. In our industrial society, our survival no longer depends on our ability to detect agency in the environment around every corner as it once did (Norenzayan 2013; Harari 2017). Autistic people may find it problematic to conceptualize a supernatural agent that they cannot see, readily interact with, or imagine its intentions (Norenzayan et al 2012). To believe in supernatural agents behind natural phenomena and human affairs, one must possess the mentalizing capacity required to conceptualize such entities and their desires in relation to them (Bering 2002; Willard and Norenzayan 2012). Rather than reach for an agent as the cause of unexplained phenomena, they may seek explanations derived from previous knowledge of the natural world to come up with a more suitable explanation. We could say that the HADD in Autistic people is weakened (Willard and Norenzayan 2012), a Hypoactive Agency Detection Device.

The study conducted by Maij et al. (2017) offers further insights into the relationship between cognitive processing and the attribution of agency, particularly in individuals with Autism. Their research focused on how Autistic individuals perceive agency by observing videos of geometric figures. The Autistic participants were less likely to ascribe agency to the movement of the figures even when an agent was present (Maij et al. 2017). This was compared to non-Autistic participants who were more inclined to ascribe agency when there was not any (Maij et al. 2017). This suggests that Autistic individuals have difficulty recognizing and attributing agency to non-human movements when they lack intentional cues. The movement of the figures activated the TOM networks in the brain, causing the non-Autistic participants to over-attribute the presence of agency. Participants who ascribed agency were also more likely to subscribe to a belief in a God (Maij et al. 2017). Supernatural believers in general are more likely to attribute intentionality to random events (Riekki et al. 2014). We see this exaggerated in modern religions wherein everything is said to bend to the will of God (do the Sun and the Moon not submit to the will of God?). The systematic thinking of Autism does not allow for the existence of minimally counterintuitive concepts to exist as easily as they do in the minds of others (Norenzayan et al. 2012). The idea that a mind could exist outside of a physical body leaves no physical body for this mind to exist within. Thus, the concept of a God would be harder to grasp, and other explanations become easier to grasp (Bering 2002; 2006a; Norenzayan et al. 2012). To the systemizing brain, the idea that a mind that exists without a body who is the force behind unexplained phenomena and has always existed has far less explanatory power than other minimally counterintuitive concepts like a baby who never grows up. For a child who never grows up may help us to unlock the mysteries of aging, senescence, and death. It is in fact easier to believe that everything just exists rather than an eternal all powerful agent popped everything into existence. The answer to everything is the answer to nothing.

This does not mean that Autistic people or people with weaker mentalizing capacities are incapable of believing in Gods or other supernatural agents (Gray et al. 2011), it simply means that in specific cases, these people would be less likely to ascribe agency and determination to natural phenomena and processes that were in fact guided by an intelligent agent (Clark and Visuri 2019). Furthermore, even if the person with reduced mentalizing capacities thinks that there is an agent behind an otherwise unexplained phenomena they would be less adept at devising its intentions and their conclusions may turn out to be atypical. When mentalizing skills are impaired, religious belief is less intuitive (Norenzayan 2013). These relationships are much less well defined in less religious countries (Geertz 2010; Lindeman et al. 2015). It may be easier for a person with Autism to believe that people are simply gone when they die.

Mentalizing deficits in Autism present an obstacle to the conceptualization of God (Norenzayan et al. 2012). It does not guarantee Atheism, but makes the acquisition of religious belief, particularly religious belief that is inline with the wider community and culture, more difficult (Bering 2001; McCauley 2011; Barett 2004; Willard and Norenzayan 2013). Caldwell-Harris et al. (2011) demonstrated that young adults with Autism were more likely to be Atheist or to create their own religious constructs. Atheists also tended to score higher on AQ tests than average regardless of an Autism diagnosis (Caldwell-Harris et al. 2011). Their thinking processes were closer to that of an Autistic person. This may help us to better explain why women over men tend to be more religious (Francis 1997; Stark 2002; Rosenkranz and Charlton 2013), as well as the religious tendencies of other people groups (Travers 1941; Epley et al 2009). If we extrapolate this back to our Paleolithic ancestors, people with mentalizing deficits (Norenzayan et al 2012) may be less inclined to attribute agency to natural phenomena. They may look for other answers to explain how the world works. They would have been more drawn to naturalistic, non-agentive explanations, and thus would have given us the first inclinings of science. They would be less likely to see agency in the actions of others around them or incorrectly attribute the agency. They conversely may have had a harder time understanding the behaviours and intentions of their peers. They may have had trouble understanding why certain things happened to them within a group setting and their own place within such groups. They would have created fewer group ties in a world where group ties meant everything. This may have led to fewer of them surviving.

In modern industrial societies where a person's survival is not as directly tied to detecting agency in natural phenomena and group cohesion, neurodiversity is better able to survive and thrive. The advancement of science has also given us a clearer way to interact with the world and to answer questions that may have been previously answered by religion. These answers focus more on processes rather than having a personal connection with a creator. This way of thinking naturally appeals to the systemizing brain.

How Do Beliefs Get CRED?

Religion relies heavily on Credibility Enhancing Displays (CREDs) to convey sincere belief in their tenets (Henrich 2009). A CRED is on the surface just some behaviour that conveys information to another person. An obvious example would be eating a certain kind of food that they know is safe, but you might not. Eating the food demonstrates that the food is at least somewhat safe to eat. This is a key method of learning for small children within a group (Henrich 2009). A key credibility enhancing display in recent history was people posting themselves getting the CoronaVirus Vaccine in 2021. By broadcasting themselves getting the vaccine they demonstrate that they think the vaccine is safe, and that they trust in the science behind the vaccine; this in turn encourages more people to get the vaccine (especially when it is people of prestige like presidents). These behaviours are often passed on from parent to offspring or from high prestige members of a group to others (Henrich and Henrich 2007). CREDs need not be costly to the performer but the costliness of a CRED under certain circumstances can add to the persuasiveness of the behaviour. A person giving money to charity obviously incurs a cost to the person, but a learner witnessing this act is more likely to give to charity themselves than if the person simply told them to give to charity (Henrich and Henrich 2007). Religion takes these concepts and uses them to convey a message regarding a person's beliefs and their commitment to them (Henrich 2009). These acts need to be costly to convey the honesty of one's commitment (Atran 2002). These refer to acts that could be dangerous or require a large amount of time and energy, and that enhance the trust of others in one's beliefs (Sosis and Alcorta 2003; Sosis et al. 2007). The more dangerous and extravagant the behaviours the greater the level of commitment (Sosis and Alcorta 2003; Sosis et al. 2007). Only someone who truly believes in these supernatural tenets would perform these acts. If they did not believe, why would they spend time, energy, and resources in committing such acts? It also creates a barrier to entry for fakers and free riders. If you did not believe that you were going to receive some kind of reward, you would be less likely to perform the task, especially the costlier it is (or if you did not truly believe you were going to be punished if you did not). The performance of these displays lets people know who they can trust (Henrich 2009). Other people performing these acts possess similar beliefs, and are thus more inclined to help one another among genetic strangers (Atran and Norenzayan 2004a). CREDs continue to be passed on from generation to generation and within generations in a group, akin to evolution (Norenzayan 2013). CREDs work because they are conveying a message, but the message is only as useful as the mind receiving it. There is a direct observable relationship between a person eating a certain food or demonstrating a skill and the efficacy of the action for the learner. When it comes to the performance of religious acts that are meant to communicate the mental states of people, not so much. When you already have difficulty understanding the mental states of others and communicating your own mental states, these CREDs may fall upon deaf ears. If you are not inclined to pay attention to what is being communicated, you would be less likely to pass on this information in the correct way. When you do not understand what is being communicated by these behaviours or why they are being communicated to you, you are less likely to perform the same actions around others. Thus, Autistic people may (unknowingly) represent a break in the chain. They may conversely perform certain rituals at inappropriate times and thus, communicate the wrong information or the correct information to the wrong people.

Religion and the Brain

Religion is integrated into our psyche as an extension of the Theory of Mind; it follows that the areas of the brain that are associated with the Theory of Mind and processing social information also have a hand in religion. The study of religion and the brain indicates that there is no specific "God" region (Jodies 2019). Much like any other experience, religion involves different areas of the brain working together to both perceive and process the information around us (Jodies 2019). It is curious that the beliefs of God often coincide with the beliefs of the believers; people tend to construct Gods in their own image (Feuerbach 2004; Freud 1930; Guthrie 1993; Hume 1793). A study by Epley and colleagues (2009) showed activation in both the Frontal and Temporal regions when reasoning about one's own beliefs regarding a given topic (abortion, affirmative action, same-sex marriage, etc...); while reasoning about the beliefs of others showed greater activation in the Temporal and Parietal regions compare-of. The scans did not show a significant difference in activation areas between reasoning about one's own beliefs and the beliefs of God (Epley et al. 2009). Having belief in a specific God with specific goals that believers can profess to others allows them to seek out other like-minded people. The practice of imagining Gods who believe and act in the same way as they do allows believers to claim a moral high ground, as their beliefs align with the all-knowing creator of the world (Epley et al. 2009). This also shows why there are so many different religions and knowledge claims about the same God.

The Temporal lobe hypothesis was first inspired by the observation that people with the condition Temporal Lobe Epilepsy tended to have intense religious experiences and consequently be more religious (Waxman and Geshwind 1975). Persinger (1983) exposed patients to a transient, focal electrical field in the Temporal lobe. Patients reported feeling the presence of a supernatural being when they were exposed to these electrical impulses (Persinger 1983; 2001; Persinger and Makarec 1987). The patients in question reported feelings of connectedness with the world as well as with the Gods associated with their cultural affiliations (Christians did not experience Buddha). Persinger concluded that religious experiences are a normal consequence of spontaneous biogenic stimulation of the Temporal lobe structures (1983). Work by Blanke et al. (2005) connected out of body experiences to the activation of the TPJ. Trans-cranial magnetic stimulation to the TPJ impaired this response (2005). This supports Persinger's work because it shows that the Temporal lobe is implicated in experiences that can be linked to religiosity and how they can be manipulated.

Schjoedt (2009) compared the brain activation patterns of Danish Christians under an fMRI Scanner. Subjects were instructed to recite the Lord's Prayer, personal prayers, and a Nursery rhyme for comparison. The FMRI results showed that recitation of personal prayers activated the left Precuneus, which is part of the left Temporal-Parietal Junction (2009). The act of personal prayer increased activity along the medial Prefrontal cortex and Temporal regions (2009). Reciting the Lord's Prayer on the other hand activated the right dorsolateral prefrontal cortex, the right Parietal cortex, the left cerebellum, and the posterior part of the Temporal cortex (2009). Finally, reciting nursery rhymes yielded a similar activation pattern to that of the Lord's prayer (2009).

The reciting of personal prayers to God had a specific pattern of neural activity which engaged areas of the brain responsible for social cognition and Theory of Mind (Schjoedt 2009; Gallagher and Frith 2003). Prayer to God involves negotiation and social reciprocity (Schjoedt 2009). The patients engaged with God as if they were engaging with another person; whereas, reciting of the Lord's Prayer focused mostly on the prefrontal cortex. It involved memory, conceptualization, and self-introspection (2009). The activation of the precuneus is inv;lved in self-referential activities (Cavanna and Trimble 2006). Reciting of the Lord's Prayer mainly draws on areas of the brain responsible for memory, while personal prayers require improvisation (Schjoedt 2009). When engaging in personal prayer, the patients created (whether real or imagined) a direct conversational line with God, which involved negotiation, and social reciprocity (Schjoedt 2009). The act of engaging with God recruited areas of the brain responsible for social cognition, self representation (Weingard 1977), and information retrieval. It was much like engaging with another person. The act of prayer allows for many people to engage with God and feel as though they have a personal unique connection (Weingard 1977; Epley et al. 2009).

Harris and colleagues (2009) asked Christians and non-Christians to evaluate the truth of religious and non-religious claims. Their study showed that religious thinking engaged different parts of the brain compared to non-religious thinking. Claims were evaluated by participants pressing a button to indicate if they thought a particular claim was true or false. FMRI results showed that belief in each statement triggered increased blood oxygen levels in the ventral and medial Prefrontal cortex, the left superior Frontal gyrus, and the Occipital cortices (Harris et al. 2009); these areas are associated with memory retrieval and problem solving (Northoff et al. 2006; D'Argembeau et al. 2008). Belief in religious stimuli (e.g.: Jesus Christ performed miracles as stated in the bible) specifically triggered a greater response in the anterior Cingulate cortex, just behind the Prefrontal cortex (Harris et al 2009). Responding to religious stimuli as true revealed a greater signal in the anterior Insula, and the ventral Striatum (Harris et al 2009); these are areas of the brain regularly linked to the perception of pain (Wager et al. 2004) in the self and others (Singer et al. 2004). There was a greater response signal in the anterior Cingulate cortex, which was taken as a response to conflict (Carter et al. 1998). Responding to nonreligious statements on the other hand produced greater signals in the left hemisphere networks including the Parahippocampal gyrus, the middle Temporal gyrus, and the Temporal pole (Harris et al. 2009). These areas are involved in memory retrieval, and semantic memory (Inzlicht et al. 2009; Diana et al. 2007). For non religious statements, participants pulled more from memory when determining if they believed something, whereas participants pulled from instinct and intuition when responding to religious stimuli (Harris et al 2009). Much of this work is contingent on the implied honesty of participants when it comes to belief and evaluation of statements.

In addition to one's conception of God, religion encompasses meditation and ritualistic behaviours. Religious rituals refer to intensive, and repetitive behaviours that foster deep faith, and collective action in adherents (Norenzayan 2013). These repetitive practices are often more about performance than they are about true belief (Azari et al. 2001). The participation in ritual activities is a means of fostering group cohesion and reinforcing belief systems (Norenzayan 2013).

Meditation, and the recitation of scriptures require high levels of concentration (Azari et al. 2001; Arumugan 2015). These tasks often require the recalling of information, concentration, and a disconnection with the immediate environment (Lazar et al. 2000; Azari 2001; Ritskes et al. 2003).

The enactment of ritualistic behaviours primarily engages the areas of the brain involved with concentration, and memory retrieval (Azari 2001). The recitation of religious subjects involved peak blood flow and activation in the Parietal circuits, compared to the reading and recitation of non-religious materials by religious subjects (Azari 2001). Meditation primarily involved increased activity in the Frontal lobe. For example, yoga meditation increases glucose uptake in the Frontal and Occipital regions (Herzog et al. 1990). The practice of Kundalini meditation (a Hindu mediation that combines deep breathing with chanting and physical movements) involves increased activation of the prefrontal cortex, the Parietal, Hippocampal, and Temporal regions (Lazar et al. 2000). The practice of Kundalini meditation is associated with reduced stress and anxiety levels (Gabriel et al. 2018; Eyre et al. 2017; Garcia-Sesnich et al. 2017), resulting in reduced oxygen demand and decreased global oxygen levels (Lazar et al. 2000). Other studies on different types of meditation also show increased activity in the Prefrontal cortex (Ritskes et al. 2003). The state of meditation involves a decreased activity in the superior occipital gyrus, associated with feelings of decreased self-awareness (Ritskes et al. 2003). This decrease of self awareness, and awareness of our immediate surroundings (Lazar et al. 2000) is often associated with—what are often referred to as—mystical experiences (Beaurgard and Pacquette 2006). The practice of these acts in large groups helps to foster a sense of group cohesion and a connection with God; however, these activities have effects which can also be enjoyed by people without a direct link to a particular religion. They use religion more as a catalyst or a medium of delivery.

Studies regarding religion and the brain show that there is no specific part of the brain that we can associate with religion. Rather, religion emerges from existing brain structures and functions; specifically those associated with determining agency, and determining the mental states of others (the theory or mind). The social aspects of religion—communication with supernatural entities, the understanding of their desires, and the belief in religious claims that are outside of classical knowledge—engages our social and language centres (Chilton and Kopytowska 2018). These are the same parts of the brain that are most affected in Autism. Social deficits related to Autism may hinder the ability to properly conceive of and communicate with a God (Norenzayan et al. 2012).

The social deficits associated with Autism may distance Autistic people from wider religious communities, thus further impairing their ability to participate and understand them. Rather than relying on feelings of being watched or on emotional connections with a God, people on the Autism Spectrum thrive better when they are given concrete information that relies on consequences to other people as a means to promote certain types of behaviours in society. People who do not possess an understanding of the deeper meanings behind ritualistic activities may still benefit from the stress relieving and social aspects of these practices. People on the Autism Spectrum may become deeply involved in ritual, and religious practices as a method of attaining community, and a sense of belonging with wider social groups. Religious rituals may also help Autistic people maintain some level of routine, and control in their lives; which can act to significantly reduce stress. These benefits may help Autistic people to better understand the utility of religion even if some of the other aspects are harder to grasp (Norenzayan et al. 2012). People on the Spectrum may as a result develop a more deistic and spiritual concept of a God, as opposed to a personal theistic God who intervenes in human affairs and dictates how we should live our lives (Clark and Visuri 2019; Norenzayan et al. 2012; Caldwell-Harris 2011). Autistic people may alternatively borrow concepts from different religions, from their family, peers, and the sciences to create their own interpretation of God. The difference in lateralization in the Autistic brain also affects how one interacts with supernatural phenomena. Decreased lateralization and the dominance of right-hemisphere over left-hemisphere thinking impacts how our brains conceptualize the environment, and thus how we perceive and contextual stimuli.

Brain Lateralization: McGilchrist's Conundrum

In his review, McGilchrist (2019) attributes religion to the right hemisphere, citing its affinity for the novel and the external. This on the surface may seem contradictory to my analysis. I described Autism as right-brain dominance in the last chapter. However, much of McGilchrist's work focuses on typical brain function, and typical hemispheric communication (McGilchrist 2009; 2019). McGilchrist describes the right hemisphere as being focused on the peripheral environment, constantly bringing in new information (2009). The right brain is focused on understanding, while the left brain is focused on manipulation of the environment (Desmedt 1977; Gitelman et al 1996). The right brain takes in novel stimulation, and the left brain chooses how to process it to make it more familiar and readily available to be called upon when needed. The left brain does this by connecting the new knowledge to what it already knows about the world. It makes the information more personable, and less alien. We could see religion as the left brain trying to familiarize and make sense of the right brain's world (Azari et al 2001). Thus, experiences only become religious when our brain relates it to previously existing religious schema (McGilchrist 2009).

However, when you are working with two right brains (an approximation of Autism), what you get is the two brain halves bringing in external information and having to filter through it to determine what is necessary for the task at hand. Rather than the left-brain creating relations and narrative, you have both brain halves trying to create context separately (Dinstein et al. 2011). This instead generates a hyper-awareness of the external, mechanical world. This manifests as difficulty processing, and prioritizing external information (Dinstein et al. 2011). This can often be seen in the sensory seeking behaviours of Autistic people, trying to take in as much information about the world around them as possible. Rather than creating a narrative of an agent who causes things to happen all around us, instead the narrative is focused on the interaction of patterns and events to create the circumstances we see ourselves in.

Summary

Religion refers to belief, and consequential reverence of supernatural, counterintuitive agents who control certain unseen aspects of our lives and the environment. This belief evolved out of our tendency to see agency behind everyday phenomena. When we did not have an immediate explanation for something in the environment, it was more beneficial to assume intent rather than the absence of intent. Those who inferred agency behind certain events that would have otherwise led to their demise, obviously lived to spread their genes; contrarily, those who did not infer agency disproportionately did not as well. This formed the basis of the Hyperactive Agency Detection Device in humans. We see this in experiments where people are more likely to assign agency where there is not any.

Humans evolved living in tight-knit social groups of a few extended family units. Within these units the ability to infer the mental states of others would be advantageous over not being able. It further allowed us to cooperate on shared goals, evade conflict and help others out when needed. Those who were unable to cooperate within these group units would have subsequently been relegated to the periphery or cast out. The ability to infer the mental states of others using body language, as well as one's own experiences, is referred to as the Theory of Mind. From inferring the mental states of other humans and animals, the Theory of Mind has evolved the propensity to systematically treat agents in the environment as capable of self generated autonomous actions that were caused by the intentions of mental states like that of humans. Thus, we infer agency behind events in the environment that may not be directly influenced by an agent. Once we have determined the presence of an agent (either correctly or incorrectly), we almost immediately seek to understand its mental states and why it is causing whatever event to happen to us. This process is referred to as the Existential Theory of Mind (ETOM).

Humans tend to infer agency in the absence of readily accessible explanations. We have a desire to ascribe desires and intentions to these agents as a means of understanding the observed phenomena. This has led to the creation of unseen, and counter-intuitive psychological agents. These agents are counter-intuitive because they require certain abilities to explain the phenomena that they cause, their attributes run counter to what would be considered typical. Their counter-intuitiveness helps them to be remembered because they violate certain physical laws that set them apart from ordinary agents or objects. The ways in which they are counter-intuitive helps us to explain the phenomena at hand and make certain predictions about the environment which we can then relate to.

The term religion comes from re-legos. It is the common belief in these unseen entities that brings people together and allows them to cooperate towards shared goals. It also tells us who we can and cannot cooperate with based on those shared beliefs. These beliefs are often demonstrated by Credibility Enhancing Displays that broadcast them to others in a reliable way that is often hard to fake.

Religion's tie to the Theory of Mind is observed in the brain, as the areas of the brain that are associated with the Theory of Mind become active when thinking about God or performing certain religious acts (Waxman and Geshwind 1975; Persinger 1983; 2001; Epley et al. 2009). These parts of the brain are also the parts most affected in people with Autism Spectrum Disorders.

This connection helps to explain why higher percentages of Atheism are seen in people with clinical diagnoses of Autism Spectrum Disorders. Autistic people are less inclined to attribute agency to environmental phenomena. When shown videos of geometric figures either moving randomly, programmed to move within certain limits, or were directly animated intentionally: Autistic people were less inclined to attribute agency where it did exist, while the control group over-attributed agency (Maij et al. 2017). Autistic people would then have a Hypoactive Agency Detection Device (we will call this HoADD) over Hyperactive. Autistic people (or people who exhibited Autistic traits and tendencies) would have been more likely to investigate the unknown. The investigation of the unknown would have led to new discoveries and innovations; it also could have led to more death and injury. These are the people who may investigate the rustle in the bushes only to get eaten by the sabre-tooth tiger, or have said the wrong thing and get thrown out of the tribe. The corollary to HADD would be the Hyperactive Pattern Detection Device (HPDD)—doesn't roll off the tongue as well. People with the HPDD would be more likely to assign non thinking patterns and processes where there are none, which could lead to false predictions (Dinstein et al. 2011).

This research is primarily limited to those who are clinically diagnosed because those are the people whom psychologists and neurologists studying this subject would seek out. Terms like "High Functioning" and "Low Functioning" are contentious in the Autistic population as Autistic people can present differently in different situations. Functioning labels tend to describe Autistic people through an Allistic lens wherein the Autistic people that are best able to fit into and exist in an Allistic world are deemed "High Functioning." These studies are often limited to High Functioning Autistic people because they require a certain level of verbal intelligence and communication abilities to discuss beliefs. It is more difficult to explain the test parameters and determine the beliefs of someone who does not communicate in a conventional manner. It is a self-fulfilling prophecy, as any Autistic person who could follow instructions and cooperate long enough with the people administering the tests to participate in the study and how it was set up would be deemed High Functioning by the criteria of the ones performing the studies.

Deficits in Theory of Mind hinder Autistic people's ability to communicate their needs and ideas as well as have meaningful connections with their peers. On the other hand, when they do make connections, they are usually much deeper and there is more president to hold onto them. The same differences in Theory of Mind neuro-programming that make it more difficult for Autistic people to properly assess the intentions of people also make it difficult to imagine agency and connect with a God. They may be overly trusting of people or under-trusting and not know when to ask for help. This can lead them to be vulnerable to abuse by caregivers or other people that may seek to hurt or take advantage of them by concealing their true intentions. This deficit in the ability to infer the mental states of others is why it is important to give Autistic people meaningful communication tools so that they can better navigate the world and express their needs. The Theory of Mind may be necessary for religion to have evolved but it may not be necessary to sustain belief in God in the modern day. Just because Autistic people may not readily create concepts of Gods and supernatural entities the same way other people do, it does not preclude them from participating in religion and forming their own ideas concerning God or gods. Even if Autistic people do not possess the mental software required to properly believe in these entities, they still live in a largely Allistic, religious world. They were most likely raised with Allistic concepts of God and had to conceptualize them within their own neurology. This may take the form of seeing Gods as an unseen creative force. They may follow religious tenets and rituals because they receive some other tangible reward for them outside of a connection with a God. Many who ascribe to a belief in a God take comfort in "knowing" that God has a plan for them and that God is always out there. For those who do not believe in a God, it may be easier to accept the apathy of a cold-dark unthinking universe. These people may take comfort in understanding that sometimes there is nothing that they or anyone can do or could have done. For some, it may be easier to believe that the universe just is, rather than an eternal un-caused and un-created God created it—that just raises more questions!

Religion's ties to the Theory of Mind may also in part explain why more women than men are religious. On the other hand, men are more often than not the leaders of major religions while more women in the modern day adopt the "spiritual but not religious" label. They are more inclined to see agency as they tend to be stronger empathizers and more people-centric compared to men. Whereas with men it often exists as a state of either-or. Women tend to have a stronger Theory of Mind and are more apt at understanding the emotions and intentions of others. Women also rely on other people and interact more with agents than men do and thus, have more opportunity to relate to and come up with unseen agents.

Given a large population of individuals with a cognitive set up prone to false agency ascription, there is a high probability that this population will develop God concepts and religion. What does that say about the Theory of Mind and the Atheist? Religion evolved to serve a purpose in our lives and increase survival, but that does not make it true. Not believing in the existence of a God does not mean that the Atheist lacks a Theory of Mind (Coleman 2015). The Atheist may still carry some of their neuro-evolutionary baggage to seek out agency in the unexplained. Just because our brain comes to this conclusion first, does not mean that it is always correct. They have learned to block the reflexive answer and search for other, more probable answers to questions of origins and the unknown. They search for answers in the real world rather than attempting to make concessions for something that might not actually be there. TOM underlies the totality of our mental life, using TOM to reason about supernatural agents is only a small portion of its utility to the human experience, thus, the Atheist would need a theory mind to function with other humans (Coleman 2015). It is not the Atheist who has a weak Theory of Mind but people who have an impersonal concept of God who may.

This also breaks the commonly held expression, "We are all born Atheist." It may be more accurate to say, "We are born-theists", or "born teleologists" as we are purpose seekers, born thinkers, and tool makers. Our thought processes are the product of millions of years of evolution, but we still have to decide what we are going to do with them. We shall next look at the evolution of religion and how it allowed humans to cooperate. We will also explore the role of religion in shaping human societies of the past, present and the future.

Chapter 4

Religion and Human Evolutionary Psychology

Everyone must live and cooperate with other humans on some level. How do people get along and know how to act around one another? How did humans adapt to living in larger and larger groups of anonymous people? How do we recognize friend or foe? Who do we want to cooperate with and who do we want to avoid? How does religion solve this problem, and how did religion evolve? How does religion aid in the transfer of information between individuals? What is religion's role in the creation and maintenance of civilization?

The True Power of a Shared Belief

Every day we run into countless strangers. How do you know that when you get into the car and drive to work you are not going to get hit by someone running a red light? We could say it is because there are traffic laws and there are consequences for breaking them. When we get into our cars, we believe that other people know these laws and that they are going to abide by them. They likely would want to get home safely as well. While at work you ask a coworker who you are not related to, know nothing about their personal life, and have no relationship with outside of work to help you. Your co-worker will help you, because they believe that you would help them in a similar situation. You both believe that you work for the company, and will receive a paycheck from the company. It is because we believe that cooperating with one another furthers us both in some way (Harari 2016).

The more beliefs two people share, the closer the worlds in their heads are, and the closer are their goals to each other become. If two people's goals are similar, the more likely their cooperation will benefit both parties. Society is built around the requirement of shared beliefs and shared expectations. To determine that people possess the same beliefs in certain situations, these beliefs must be communicated in a way that is unmistakable (Atran and Norenzayan 2004a). While at work, it is the uniform, the employee badge, and the punching in and punching out that communicates a set of shared beliefs. Religions often involve a set of visual features meant to communicate one's adherence to them (be they symbols, or pieces of clothing). People of different cultural groups often wear similar clothes, create similar art styles, and perform certain rituals to communicate their belonging to a wider group. If one does not communicate these traits correctly, people around you will be less likely to discern their beliefs, motives and whether they should help you, or if you will help them. Religions use what cultures have already created to discern a shared history and elaborate it to communicate shared belief systems. The more elaborate the signal, the more you stand to gain from getting it right, and the more you risk by getting it wrong (Norenzayan 2013; Crespi and Summers 2014).

Building on the HADD, once we have decided the presence of an agent (be it human or otherwise) we must somehow decipher its intentions in the scenario—am I in danger? Likewise, we must be able to communicate our intentions to said agent quickly and accurately (so that the agent detected knows if it is in danger or not). However, as soon as a method of communication has been determined is as quick as the same method will be bluffed (Irons 2001; Sosis 2004). Going back to our analogy, a non-poisonous species would benefit from having similar colourations to a poisonous species when faced with a predator. To fight off deception, these signals must require a large amount of commitment to make them harder to fake (Irons 2001; Sosis 2004; Atran and Norenzayan 2004a; Murray and Moore 2009). The more work one must put into creating the signal, the more likely the signal, when given, is to be genuine (Atran and Norenzayan 2004a). This is where religion comes in: the set of rules, rituals, and other behaviours are tied to a set of beliefs which are typically tied to some form of supernatural watchful deity and an afterlife belief (Irons 2001; 2008; Sosis and Bressler 2003; Atran and Norenzayan 2004a; Sosis 2006, Norenzayan 2013). You also need to throw in some nonsense beliefs that are not directly related to morality to tell yourself apart from other groups (these people don't eat pork, and these people don't eat beef). Would you go to church every week, fast during the day for an entire month, or cover yourself from head to toe if you did not truly believe that God is watching you? These behaviours provide accountability: I see this person at church every week, they helped my neighbour fix their roof, they give to charity; I can trust them! You see a person in uniform, and you automatically know the role they play in society and their intentions. You could forge all your tests and your degree and get caught and lose everything and potentially go to jail, or you could just get the degree honestly and keep your job and avoid all the anxiety of keeping up the charade. Religions also typically come with a mythology surrounding them that require a level of commitment to study and recall this information (Norenzayan 2013). To properly understand the rules, one must pay attention to the small details. Prior to the written word, these mythologies were passed down orally and through the participation in ritual, and thus the participation in activities ensured commitment (Atran and Norenzayan 2004a) to the belief. This package of morals and hard to fake signals provided a method to discern friend or foe and to discourage deception and free riding (Atran and Norenzayan 2004a). When it is easier to do the work than to pretend that you did it, it becomes beneficial to be honest (Irons 2001; 2008; Murray and Moore 2009; Atran and Norenzayan 2004a). Those who correctly determined the intentions of others were more likely to survive and help others who believed as they did to survive and thrive over those that did not. Meet a person with a gun in a dark alley and stretch open your arms to hug them. A shared set of beliefs and morals in a supernatural watcher(s) reduced interpersonal anxieties and ensured greater cooperation within communities throughout our evolution (Norenzayan 2009; 2013). If we think we are going to paradise, then we will work together to achieve it. This insurance of cooperation allowed humans to live in larger and larger groups and to accomplish more than what we could otherwise achieve (Harari 2016).

Rather than hold individual people's relations to us in our heads, we could instead hold these symbols in our heads. These symbols allowed us to determine our relationship with other people in the group, even if we knew very little or nothing about them as individuals (Norenzayan 2013; 2014; Harari 2016). The higher the population density of an area, the more cogs in the machine, the more levels of government that you need (Harari 2016). Opposed to seeing people as individuals, you begin to see people as larger groups and what those groups of people mean to you in different contexts (Thomson et al. 2011). The larger the group, the greater the potential anonymity and the greater the need to know who to cooperate with (Norenzayan 2013). Religion facilitates us in predicting shared beliefs (Norenzayan 2013). The better we are at determining the shared beliefs of others, the better we are at discerning who to cooperate with and to what extent. The increased morality that religion provides us reduces the anxiety of living in large groups with virtual strangers, which in turn allows groups to become larger and larger (Norenzayan 2013). The larger and larger groups become, the fewer people in proportion to group size are required to secure basic resources. Larger group sizes allow people to specialize and develop new skills, which creates increased roles in the group (Harari 2016; 2017). With more specializations groups can become even larger to facilitate these new roles, and that leads to a greater need to determine the intentions of others quickly and accurately (Harari 2016; 2017). Thus, people developed more elaborate visual identifiers to communicate their affiliations and intentions which creates more elaborate religious behaviours, rituals, and beliefs. In most cases, evolution reaches a physical threshold and stabilizes: the taller the giraffe gets, the more force is placed on its limbs. Where is the threshold in this case? What are the stopping mechanisms to human group size?

If we do not believe in these shared beliefs, then the very system breaks down. You cannot trust people when you get into that car—I have seen that one of the most difficult things for Autistic people is learning to drive. If you are unable to perform the required tasks and behaviours that communicate your beliefs to others, then people around you do not know to trust you. These people may not readily pick up on what someone is trying to communicate to them through outward signals. Some people may fail to properly grasp the significance of these rituals, and thus perform them incorrectly, or not at all. It takes more time for people with this different mindset to become integrated into society because they do not spontaneously connect with the symbols being communicated. They may be treated as outcasts by others for not being able to properly communicate the correct belief at the right instance and to the right person. They may more easily improperly discern friends from foe. They may be led into dangerous and even fatal situations by not knowing who to trust. Because they failed to integrate into the larger group, people will be less likely to help them in such situations. They will appear as a foreigner in their own land and will be less likely to successfully pass on their traits.

Survival of the Friendliest: Human Self Domestication

Domestication refers to the process of altering the traits of animals to suit the needs of humans (Shilton 2020; Wrangham 2019). The process tends to select for reduced aggression and tolerance towards humans (Shilton 2020; Wrangham 2019; Trut 1999; Belyaev 1979). This tolerance of being around humans has led to an ability to cooperate with humans as these animals became more useful to us (Hare 2002). Key physical traits of domestication include reduced sexual dimorphism, decreased dentition, reduced cranial capacity, reduced facial projection, neoteny, and reduction in strength (Beylaev 1979; Trut, 1999; Trut et al. 2006). Endocrinologically, domestication has resulted in decreased reactivity to androgens, and increased production of serotonin in the brain (Agnvall et al. 2015; Cieri et al. 2014; Trut 2009; Plyusnina et al. 1991). The interplay of these chemicals in the brain has caused a cascade of endocrinological events that have led to decreased brain size, reduced facial projection, neoteny, an increased learning period, reduced sexual dimorphism, and other distinct traits that we see in domesticated species. This in turn further perpetuated decreased aggression, increased tolerance and prosociality towards conspecifics, and cooperative communication tendencies (Trut 1999; Trut et al. 2007). This set of traits is referred to as Domestication Syndrome (Beyleav et al. 1979; Leach 2003; Hare and Tomasello 2005; Wilkins et al. 2014; Agnvall et al. 2017). In the case of Human Self Domestication, we are the animals that were altered to better suit our needs (Hare 2017).

Serotonin and oxytocin are key chemicals in the domestication process (Cieri et al 2014; Henrich 2015). If you are happier, you are less anxious and are thus less likely to attack someone (Cieri et al. 2014). Bonding and sociability encourage the production of serotonin which reinforces these characteristics and its production (Cieri et al. 2014). The increased receptivity to these two chemicals encouraged social responsiveness and expanded the developmental window for social learning; this is also seen in domesticated foxes (Belyaev et al 1985; Gogoleva et al. 2008). If you are friendlier towards humans, you are more likely to cooperate with them (Hare 2017) and get rewarded. If you are happy, you are not thinking about survival (Hare 2017; Shilton 2020). Increased serotonin receptivity and production ultimately leads to decreased facial projection and restricted cranial capacity (Cieri et al. 2014). Serotonin's effect on cranial size and development is notably seen in women who took antidepressants affecting serotonin levels during pregnancy (Alwan et al. 2007).

It is important to note that there may be other factors that would have led to a decrease in the average brain size for humanity. Having a much larger sampling pool may naturally pull the average down, compared to the limited pool of our fossil ancestors. As we began to cooperatively communicate and create ways to store information, the average person was no longer required to hold as much information in their head. Small bands of hunter-gatherers would have been required to hold comparatively more knowledge individually for survival and attaining resources than the average person in industrialized society. The decreased need to hold information would have led to a decrease in individual brain capacity, while the total knowledge capacity still grew. Guess the human brain can only get so big. We may have reached an evolutionary tipping point where a larger cranial capacity is no longer increasingly beneficial. If you have just as many if not more children with a smaller cranial capacity than with a larger one, then evolution will select against it. Interestingly, there is an observed reversion of brain size in Dingos compared to domesticated dogs (Smith et al. 2018).

Traits for prosociality in humans were selected for as the requirement for interacting with other humans became more vital to our survival and thriving. The two major traits that separate humans from other great apes evolutionarily are bipedality and brain size. Increased brain size and living in larger communities facilitated cooperation. The ability to cooperate, and to cooperate flexibly (Hare et al. 2012; Hare 2017), selected for prosociality and against aggression (Hare 2017; Wrangham 2019) in a positive feedback loop. We became better able to read facial expressions and judge the intent of others. The increased cooperation combined with living in increasingly close quarters made reactive aggression less effective as a response (Wrangham 2019). For if one were to react aggressively towards another person for a transgression, a much larger organized action could be mounted in response against the culprit. The advent of lethal weapons made reactive aggression particularly less effective (Wrangham 2019). Run after someone with your spear, and ten people run back after you with theirs. The requirement of cooperation would have facilitated the evolution of more complex language (Thomas and Kirby, 2018); you need to sort out your differences somehow (Progovac and Benítez-Burraco 2019; Benítez-Burraco and Progovac 2020). This in turn selected more for submission and collectivism over defiance and individualism (Hare 2017). In the case of domestication in non-humans, those individuals who submitted to humans were more likely to be chosen to reproduce. In the case of human self domestication, those who submitted to figures of authority, followed social and cultural norms, and did not draw attention to themselves were more likely to remain within the group and pass on their genes over others (Wrangham 2019). With cooperative communication came conspiracy, and the formation of coalitions to enact punishment on those that exhibited reactive aggression or other unfavourable behaviours (Wrangham 2019). They could more easily become ostracized from the group or killed if necessary for becoming a threat. This would also allow women to select for less aggressive and more submissive men (Wrangham 2019). They could form large groups of women that would look out for one another and retaliate on any despate males (Wrangham 2019). This would begin to instill a selection away from violence and a sense of acting in right or wrong ways. The use of birth controlling methods would also aid in this selection process to actively select against aggressive traits.

Domestication can be thought of as a convergent process, selecting similar genes independently in different species based on selected behaviours (Theofanopoulou et al. 2017). Genes that humans share with other domesticated animals are typically involved in brain development and function (Theofanopoulou et al. 2017). These genes are implicated in learning, developmental plasticity, and in neurotransmitters (Theofanopoulou et al. 2017). Humans share the most genes with that of dogs (Theofanopoulou et al. 2017) over other domesticates. Dogs are also thought to have partially domesticated themselves out of a mutualistic relationship with humans rather than simply livestock (Cagan and Blass 2016). These genes are not shared by other domesticates and great apes, nor with archaic humans (Theofanopoulou et al. 2017; Hare et al. 2012; Okanoya 2017), indicating true convergence.

The selection for prosociality and against aggression would have led to changes in the reactivity of Hypothalamus-pituitary-adrenal-axis (HPA axis) which ultimately shaped our brain to what is seen in modern humanity (Theofanopoulou et al. 2017; Cieri et al 2014). The increased serotonin and decreased sensitivity to testosterone would have led to a generally happier disposition and resulted in reduced cranial capacity compared to Neanderthals and early modern humans (Ponce de Leon et al 2008). As we came to tolerate one another more and more, and live in larger and larger groups. We were better able to share information, learn from one another, and innovate. Less of our neural capacity was devoted to aggression and more was dedicated to learning and growing. Unfortunately, we still retained much of our aggression, but it transitioned from reactive to proactive, this combined with cooperative communication is what ultimately led to organized warfare (Wrangham 2019). Selection against reactive aggression, and selection for cooperation, prosociality, sophisticated communication, and emotional control in human evolution closely mirrors the process of domestication (Wrangham 2019). This has given humans a morphological and genetic profile parallel with that of other domesticated animals. But what does religion have to do with this?

The Abrahamic religions often use the metaphor of domesticated species to describe the relations of God and humans. *Straying away from the flock; a horse charging into battle.* The most famous might be: *The Lord is my Shepherd.* As a shepherd tends to their flock, God tends to *His* people. People come together based on a shared belief system, like being herded. Those humans with higher serotonin levels would be more inclined to associate a positive experience from interacting and cooperating with other humans over the alternative. Eventually, the proclivity towards gathering would be linked to the generation of happiness. Religion became a way for people to generate happiness through stories and engaging with people who share beliefs. The belief in a God that watches over you would have encouraged people to cooperate better, and not stray from cultural norms. It would have kept them in the group behaving in a way that is acceptable to more humans (Norenzayan et al. 2016; Norenzayan 2013). It teaches them that there is always something watching over them, like a shepherd minding his flock. When people are watched, they tend to follow social norms and act more morally than they would otherwise (Norenzayan et al. 2016; Norenzayan 2013). Many of us refrain from certain acts in public that we would do at home. Not only could you be punished with ostracization and the loss of security in this life, but you would have consequences in the next one as well. The correlation of being watched and acting morally has become so ingrained in our evolutionary survival that we adjust our behaviour even to the illusion of being watched (Norenzayan et al. 2016). People who could follow authority and had less reactive aggression would be selected for. Thus, genes in line with the domestication process would have been selected for in these settings. A God is the ultimate in authority. Our shared belief in a God has created a celestial watcher who domesticated us for survival in a human world.

Religion takes the domestication process of humans even further. With some selecting people who possess the traits that would make them more likely to propagate their religion. It selects who mates with who (Slyke and Szocik 2020; Buunk et al. 2012; Badahdah and Tiemann 2009); how you will raise your children (Norenzayan 2013), how it moves, and how you must behave around each person.

Domestication allowed us to utilize animals and rid us of our anxieties regarding scarcity. Human domestication reduced our anxieties of being around one another in large groups with minimal privacy. It allowed us to create moral systems that gave us a code for effectively interacting with one another. Domestication produced modern human behaviours, not shared with our ancestors (Theofanopoulou et al. 2017). Domestication selects for adaptations for living with humans; humans also need to live with humans. Domestication created an entity that made us more aware of ourselves. Did morals come from God, or did God come from morals? Human domestication favoured the development of religion; religion helped to reinforce the human domestication process. The domestication process was instrumental in the evolution of the modern human species (Hare et al. 2017).

Letting Our Anxieties Run Wild

Much of human evolution is driven by a desire to minimize anxiety with certainty. This mechanism has led to certain traits running wild in one direction in a positive feedback loop. This is exemplified in the HADD, where detecting an agent was immensely more adaptive than not detecting one, even when one was not there, which led to detecting agents everywhere. This is also true when it comes to sensing when we are hungry. In times of starvation punctuated by feasting, it is beneficial to know when you are hungry (Thomson et al. 2011; Von Hippel and Trivers 2011), but not as beneficial to know that you are full. It is also beneficial to eat as much as one can during those times of plenty and worry about the consequences later. The desire to minimize this anxiety led us to the great inventions of food storage, agriculture, preservation, and finally mass production. Unfortunately, in the modern day, this has led to overwhelming rates of obesity and other maladies related to over-consumption. Not to mention the general greed and anxiety that plagues our everyday decisions. Evolution has not been kind enough to give us a stopping mechanism (Thomson et al. 2011).

Religion has taken our fears related to death, and uncertainty and magnified them. What is going to happen when I die? When the people closest in my life die? When the world changes around us, our brain must compensate for this change. Loss of control often meant loss of life. But in the modern world, loss of control is a few bad days that simply feel like you are going to lose your life. Giving a person the illusion of control allows them to slip back into life when they feel the overwhelming anxiety. Even if we are not in control, at least someone is. Even if we don't know what is happening to our children, and those we care about, someone does. An eternal parent who will take care of me and show me the way does (Thomson et al. 2011). Religion gives us an answer when we don't have one, even if that answer cannot properly be explained.

In the world of our ancestors, being ostracized from the group almost certainly meant loss of resources and death. In the modern day, the things that affect our lives the most are those that disrupt our access to resources (those resources include group associations and connections). You might not die from losing one's status in the group or being ostracized from that group in the Western World, but your body still feels the loss. Thus, we have become genetically programmed to avoid this at all costs. That genetic programming is anxiety. Hormonal and neurochemical changes related to anxiety and depression affect the developing fetus and can ultimately impact genetic expression (Lebowitz et al. 2016; Bartlett et al. 2017; Schiele and Domschke 2018). Stress causes the HPA-axis to release more cortisol and androgens, which in turn would impact the development of the fetus, the activation of its HPA-axis, and the activation of gene expressions (Van Goozen et al 2000; Hauth et al 2000; Hauth et al. 2014; El Baz et al. 2014). Anxiety influences our life choices; those life choices ultimately influence the transmission of our genes in both direction and in speed. Our fear of ostracization is so strong, that our anxiety has pre-programmed us to modify our behaviours to avoid it (Marks and Ness 1994; Zuccala et al. 2021). The Theory of Mind allowed us to build a social map to avoid unrest from our peers. The longer we were able to cooperate with our peers and not set off their anxieties: the longer our anxieties would not be set off by them. Being part of a group made our lives easier, more predictable, which provided neurochemical feedback. The absence of that predictability would trigger another neurochemical cascade that feels like it is crushing us. Those that would work the hardest to avoid such a feeling would be more likely to pass on their genes (Marks and Ness 1994). For some this may also take the form of risk-taking, to win favour in the group. Risk-taking in the hunt and in competition may win one favour in access to mates or to mate selection. Thus, we would evolve the ability to read people's cues and emotions to maintain social bonds. Religion takes that map and turns it into an instruction manual. Rather than simply giving us a general idea of which direction to go, it tells us in clear words what to do and what not to do in every situation. Because not knowing gave us fear and anxiety that would often lead us to our demise (von Hippel 2011).

> *Do not cheat, do not steal, share your wealth whenever you can. Take care of your family. Wear these clothes to communicate that you are following the same manual. Perform this action now to truly connect with this person and their family.*

In addition, it gives you the reward of eternal paradise, granted by an all-loving and all-knowing entity as a reward for following this manual (Norenzayan 2013). When you are building something, following the manual is the difference between paradise and eternal hellfire. Our genetic programming tells us to follow that manual because being a part of the group is a slice of that paradise, but losing that paradise is the hellfire (Norenzayan 2013). Those who did not possess the genetic programming that would allow them to avoid the anxieties of others as insurance of one's own anxieties would be less likely to achieve a minimum status within the group. Those people would be cast to the peripherals of that group, and would have less access to prime resources. To reduce anxieties those outcasts would naturally seek out one another. There is always someone who loves an oddball. Perhaps an affinity for outcasts could also be genetically programmed into some as a safety net. They would provide each other warmth when no one else would. If you don't have the inclination to properly pursue a healthy relationship (the map), those relationships that one would form would be more ephemeral. The cycle would repeat throughout those people's lives and haunt them in their sleep. In modern times those outcasts would be drawn to seek each other out. The sheer number of them combined with our living in large urban centres would mean that they would be more likely to run into one another than they would have in the vast wilderness of the Paleolithic. Their access to resources is less scarce; those that would normally have not passed on their genes may now have more opportunity.

You would not be drawn to the instruction manual if the map in your brain did not tell you to be drawn to the instruction manual. What if the map was upside down? The instruction manual may very well seem pointless to you. Thus, you would wander through the group not knowing how to interact with anyone and not know why everyone else is acting a certain way. The ways these people are acting seem queer to you. You would not know how to properly engage with the other people around you (even if you may still want to). You would even appear to others that you do not wish to properly participate because you are not producing the proper behavioural signals. This would lead to increased anxiety in social situations and the only method to reduce them would be avoidance. This would only lead to further isolation. Thus, those traits would become weeded out of the gene pool.

The strong desire to minimize our anxieties may have contributed to the overwhelming prevalence of anxiety as a mental health concern in modern-day. People simply have too much of it; it is what keeps us alive, even if we fully know that we are not going to die. Those without the capabilities to reduce those anxieties would be more likely to encounter them and less likely to form the bonds necessary to pass on their genes and raise healthy offspring. Our intelligence might simply be our own undoing. We are so smart that we realize Darwin's genetic race is simply an illusion. By giving us the manual, religion prevents us from letting the existential anxieties that can only come from such environmental awareness run out of control. Just follow these steps, and your life will have a purpose, you will have value. You will cease to be simply dust in this universe. There may be a threshold for human intelligence, as those who are too smart do not seem to reproduce as well as those just beneath them. Our evolutionary programming on its own may not be enough to stop it. Just be fruitful and multiply. You don't need to know, just do. Follow this book and you shall do best for yourself and for your species. How do I know? Because this book is the summation of humanity attempting to turn the pictures in its head into an easy-to-follow manual.

From Genes to Memes

Genes are the smallest units of evolution (Dawkins 1976), and organisms are the vehicles who house these genes. For genes to propagate in a population, the organism must survive long enough to reproduce (and succeed in doing so). Genes that provide some sort of reproductive advantage are more likely to propagate and at a higher frequency than genes that do not. Inclusive fitness refers to a particular group better surviving at the expense of less suited groups (Crespi and Summers 2014). The traits that make that group more successful are more likely to remain within that group and thus, the group becomes the primary vehicle for evolution rather than the individual (Crespi and Summers 2014).

Natural selection is a rather inefficient process to propagate genes. Natural selection relies solely on organisms surviving through changing environments for certain variants of genes to become more common through time. It can take many generations for the favoured allele of a given gene to become prominent in a population. Short of catastrophic events, organisms wander around, and mate with conspecifics, in an attempt to produce offspring that will survive to do the same. Rather than create a desire to have offspring, evolution has created a desire to have sex. Sex feels good and having offspring is energetically taxing. The concept that sex equals offspring to the organism is superfluous. The offspring inherits the traits of its parents, which are adapted to the environment one generation behind the current. It is this lag that continues to push evolution forward, always chasing the environment. If we could speed up this process, then evolution would be much more powerful. We see this in domesticated species. Through careful selection, we have produced the entire variability of domestic dog breeds in 15000 years from the wild Eurasian wolf stock. What if rather than using organisms as the vehicles to spread genes, we use them to spread memes?

A meme refers to a piece of information that moves through a population by non-genetic means (Dawkins 1976). Memes require a mode of transportation and a method of understanding. The evolution of human language allowed for faster understanding, complexification, and transmission of information in populations (Progovac and Benítez-Burraco, 2019; Benítez-Burraco and Progovac, 2020). The true value of a meme is its ability to change the behaviours of the individuals spreading it, and modify itself as it travels (Dawkins 1976). Memes compete to reach the most people in the shortest amount of time possible. They accumulate more information and change as more people hear of them and add their own knowledge to the pool. Memes are like genes, but memes do not need sex to propagate. They can spread through a group both vertically through consecutive generations and horizontally through members of a population. They do not need to wait to be recombined in a human body. Genes take generations to change behaviours and only one generation at a time. Memes take moments to change behaviours and can work in multiple generations at any point in an organism's life. Rather than create a child, you create a packet of information that changes, multiplies, and moves through a population, like a virus.

Be fruitful and multiply. Those who hear the phrase *"be fruitful and multiply"* can decide to act on it or not. The individuals who encounter the phrase now can pass it on. Why should I be fruitful and multiply? Because this will lead you to a good life! You will have more company, you will have more intimacy and sex; this will contribute to your overall happiness. Those who heard this meme and were able to act upon it would have more offspring, and would thus have more opportunities to pass on this information and modify it. *Be fruitful and multiply*, by how much? What is a good number? As many as one can! As many as you can provide for. If you have more offspring than the family who did not hear this phrase, then the phrase will spread. If they can project success and happiness in carrying this meme, more people will be influenced by it and will hence follow suit. Someone may walk by your smiling family and remember the phrase, *"be fruitful and multiply."* By seeing how happy you are, they would be more inclined to embrace the message. The behaviour becomes part of the meme. Larger families would become more and more successful at spreading this meme. Their genes would come along for the ride. Genes that would make a person better at spreading this meme would get passed along with it. Of course, people could manufacture counter memes. *"You can be happy without children. More time for yourself and less stress in your life,"* someone might say. That phrase is very true, and many people have found happiness in the absence of offspring. This meme would have a harder time spreading than the former. Fewer people would receive it and pass it on. That meme would produce fewer vehicles to carry it.

Live long and prosper. What does *prosper* mean? The statement is much more open ended than our former example. If one is to live a long life, they may be inclined to take fewer risks. Prosper can mean many different things to different people. Prosper may look like having a large family to some people. Prosper could simply mean reaching one's fullest potential and not reproductive potential. If the meme does not directly lead to the greater production of offspring via the changing of behaviours, then it may not be able to spread as well to new generations as one that does. Perhaps the meme could be disseminated to large groups of people continuously. Prosper despite others or help others to? If everyone is prospering, then I am more likely to prosper. The manufacturing and spreading of memes requires a level of Theory of Mind to properly understand how one's behaviour impacts others. *"Be fruitful and multiply"* impacts both the survivability and the reproductive output of the individual, making it easier to spread, and easier for genes to use over other memes. Memes take advantage of the ability to make someone spread them effectively (Dawkins 1976; Blackmore 2010). In our world, that is sex.

Be memorable; be spreadable. Memes compete with one another for space in our brains. They compete to change the behaviour of individuals, and they compete to move through a population faster, and to as many people as possible. Memes would change and adapt to be better dispersed by the people carrying them. Changing peoples' behaviours changes the environment that the memes must move through. The interaction of the information and the change in behaviours creates a fluid cultural environment for people to interact with one another and pass on their genes with their memes. The genes that are better at spreading memes will influence which memes get spread. Many different memes will be dispersed in experimentation, and new ones will arise to take over those that die out. Genes for survival may begin to divorce themselves from the physical environment as the cultural environment becomes more important to survival. Extreme events, migration and climatic shifts would still play a role in selection; one can always wear a coat. That coat would become a meme, those who wear coats would be more likely to survive. The genes that make someone more inclined to wear a coat or change their behaviour when they see someone else wearing a coat would be the ones to get passed on (Blackmore 2010). If wearing a coat is energetically and genetically more efficient than growing a fur coat but produces the same survivability then wearing a coat will spread over growing one. If someone tells you to wear a coat and you put on the coat, while the other person does not and dies, it is your genes that get passed on. With this, memes that incur some kind of survival advantage are the ones that survive in the population. Memes would select the genes that are good at following the memes, breeding obedience over obstinence in a population.

As certain genes that are either close together on the chromosome, or ones that aid in adapting to related conditions may travel together in the human vehicle, so may memes conglomerate. Memes change as they spread. *They are watching you. Your family is watching you. Everyone is watching you. Your ancestors are watching you. He is watching you!* If humans did not possess the HADD, they would not be inclined to assume that they are being watched. If they did not live in group societies of people looking out for one another, wherein people relied on one another for survival, then they would be uninclined to change their behaviours accordingly. You don't want to be left alone in the wilderness, then follow our memes.

You should *be fruitful and multiply* because *They are watching you,* because *He is watching you. Do not steal,* because *He is watching you. Share your resources, you will get it back.* If you share resources, others in the group will watch out for you. *He will watch out for you.* Carry this item so that people can identify you as a member of their group (or not). *Get to Paradise, there is life after this one! You do not want to be left alone? You do not want to go to Hell?* These memes will tend to migrate together and become associated with one another. Eventually, people begin to associate memes with others in their heads as well as the people spreading them. These memes become messages to live by. Those who share our memes, share our beliefs, they are part of our group, and we can trust them.

People are rather clumsy vehicles for carrying memes, much like they are clumsy at carrying genes. People forget and change the meanings of memes; they add and subtract words and actions to the message. They might not encounter the right people to share them with, or they simply die before they can spread them. You need a way to preserve these memes. Writing and pictures allowed us to collect these memes in one place and preserve them outside of our minds. The advent of writing allowed memes to be collected and dictated to many people like never before. This way memes were preserved in their current state for longer. The person (or persons) writing down the memes get to choose which ones are more important over others. The invention of the Printing Press allowed for text to be copied accurately and disseminated to the masses. Now people have a clear method to follow those memes if they so choose and can always refer to them if need be. People can better determine who is following the memes better, and thus how to treat someone accordingly. We have memes for treating someone who follows them and those who do not. The following of these memes brings people together to spread them and keeps people in line to survive. If you follow them correctly, you will be accepted into the group and the memes survive with you. Follow these memes and maybe you will get to paradise.

If writing gave memes a superior vehicle to humans, then technology is a superior vehicle to writing. With the internet, computers are hooked up to a grid, allowing memes to spread to millions of people across the world in seconds. What makes a meme easier to spread changes to fit the vehicle. Do more eye-catching memes spread faster? What makes a meme more eye-catching? Pictures, or words? How many words? What is the perfect meme? What gets a human to want to send these memes? All the person must do is click and send. The behavioural alteration ability of memes has become more minute and focused; What is going to get this person to spread this packet of information? The elaboration of memes from fragmented pictures and texts to high-definition pictures and algorithms increases their ability to change and to change minds. People can change one word or one aspect of a meme to change its meaning and that gets sent to millions of people in an instant. Those millions of people can do just the same. What divides us can bring us together and divide us again (differently). The meaning of the meme to a person impacts how they send it and who those people send it to, forming groups based on how memes are interpreted. Technology has changed how humans interact with memes, but also how memes interact with humans.

Memes are discrete pieces of information that are passed through a population through non-reproductive means. They are passed on via communication between individuals. If one gene encodes for one protein, then a meme would code for a concept or a behaviour. Memes can move within generations and between families in a population, unconstrained by reproduction. Memes that influence one's reproductive output would consequently impact genes. Memes that could impact behaviours to help them spread faster would survive over others. In this way, memes begin to alter the evolutionary environments of humans to be more human-centric. Memes can be combined and altered to change their message. Different messages impact behaviour differently, and lead to differential spreading. Memes would select for genes that would make a person better at spreading memes. With the invention of writing and later technological advances, memes could be preserved and passed on more rapidly and to more people. More people introduced more opportunities for the memes to acquire new information and shift into new memes. This led to further competition which would have continued to alter human behaviour to spread them. The ways in which memes are spread impact the behaviours of those spreading them and thus, impact how they are spread.

Religion: The Bridge to Civilization

The hallmark of civilization is the ability to live and cooperate in large groups of largely anonymous people (Norenzayan 2013; 2016; Harari 2016); contrarily, for most of its evolutionary history human beings lived in relatively small bands of foragers that were largely related by intimate bonds (Norenzayan, 2016). As population densities increased the chances of encountering (potentially hostile) strangers increased while the chances of cooperating with kin declined. Living in larger groups required an ever-increasing level of cooperation and an innate trust in individuals of both kin and non kin relations. With increased need to cooperate with strangers came increased opportunity for non-reciprocal interactions and free riding. How did humanity progress from living in small bands to living in large complex and interconnected societies of today?

Gobekli Teppe, residing in Turkiye, is thought to be the world's oldest large-scale religious structure (Schmidt 2010), dating back to 11500 years ago. The structure was likely built by semi-nomadic foragers prior to the advent of large-scale agriculture and animal domestication (Norenzayan 2016). The structure likely served as a meeting place for travelling bands to exchange information and trade goods (Norenzayan 2013; 2016; Schatz 2022). The construction of Gobekli Teppe likely required a high level of cooperation, organization, and commitment from many people over many years to create. How did a proto-agrarian society create such a structure?

Religion provides the foundation for the human organization required to build such structures. A shared belief and values system based on cooperation and an appeal to supernatural entities allows people to work together on large projects. Sosis (2000) showed that religious communes from the 19th and 20th centuries had higher longevities and tended to be larger than those that were based on secular belief systems. Knowing that others believe in what you believe in makes people more willing to trust and cooperate with one another to create such structures and societies (Sosis 1997; 2000 Rappaport 1999; Norenzayan 2013; 2015). Once the structure was built, it likely stood as a beacon for people from different groups and regions to come together and share ideas (Schmidt 2010; Norenzayan 2013 Schatz 2022). People in the area had began working together to domesticate animals, cultivate plants and were moving towards a primarily sedentary lifestyle during the time of its construction (Schmidt 2010; Norenzayan et al. 2014; Harari 2016); the construction of such a large structure likely reinforced some level of sedentism. Without a common belief system, it would have been much harder for large numbers of primarily unrelated people to settle in one area and work together towards common goals (humans must first become domesticated). Large-scale civilizations could only form based on large-scale cooperation, which would only be successful based on the acceptance of shared beliefs and the Theory of Mind to know such beliefs.

It was this exchange of ideas that likely led to the domestication of plants and animals and ultimately the building of large societies that are the hallmark of civilization. This organization of people is repeated in early civilizations with the building of large structures such as the Pyramids. Large groups of people coming together with a common goal and a common belief that building such structures serves a purpose to both the now and the afterward. But if religion is so integral to the conception and continuation of civilization, how have we managed to move away from it in modern society?

The New Age of Atheism

Religion has provided the basis for human cooperation; however, rising levels of economic wealth and social safety nets have led to increasing secularization in the post-industrial world (Norris and Inglehart 2004; 2011). With increased mixing of different belief systems, it has become less and less likely that you will run into someone who shares the same religious beliefs as you. Humans needed another way to determine who is a cooperator and who is a free rider. Rather than a supernatural watcher, we have created natural watchers and rather than promising reward and punishment in the afterlife, we are able to offer them in the present life. Watchful eyes from above have primed people to act in a way that fosters cooperation. Religion allowed humans to set rules that govern how people ought to behave around one another in exchange for rewards and punishments. The ability to trust one another has allowed humans to create institutions that act as the Gods watching over us (Harari 2017). People act similarly when they think they are being watched by an all-powerful God or by an all-powerful government (Sharif and Norenzayan 2007; Norenzayan and Gervais 2013). Reminders of the state encourage prosocial behaviours (McKay et al. 2011; Piazza et al. 2011; Pichon et al. 2007; Randolph-Seng and Nielsen 2007; Shariff and Norenzayan, 2007), as reminders of a God do. Rather than believe that one will be punished in an afterlife for not cooperating, one will be punished in this life if they do not behave by the rules laid out for by society.

Rather than living in a world of unpredictable natural events that left us at the mercy of a God; modern civilization has cultivated a level of security that has rendered a belief in a God less necessary (Gervais and Norenzayan 2013). We are no longer left to the mercy of the elements; technology has allowed us to harness the environment to our will. We no longer must worry that if we do not act in a certain way that we will be punished in the afterlife; rather, we worry that we will be punished in this life by systems of law. Instead of the belief in a common God who will send us to paradise if we obey it and help one another, it is the common belief in government systems that determines whether a person will cooperate or not.

In the past, religion offered an answer to questions regarding the origins of life and the interconnectedness of events. It provided a framework for trusting one another. If I know that someone believes in the same Gods as me then they are more likely to help me. With a decreasing reliance on religion as a means for cooperation, we needed another system of determining who to cooperate with and who not to. The advent of money as a universal trade good has created a system that allows us to track cooperation. If I give this person money, they will cooperate with me because they know that they can give that money to someone else in exchange for goods and services later. Instead of relying on one person to reciprocate acts of altruism, we rely on the value of money to reciprocate services provided by civilization. Eventually, that altruism will come back to us. When I order a meal from a restaurant to my house on a food ordering application, I am confident that I will receive it based not on any shared belief in a God but because I paid money for it and that the person on the other end believes in the value of money to provide goods and services if they complete the task. If I do not receive my food, I can get refunded, or the app will send another person and there will be consequences for the person who failed at the task. I am relatively certain that I will not be poisoned by the food I receive based on the reported reputation of the merchant. Replace fear of retribution from a God with fear of loss of reputation, resources, and freedom; and the need for fear in God decreases. If I give this person money, they will cooperate with me because they can gain resources to survive better and have less fear about shelter and food. If I do not cooperate with this person, I will be denied resources to participate in society. If I cooperate with the laws laid out by government systems, I will not be punished and I will be rewarded. We have replaced the fear of God with the fear of rule of law and we have cultivated a species that seeks pleasure and avoids punishment or pain (Norenzayan and Gervais 2013; Norenzayan 2013). If I want other people to help me, grant me resources, and to not be punished then I must act in a way that is consistent with the regulations laid out by systems of government. Without this reliance on religion, people are less inclined to display their religion as a signal that they can be trusted (Gervais and Norenzayan 2013).

In a world marked by uncertainty, where the prospect of our next meal or even the assurance of seeing another day was far from guaranteed, the belief in a higher power governing the universe worked to minimize our fears of the unknown.(Norenzayan 2013). Advances in science have answered many of the questions that religion once did, and we thus seek out supernatural explanations less and less. With more certainty in life, the less the HADD is activated (Norenzaya and Gervais 2013). With HADD less activated, the belief in supernatural entities is less of a necessity to people. Genes for HADD become less prominent in the population which makes their indicators of belief less common. On the other hand, genes for detecting systems and cooperating within these systems become more common in a world controlled by social systems of government rather than a God.

In contemporary society, the foundation for guiding behaviours and fostering unity among diverse individuals no longer relies on a belief system centred around a deity; but rather, in the collective agreement upon a set of rules and norms (Harari 2016; 2017). Instead civilization is built from the man-made systems that regulate conduct and maintain social order. The higher power, then, is perceived as the collective consciousness of humanity itself. This is a recognition of our capacity to shape and govern our destinies through mutual cooperation and adherence to agreed-upon norms. The shift from relying on religious doctrine to human-generated frameworks underscores the evolving nature of social organization and the emergence of a pluralistic society wherein diversity of belief is accommodated within a broader framework of shared human values and principles as opposed to a God (Harari 2016; 2017).

The advent of social safety nets has decreased reliance on supernatural entities; instead of wondering where our next meal is coming from, we know it will be provided for by government services if we need it. Rather than hope for a successful yield, we can go to the store and simply get food. Technology has allowed us to harness the elements so that we know where our next meal is coming from with increased certainty. Yet if it were not for religion, pushing humans to cooperate, then we would not have created the institutions that provide resources and security to people and remove the fear of God from their thoughts (Harari 2016; 2017).

Rather than distrust Atheists, our mistrust falls on those who do not participate in society. We have a mistrust for people who do not follow the rules of society and people who do not work or earn money. Their inability to earn money indicates that they do not reciprocate to other people to uphold the institutions that people rely in to provide resources. They are not performing the signals that tell us that we can trust them. How do we know this, they beg for money rather than work for it. They walk around in shaggy clothes all day. Having money is a hard to fake signal of cooperation; if they have money, then they must have earned it. They are given money by the government rather than providing a service to it, and thus to humanity. The system will give you the bare minimum to survive, but you're on your own for anything else. They can't provide a service to someone else, then they cannot provide a service to me, and thus they should not be rewarded with my trust, money or cooperation. This also includes people with disabilities who cannot work and are receiving government assistance. Rather than distrust those who do not believe in a God, we mistrust those who do not abide by the rules of civilization; having money is a strong indicator of whether they abide by these rules, and participate in civilization.

With industrialization and social safety nets, secularism has become more prominent. A shared belief in a God is no longer a guarantied indicator of cooperation. Technology and increasing surveillance have delivered the threat of punishment in the hereafter to this life. Modernism has allowed us to achieve a paradise in this plane of existence rather than the next (Harari 2016; 2017). You no longer need to pray to a God to get what you want; with hard work, and some social safety nets, paradise can be achieved in the here and now. In the industrial world where secularism is on the rise: fewer and fewer people are at risk of going hungry, or losing the roof over their heads. Rather than relying on a God to watch over them, systems of government keep them safe. These systems of government do not require the costly signals of commitment widespread in religion. These systems require the costly signal of achieving money to increase standards of living.

Summary

The likelihood of encountering people not within our immediate kin groups increases with ever increasing population size. Increased interactions required a system of how to interact with and cooperate with one another. Religion provided a set of moral rules regarding how to interact with people based on the reception of reward and punishments. The human capacity for religion evolved to facilitate intra-group cooperation, and dictate inter-group interactions.

When people share similar beliefs, they are more likely to work together to attain the same goals. We were able to discern these goals using the Theory of Mind. The belief in unseen agents that play a role in the lives of humanity provided a survival advantage, and thus spread throughout the population to a point that you could be reasonably sure that people we encountered believed in some form of unseen entities. But which entities did the person believe in? Was the question. Costly hard to fake signals evolved as a method to discern who possessed similar beliefs from one another. If two or more people were displaying the same costly signals, it was more likely that they held similar beliefs, and would be more likely to cooperate with one another. The costliness of the signal showcased genuine belief because the person would be less likely to expend that level of energy if they did not believe they were getting something out of it from an all-seeing God.

The ability to cooperate with one another in turn facilitated population growth and encouraged more cooperation with more and more people. This in turn required more and more elaborate forms of communication. These signals could be imitated and passed on both through generations as well as laterally between unrelated people in a process resembling evolution through natural selection. Because this communication did not rely on genes for reproduction, it could spread much faster than traditional evolution. It had the potential to change human behaviour more quickly. Increased population centres habituated people to one another, which encouraged docility and cooperation over hostility. People that were more likely to cooperate, were better able to share resources and their genes got passed down over more conflict prone and cooperation averse individuals. This led to an evolutionary phenomenon that mirrored the domestication process of other animals. Human brain size decreased because information could now be shared rather than having to be stored by individuals. Religion selected for individuals that would be better able to spread it. The proclivity towards religion became embedded in our genes.

Once humans were living in closer quarters and cooperating with one another, we were able to better share information regarding technology and the acquiring of resources. This exchange of information allowed human populations to become more sedentary. Increased sedentism led to higher population densities and the organization into the civilizations that we know today. Whereas pastoral and non-agricultural human societies have less organized religious systems (Harari 2016). These civilizations created systems of government and rules for cooperating with one another in the absence of shared belief systems. The development of systems of government decreased the need for religion as a means for governing people in society. A decreased reliance on religion, and increased security of resources, decreased the prevalence of HADD in the population. This decrease facilitated the decrease in overall religiosity in more developed parts of the world. Increased wealth and security decreased reliance on God. Modernism's *want it, go get it* principles brought paradise to the here and now rather than the afterlife. Humanity has ascended so high that it kicked the ladder of religion out from under it (Norenzayan 2013). The kick was not a swift one; pieces of the ladder still linger. Religion evolved to help people cooperate and create systems that no longer need it as its foundation. With a decreased reliance on religion, Atheism would have become more common as we were no longer required to detect the presence of unseen agents in our day to day lives as a means for survival.

Atheists and Barrett's Beer Goggles

Religion is the result of unconscious mental activities working together (Boyer 2003). These states are what allow us to make quick decisions and operate in a social world. The creation of and interaction with supernatural agents is a consequence of normal neurological functioning (Barrett 2004). Religion provides us with answers that we would otherwise not have access to. Why are we here? Where are we going? Why do certain things happen around us? It gives us an illusion of control in the chaos of life. Randomness is unpredictable and leaves us with anxiety regarding the future; in the pre-scientific world, anything that is not controlled by an agent may as well be random (Barrett 2004). Even if we are unable to predict the actions of a supernatural agent, its mere existence gives us the illusion of control. Even if we do not know why things are happening, at least someone does. This decreases anxiety in an unpredictable world. The things that we believe in are shaped by our Belief Forming Faculties—our BFFs (Barrett 2004; Barrett and Church 2013). These refer to how we take in information around us and make sense of it. This does not always lead us to the truth, but simply to the answer that best suits the situation at hand. I guess our BFFs are not actually our best friends forever.

The Cognitive Sciences of Religion (CSR) claims that humans are evolutionarily hardwired to seek out and believe in God concepts and religions (Barrett 2004). As human populations grew and people lived in closer quarters, religion became a more integral part of our lives. Barrett's 2004 book: *Why Would Anyone Believe in God* Describes to the reader the inevitability of religious belief. Left to their own devices, humans simply conjure up these agents to explain the world around them, and to give authority to what we say. Once we start believing in these agents, they start popping up everywhere (Barrett 2004). After reading Barrett's work for my research, I came away from it convinced that he was an Atheist. After all, you wrote the book about why people believe, surely you must accept that this is a product of human evolution and not divine intervention. It is not that God does not exist, but that humans have unconsciously moulded the concept of a God to suit our needs and religion has subsequently moulded the needs of humans to accept it. Only after reading a review of the book by David Eller (2010) did I realize that Barrett was a believing Christian. This became even more obvious upon reading Barrett and Church's 2013 paper entitled: *Should CSR Give Atheists Epistemic Assurance? On Beer-Goggles, BFFs, and Skepticism Regarding Religious Beliefs*. The authors use the analogy of beer-goggles as our filter for how we understand the world. Is everyone else walking around in beer-goggles and only the Atheist sees the world for what it is? Or is the Atheist the one wearing the beer-goggles? The authors argue that since the concept of God is so pervasive in humanity, then it must be true. God has implanted this concept, and the need to seek *him* out, into the minds of humans (2013). Barrett thus argues that it is the Atheist who is wearing the beer-goggles, while everyone else is sober. The alternative of course is that humans are simply programmed to seek out agency, and the

Atheist is the only one who sobered up long enough to see the Earth for what it truly is.

Barrett and Church (2013) argue that to not believe in a God the Atheist rejects what everyone sees as obvious, and what even their own mind sees as obvious. They must deny their unconscious agency detection device at every single turn. If you cannot trust your own faculties, then what can you trust? Thus, they argue that the Atheist must practice as much skepticism with everything else in their life as they do with their belief in a God. If they do not know how they can know anything, then they are not justified in their belief. After all, if there are no Gods, then natural selection has endowed us with BFFs that are unreliable regarding finding truth in our environment (Barrett and Church 2013). The authors are attempting to justify the conclusion that God (indeed the Christian God) exists using the cognitive sciences of religion, and then projecting that onto the Atheists.

Barrett and Church are putting the cart before the horse. They are trying to rationalize their already held beliefs using cognitive sciences, and then saying, "you Atheists are not so smart (Eller 2010)." This is not good science. Barrett and Church seem to be ignoring that virtually everyone who is an Atheist was raised with some form or religion in their lives, and thus has some religious baggage to shed when it comes to forming beliefs and navigating the world. In a weird sense, they are teaching us how to be good Atheists because they are telling us to be more skeptical. The Atheist could simply throw his accusations right back at them by starting with the premise, "I do not see any direct evidence for a God, and the CSR seems to merely be an evolutionary byproduct of our hyperactive agency detection. If there is a God and this God wants us to know that *they* exist, *they* could do a lot better than CSR".

We could start by re-evaluating some of our beliefs, as well as the beliefs of others, to see what works and what does not. We could consciously modify our BFFs more scientifically. Religious beliefs are very reflexive. It is only when we begin to reflect on them that we are able to modify our beliefs, and thus our behaviours (Boyer 2003). CSR is a byproduct of our ability to recognize and form beliefs about other minds; these beliefs are not always correct. By just acknowledging this fact, we can begin to determine when they are or are not correct. From there they can be modified accordingly. This may be easier for the Autistic person because they already know that they have difficulty forming accurate beliefs about the minds of other people, and thus may already be more skeptical. We can recognize that CSR evolved out of ordinary human faculties responding to ordinary human environments. The industrial, scientific world of the 21st century is far from an ordinary human environment. Science has allowed us to conceive of the very small and the immensely large, and do things that we never thought were possible. Evolution is not a search for the truth, or for the best route, it is a search for the path that leads to the passing on of genes. So we can give our brains a break when it comes to understanding how the universe works, we were not made for it. Even if the science we use to learn and understand the environment is flawed, it is the best we got. Science is self correcting, unlike our BFFs, and unlike religion. My BFFs may be faulty, but I must live in this world, work with what I have, and make the most of it.

Atheism is merely the state of not being convinced of the existence of a God. The tendency to believe in God claims as a means of connecting with a cold and dark universe, and as a means of fostering human cohesion is hardwired into our cognition via normal cognitive processes. And into our genes. This still puts the burden of proof on the believer to show that our faculties were indeed correct. Until then, we can only use what we know to come to the best conclusions about the world around us. Even if this did point us to God, it does not point us to a particular God, or to the practices and claims of religions. That God exists does not follow from hyperactive agency detection registering a false positive naturally and easily (Atkinson 2020). Humans have evolved to seek out sugar and fats as a source of energy. In a world where we did not know where our next meal was coming from, concentrated sugars and fats were highly sought out items. This has unfortunately led to an over-indulgence of fat and sugars in modern society. Perhaps humans are simply not wired for the worlds we live in. Perhaps if we were, we would not gorge ourselves on cakes, candy and potato chips.

Chapter 5

Autism and Human Evolution

Autism is not a new phenomenon. Where did Autism come from? Our closest relatives in the animal kingdom exemplify the differences between Autism and Allism; between empathizing and systemizing. How did Autism evolve and why has this condition been maintained into the present day? What is the role of having diversity of minds in a population? Why is Autism in conflict with religion?

Lessons from our closest Kin

Chimpanzees (*Pan trogledytes*) and Bonobos (*Pan paniscus*) are biologically our closest relatives in the animal kingdom (Gibbons 2012; Langergraber et al. 2012; Mailund et al. 2012; Prufer et al. 2012), and are closely related species to each other (Prado-Martinez et al. 2013). Yet their behavioural and social structures are quite different. Their differences focus on group social structure, their usage of tools, and in cognition. (Herrmann et al. 2010; Furuichi et al. 2015). These differences reflect their evolutionary ecology (Furuichi et al. 2015). Their differences place the two species on opposite ends of the spectrum of systemizing and empathizing.

The Chimpanzee range is spread out along the north, eastern and western banks of the Congo River and into the Savannas of Central and Western Africa (Basabose 2005). Chimpanzees live in much more varied habitats from rain-forests to drier forests, and savanna habitats (Basabose 2005). Chimpanzees spend more time on the ground compared to Bonobos who spend most of their time in the trees of rainforest habitats (Coolidge 1933; Malenky and Stiles 1991; Malenky and Wrangham 1994; Doran et al. 2002; Hvilsom et al. 2013; Furuichi 2015). The Chimpanzee range overlaps with the range of Gorillas, leading to competition for resources (Wrangham 1993; Doran et al. 2002; Hvilsom et al. 2013). The Chimpanzees have a varied diet consisting of fruits, tubers, nuts, insects and meat sources from monkeys and other small animals (Stanford 1998; Doran et al. 2002; Newton-Fisher 2007). This variability in habitat and seasonality of resources in Chimpanzee habitat increases resource competition and requires a more varied diet to accommodate (Doran et al. 2002). Chimpanzees spend a greater amount of time foraging for food alone (Wrangham 1993; Eggleton and Vane Wright 1994; Doran et al. 2002) compared to Bonobos. The ancestral range of Chimpanzees experienced greater drying and fragmentation during the late Pleistocene compared to the ancestors of the Bonobos living on the opposite side of the Congo River (Won and Hey 2005; Gruber et al. 2012; Furuichi et al. 2015). Chimpanzee groups are characterized by strong male-male bonds (Goodall 1986; Doran et al. 2002). Chimpanzees engage in male-male competition and warfare more often than Bonobos as seen in male-male coalitions and aggression both within and between groups (Goodall 1986; Wrangham 1993; Furuichi 2011; Wilson et al. 2014). Female Chimpanzees spend a greater deal of time foraging alone or with offspring compared to Bonobos (Doran et al. 2002; Wrangham 1986).

Bonobos and Chimpanzees diverged from a common ancestor between one and two million years ago along the shores of the Congo River (Prado-Martinez et al. 2013) in Central Africa. Bonobos are restricted in range to the forested habitats south of the Congo River in the Demographic Republic of the Congo (Hvilsom et al. 2013). The Bonobo habitat is overall wetter with less seasonal variability than the Chimpanzee habitat (Doran et al. 2002; Hvilsom et al. 2013). The Bonobo diet consists almost entirely of tree fruits (Doran et al. 2002). Bonobos are much friendlier and more socially tolerant than Chimpanzees (Hare et al. 2007). They outperform Chimpanzees in tasks involving group cooperation (Hare et al. 2007). They tend to live in larger groups than Chimpanzees (Furuichi 2009). Due to the greater stability in food resources, Bonobos are more inclined to share food over Chimpanzees, who more readily compete for resources with one another (Herrmann et al. 2010a; 2010b; Hare et al. 2007). Bonobos engage in sexual activities throughout their fertility cycle; they use sex as a form of communication, bonding, and conflict resolution (Wrangham 1993; DeWaal 1995). Bonobos form strong female-female bonds; females spend much more time grooming one another, and feeding together (Wrangham 1993; DeWaal 1995; Kano et al. 2015) than do Chimpanzees.

Both species are known to use tools both in the wild and in captivity (Gruber et al. 2010). Chimpanzees use tools primarily for extraction feeding.

Their usage of tools includes sticks for retrieving ants and termites, stones to crack nuts, and fashioning sticks into spears to hunt monkeys and other small animals (Hermman et al. 2010a; Gruber et al. 2010; Furuichi et al. 2015; Koops et al. 2015). Chimpanzees more readily manipulate objects into tools compared to Bonobos. They use tools more frequently, and in more varied ways than Bonobos do (Koops et al. 2015; Furuichi et al. 2015). In Chimpanzees, tool use is negatively correlated with the availability of ripe fruit in their habitat (Yamakoshi 1998; Furuichi et al. 2015). Bonobos on the other hand use tools mainly for grooming one another and in social communication (Ingmason 1996; DeWaal 1986; Gruber et al. 2010).

The availability of insects and nuts is similar in both Bonobo and Chimpanzee ranges, lending to the same opportunities for tool use; however, the increased abundance of ripe fruits in Bonobo environments reduces the necessity to develop extractive tool use compared to Chimpanzees (Furuichi et al. 2015). The ancestral range of Chimpanzees experienced more drying and fragmentation during the late Pleistocene leading to increased scarcity of fruits (Won and Hey 2005; Furuichi et al. 2015).

Because Chimpanzees readily use tools in the obtaining of food, they perform better in tasks involving object manipulation in space, and problem-solving involving causality (if a then b) compared to Bonobos (Herrman et al. 2010a; Koops et al. 2015; Staes et al. 2018). Bonobos on the other hand tend to perform better in Theory of Mind tasks and gaze following than do Chimpanzees (Gruber et al. 2010; Koops et al. 2015; Kano et al. 2015; Furuichi et al. 2015). In lab tests, Bonobos tended to focus more on the face and eyes compared to Chimpanzees (Kano et al. 2015). Chimpanzees tend to have higher brain grey matter volumes in the motor and visual cortices and in the hippocampal regions (Staes et al. 2018). This is consistent with their propensity to manipulate objects for foraging (Staes et al. 2018). Bonobos have higher grey matter in regions involved in social cognition such as the amygdala, and the dorsolateral Prefrontal cortex (Staes et al. 2018). Bonobos also have smaller brains than Chimpanzees (Staes et al. 2018), which supports the Bonobo self domestication hypothesis (Hare et al. 2012).

Bonobos and Chimpanzees are very closely related species that have evolved along different trajectories in response to environmental factors. In response to a more varied environment that is more prone to food scarcity,

Chimpanzees evolved the use of tools to access a wider variety of food sources. Consequently, they possess a better understanding of manipulating objects in space and causality compared to Bonobos. The ancestors of the modern Bonobo evolved in an environment where there was an abundance of food. This abundance released them from food competition, and allowed them to evolve along a more social trajectory. The Chimpanzee and the Bonobo represent the evolution of systemizing and empathizing modes of cognition respectively. The different evolutionary paths of these two sister species may lend us insight into the evolution of systemizing and empathizing in Humans, and thus, the evolution of Autism in humans.

Looking at Our Own Evolution

If conditions like Autism were overall detrimental to the Human species, then we would see their numbers gradually decrease over time much like the genetic frequencies for physical ailments. Yet, Autistic traits have persisted in the Human population and do not seem to be going anywhere. Autism is likely the additive result of hundreds to thousands of alleles with a small effect size (Polimanti and Gelernter 2017) in the right combination along with hormonal levels in utero acting upon one another resulting in variations of the condition (Benitez-Burraco 2018; Baron-Cohen et al. 2015).

Genes involved in the typical development of the Human brain are also involved in the pathogenesis of mental conditions (Vallortigara and Rogers 2005; Striedter and Northcutt 2019; Leisman et al. 2022). This includes genes for neuronal migration and brain development (Okensberg et al. 2013; Fatemi et al. 2005). Gene variants in Autism tend to contain both nucleotide deletions and duplications; leading to the downregulation of key proteins involved in brain development (Quintero-Rivera et al. 2010; Wang et al. 2018; Merner et al. 2015; Fukuda and Watanabe 2019; Labonne et al. 2020; Meltzer and Van de Water 2017; Xu et al. 2014; Pauly et al. 2023). Single Nucleotide Polymorphisms in the AUTS2 gene, involved in normal human brain development, occur in Autism (Okensberg et al. 2013). Differences in this gene are linked to the Human-Neanderthal split (Green et al. 2010); Neanderthals exhibit the ancestral phenotype and mutations in this gene were selected for in the evolution of modern humans (Green et al. 2010). Polymorphisms of this gene in ASD are closer to the Neanderthal variant (Green et al. 2010). This gene is evolving rapidly in humans (Green et al. 2010; Pollard et al. 2006; Prabakar et al. 2006) with multiple polymorphisms. The enrichment of Neanderthal alleles is associated with the neuronal connectivity pattern of Autism (Friston 2004; Keehn et al. 2013; Gunz et al. 2019; Nair et al. 2020). Enrichment of rare and uncommon Neanderthal-derived alleles are found in Autistic people and their siblings (Pauly et al. 2023). Genetic variants displayed in Autism are associated with high intelligence (Crespi 2016). The period of Neanderthal admixture into the modern human population is associated with key innovations in human prehistory (Bar-Yosef 2002; Greenbaum et al 2019), like the separation of dwelling spaces. Neanderthal DNA accounts for 1-5% of modern human diversity (Reich et al. 2010; Prufer et al. 2014). Neanderthal alleles have been under purifying selection in modern human populations; however, some of them may be under weak positive selection (Pauly et al. 2023). The allele variants associated with Autism are closer to the ancestral state of modern humans (Green et al. 2010). The presence of Neanderthal alleles in Autistic individuals may give us clues to how Neanderthals and earlier human species behaved.

Viewing Autism not as a solitary condition but as a complex genetic network of alleles offers a nuanced perspective on its evolutionary significance. Polimanti and Gelernter (2017) propose that these alleles, which may have conferred individual advantages in specific evolutionary contexts, could also manifest as detrimental phenotypes when combined in certain configurations. The same mechanisms that contributed to the evolution of the Human brain are likely to be involved in the pathogenesis of mental illnesses (Agnati et al. 2012; Nettle 2012; Nettle and Bateson 2012; Polimanti and Gelernter 2017). Autism-related alleles have been conserved throughout evolution (Okensberg et al. 2013). The gene alleles that code for Autism are involved in critical processes such as brain development, neuronal migration, and neural protein synthesis (Okensberg et al. 2013). Autism emerges as an extreme manifestation of a polygenic predisposition for systemizing behaviour, characterized by obsessions and developmental differences (Baron-Cohen et al. 2007). Within populations traits for a propensity towards systemization can be selected, which may lead to the expression of the condition in some individuals. This perspective reframes Autism not as an aberration but as a complex interplay of genetic predispositions shaped by evolutionary forces, shedding light on its multifaceted nature and evolutionary origins.

In families of Autistic individuals, genes implicated in the expression of Autistic traits are associated with years of schooling, childhood intelligence, lifelong learning, and openness to new experiences (Polimanti and Gelenter 2017). People with Autism Spectrum Conditions are overrepresented in the fields of mathematics and engineering (Baron-Cohen et al. 1998). Parents of Autistic children are twice as likely than average to work in engineering (Baron-Cohen and Hammer 1997; Baron-Cohen 1998; Baron-Cohen et al. 2007). Traits that make someone a strong systemizer may have led to innovations in technology in the past (Spikins 2009). Mental rotation, a skill that Autistic people score above average in, involves imagining an object from multiple angles in space. This skill would have proven useful in the manufacturing of stone tools and other prehistoric implements (Spikins 2009). A lengthened learning period would allow for more information to be taken in, and for skills to be honed. People with Autism Spectrum Conditions tend to have increased sensory and visual-spatial abilities, enhanced synaptic functions, increased attentional focus, high socioeconomic status, and more deliberative decision-making (Baron-Cohen 1998; Richards et al. 2020; Leisman et al. 2022). These traits may have proven useful both in our evolutionary past, as well as today. The investigation of natural systems would have led to innovations and better predictions of weather, and migrations patterns that would have proven beneficial in our evolutionary past (Baron-Cohen et al. 2007; Spikins 2009). Perhaps some people with these traits may have had decreased fitness in some areas; but overall, genes for systemizing would have persisted in the population. Genes for systemizing would be more prominent in the immediate family members of Autistic individuals; these genes would have persisted in the population but not fully expressed in some over others (Baron-Cohen 1998; Baron-Cohen et al. 2007). This would have contributed to the prevalence of the Autistic phenotype in the population. People with strong systemizing abilities would tend to select mates with similar aptitudes which would have further perpetuated those genes in the population (Nordsletten et al. 2016; Richards et al. 2020) over others. These genes would concentrate in small pockets in the fields of engineering and sciences. (Baron-Cohen 1998; Roeflsema et al; 2012).

In the industrialized world of the 21st century, people are increasingly relying on technology. New innovations and ideas in the worlds of sciences, technology, engineering, and mathematics are constantly being developed and explored. People with a genetic propensity for systemizing pose an advantage in this world that they may not have in a past that relied more on socialization and social connections. In many ways technology has bridged the gap. It allows Autistic people and people who are not strong empathizers to communicate and form bonds with other people where they would have been left socially isolated in the past (Silberman 2015). If people with Autistic traits are more likely to have Autistic children (Toth et al. 2007; Lomelin 2010), then it is not a stretch to predict the increased prevalence of Autism and people with broader Autistic traits in future generations. The mixing of formerly disparate groups and cultures introduces new combinations of traits into the human population that may have not been seen since our ancient past (Lehman 2010). This mixing may lead to the presence of new or formerly rare conditions that may prove beneficial or detrimental in the human evolutionary landscape (Lehman 2010; Leisman et al. 2022).

Frequency Dependant Selection

Frequency dependent selection refers to traits that are selected for or against depending on their relative occurrence in a population. This type of selection helps to reinforce variability in a population and allows individuals within a species to specialize (Hunt and Jaeggi 2022). With environmental variation, individuals within a species adapt to occupy a variety of niches. As niches fill up, adaptations for that niche will begin to be selected against due to competition for resources within limited space. Competition forces individuals to take on new roles and shift the frequency of available traits within a population (Hunt and Jaeggi 2022).

In a population with a frequency of systemizers and empathizers existing on a continuum, traits for one extreme or the other would be selected for under different circumstances. Systemizers would be selected for their ability to harness new information, identify patterns, and investigate new phenomena; while empathizers would be selected to communicate the information to other members of the population in a way that is easily integrated into the knowledge of other people. In a Stone Age society having one person to track the weather and migration patterns of animals for hunting would be sufficient in a band of hunter gatherers. In fact, having more would likely not increase the efficiency of hunting enough to select for it at a higher frequency than one per a given group of size x (Hunt and Jaeggi 2022). Traits are selected to maximize their usefulness in a population and to fill available niches (Hunt and Jaeggi 2022). Likewise, if a population became fixed on empathizers one could imagine that there would be less innovation and knowledge regarding natural phenomena. Individuals would begin to specialize to fill available niches, with Autism representing one extreme of specialization (Hunt and Jaeggi 2022). Over time, adaptation can lead to maladaptation when conditions change. The niche that it is adapted for is too small, that it cannot function in surrounding conditions with other individuals (Hunt and Jaeggi 2022). Once all niches of a certain type are filled, individuals may need to adapt to open niches that may change with each generation (Hunt and Jaeggi 2022). As individuals mate with one another in a given niche then more specialized individuals would be present in subsequent generations. However, availability of resources (roles in a community) and mates may limit the frequency of individuals with a given set of traits specialized to a niche of defined size. Having individuals with a variety of traits and specializations encourages cooperation with one another as individuals interact to obtain resources (Hunt and Jaeggi 2022).

The systemizing brain is one more prone to the investigation and understanding of the exterior world. This drive to investigate new phenomena leads to discoveries and innovations. In our early evolutionary past, this drive would have been limited by the inherent danger of the new phenomena. People who were less inclined to investigate new phenomena, and be more wary of suspected danger would be able to protect others by warning them of danger. This creates a balance of wariness and curiosity in a group (one watches out while the other investigates). With increased knowledge and the invention of new technologies that were developed by investigation, the world would have become a more known and safer place. As we conquered more of the unknown around us, it would become safer to investigate more phenomena. This process would allow traits for investigation and systemizing to proliferate with each passing generation. In the 21st century where investigation endangers one's life a whole lot less: genes for the investigation, systemizing, understanding, and the acquiring of new knowledge could be selected for at greater frequencies.

If more niches were to open in systemizing, we could see Autism Spectrum Conditions increasing in frequency to occupy these niches. This is observed in regions with a higher concentration of jobs in the sciences and technology fields (Roeflsema et al. 2012). With increased scientific discovery and advancement in technology, one may expect more niches around systemizing to open and thus, we could see an increase in the prevalence of Autism Spectrum conditions and an overall increase in the prevalence of Autistic traits in the wider population in the future(Crespi 2016; Hunt and Jaeggi 2022).

Revisiting Domestication

Domestication refers to the process of selecting for features that habituate wild animals to the presence of Humans. Human Self Domestication refers to the observation that humans possess many of the same traits seen in other domesticated animals. Domestication exists on a spectrum with some individuals being more docile around humans than others. Domestication can also be reversed in a process of feralization. The feralized animal is not wholly like its wild counterparts but exhibits traits that are in between, reflecting the domestication process in reverse. The amount of contact an individual has with humans along with its genetic make-up play a role in its domestication. Different factors go into making a species easier or harder to domesticate.

Across animal species: the process of domestication typically favours traits of tameness and discourages aggression. Humans have repeatedly attempted to domesticate the zebra with little success (Diamond 2012). Unlike some other domesticated animals, zebras have demonstrated a natural wariness towards humans, which can be attributed to their prolonged coexistence with large predators in Africa (Brubaker and Cross 2015). This heightened sense of vigilance, coupled with inherent aggressiveness, particularly among male zebras, poses significant hurdles to domestication efforts. Notably, zebras exhibit a shorter flight initiation distance compared to horses, indicating a heightened sensitivity to potential threats from humans (Brubaker and Cross, 2015). These behavioural traits, combined with the species' territorial nature, have rendered zebras challenging to domesticate and even to breed successfully in captivity

(Lasley et al. 1994). Just as certain species exhibit varying susceptibilities to domestication; likewise, certain individuals within a species are more or less susceptible to domestication. Many of the genes that play a role in domestication are expressed differently in Autism (Benitez-Burracco et al 2016; Niego and Benitez-Burracco 2019).

Domestication played a role in the acquisition of language (Benitez-Burraco et al. 2021). Constantly being in close contact with one another necessitated the development of more sophisticated forms of communication (Benitez-Burraco et al. 2021). As aggression decreased language would have evolved as a means of conflict resolution (Benitez-Burraco et al. 2016). Individuals who were raised without contact with Humans exhibit many traits presented in Autism (Niego and Benitez-Burraco 2021). These individuals tend to exhibit high levels of reactive aggression, deficits in language skills, and in language acquisition (Wilkins et al. 2014; Kapoor 1973). Altered states of candidate genes for domestication tend to be over-represented in developmental conditions associated with different brain states (Benitez-Burracco et al 2016; Niego and Benitez-Burracco 2019). Considering Autism impacts a person's abilities to communicate and readily form social bonds with others, it stands to reason that this condition would be resistant to the domestication process (Niego and Benitez-Burraco 2019). Aggressive behaviour is more common in children with ASD (Farmer et al. 2015; Mikita et al. 2015). People on the Autism Spectrum tend to exhibit increased anxiety (Benitez-Burraco 2016; Park et al. 2016), and elevated levels of glucocorticoids in blood plasma (Hamza et al. 2010) around other Humans. Elevated glucocorticoids indicate that Autistic people exhibit higher stress levels compared to typically developing individuals around others. The domestication process involved reduced levels of stress hormones in plasma, and a decreased stress response from the sympathetic nervous system (Deacon 2010; Wobber and Hare 2009; Hare 2017). Autistic people exhibit increased stress levels around other people for longer durations and generally take a longer time to recover (Spratt et al. 2012). Individuals on the Autism Spectrum exhibit decreased oxytocin levels and oxytocin receptivity (Moerkerke et al. 2021). Levels of oxytocin reduce stress around other individuals and reinforce bonding behaviours (Moerkerke et al. 2021). Domesticated animals show increased levels of oxytocin compared to their wild counterparts (Wilkins et al. 2014; Theofanopoulou et al. 2017). Abnormal features of domestication exhibited in Autism also include abnormal ear shape and a larger overall brain size (Wilkins et al. 2014; Niego and Benitez-Burraco 2021). Candidate genes for domestication are dysregulated in the blood of individuals with ASD (Benitez-Burraco 2019).

The differential expression of genes involved in the domestication process play a role in the manifestation of the ASD phenotype. Human domestication evolved to allow individuals to better cope with constantly being in close quarters with other individuals. Autism involves the abnormal expression of these genes, producing a phenotype in Humans that is genetically closer to the ancestral Anatomically Modern Human condition. Autism is not a new condition (despite what increased numbers might have you believe), instead Allistic traits likely evolved as Humans continued to live in closer association, cooperate with one another and developed complex language (Benitez-Burraco 2016; 2019). We moved away from systemizing to better understand the external world to an empathizing method of cognition that seeks to understand the internal world of the human mind.

Autism and Religion

The belief in unseen agents requires a cognitive faculty that seeks to attribute purposeful intentions, wishes, and emotions to the minds of others (Norenzayan et al. 2012; Keri 2023). Autism refers to the impairment in attributing mental states to others' minds (Norenzayan et al. 2012). Thus, Autistic deficits in Theory of Mind constrain belief in a God (Norenzayan et al. 2012). Alone in a dark forest, the Autistic person is less inclined to intuitively assign agency to an unknown rustle in the bushes. Rather than assign agency and know how to handle the situation from there, they would be more inclined to seek out non agentive explanations. This tendency to assign non-agentive forces to phenomena led to a predisposition to investigation of the unknown, and an Atheistic worldview. This would lead to new discoveries of how the world works, but it would also lead them to getting killed much more frequently. The natural inclination away from assigning agency would have led to a disconnect with these invisible agents and thus, with the people who did *see* and interact with them.

The TPJ is activated when a person is engaged in religious thinking; this is the same part of the brain that is strongly affected in Autistic individuals. The mirror neuron system is responsible for generating the same emotional state when observing or performing an action (Baurer 2005; Yates and Hobson 2020). Impairment in the top-down regulation of mirror neurons in Autistics leads to a disconnection in the mimicry pathway, and thus a disconnection to the emotional states of others (Bauer 2005; Yates and Hobson 2020). The lack of mirror neuron activity in the Inferior Frontal gyrus when imitating observed behaviour and emotional expression (Dapretto et al. 2006) leads to difficulties with imitation, empathy, social cognition, and sharing experiences later in life. The lack of neuronal activity in this pathway creates a disconnect between other people when observing behaviours and emotional states. They are less likely to experience the same emotional state when imitating behaviours and thus, are less inclined to imitate. This disconnects them from the people around them and thus, from the agents they are communicating with using these behaviours. Those that did assign the same agency to certain phenomena would naturally have something to communicate with one another about. This would further isolate the individuals who did not assign agency to a given phenomenon. Slowly, language would form around different phenomena to better understand it. Those that did not would have had to develop an alternative strategy to not let themselves become isolated from the group. They would have to contribute in another way; the inclination for investigation and to solve problems would have proven useful to individuals around them, and they would share their ideas to communicate with and connect with other individuals.

Developmental deficits in mentalizing disrupt the intuitive understandings of religious representations about intentional agents; however, deficits in Theory of Mind do not fully explain the wide range of religious beliefs held by Autistic peoples. Theory of mind does not develop linearly in Autism, rather; Theory of Mind develops more systematically through trial and error with other people around them (Hwang et al. 2007). Autistic people would be able to use trial and error systems to discern what people around them thought and felt in situations and from there be able to reason about Gods through them. Autistic children would learn about concepts of Gods and other unseen agents from people around them. They would learn of their traits and desires to form their own opinions of what they are and integrate this information with their understanding of the world. Some may conclude that these unseen agents simply do not exist because they cannot be interacted with, and everything attributed to them can be explained using non-agentive explanations. The literal brain of the Autistic person may find it hard to hold such counter-intuitive concepts as minds without physical bodies. All that they know of minds is that they require physical bodies to exist. Others may conclude that these unseen agents are immaterial forces of nature personified. The studying of religious doctrine can become a special interest of Autistic people and a way for them to connect with the greater community. Learning religious practices, and participating in ritual could be an acceptable expression of Autistic special interest and repetitive behaviours; as well as to mask Autistic traits to better blend into the community. Participating in the repetitive rituals of religion could be a way to relieve anxiety in the Autistic person, and give them a sense of control (Joliffe et al. 1992). An Autistic person's knowledge and connection with the natural world may be attributed to a connection with a God or Gods by their peers—especially in times before modern science. They would come to understand their knowledge as a gift from God. Autistic people would further integrate these God concepts into their wider understanding of the world; these concepts of Gods may in fact be more like early Human concepts of Gods rather than the monotheistic Big Gods of today (Lehman 2010). These God concepts would also be integrated into the God concepts of the greater society and would change with peoples' changing ideas.

As Autistic traits become more prominent in the population, we will gradually observe a movement away from religion. But as the population becomes less religious, the religious minority will become outcasted by society. They will draw further into their groups to seek refuge. From there they may become more radicalized and fight back against the rising irreligious to remind them of what was left behind. Just as some people may struggle with accepting such a top-down structure to the universe, it may be equally hard for some to grasp a universe without these unseen agents guiding it and looking out for them.

Summary

Chimpanzees and Bonobos represent opposite ends of the spectrum of systemizing and empathizing. Their social structure, problem solving abilities, and understanding of tools reflect this difference in cognition. As a result, Chimpanzees possess a better understanding of space, and cause and effect; while, Bonobos perform better at Theory of Mind tasks, and nonviolent conflict resolution. These two sister species demonstrate how different physical and social environments can lead to different outcomes in social structure and intelligence. Similarly, different environmental and social pressures would have led to differences in systemizing and empathizing on the individual level rather than the species level in Humans. Humans are equally related to both Chimpanzees and to Bonobos; studying these two species may lead to a better understanding of our evolutionary past.

Looking at our own evolution, Autistic traits have likely been present in populations throughout human history. Autism is the additive result of hundreds to thousands of alleles with a small effect size working in concert to generate a wide range of phenotypes. Variations in genes involved in the typical development of the Human brain are involved in the pathogenesis of mental conditions. There is an overrepresentation of Neanderthal-specific alleles involved in brain development in Autism. Are we to the Bonobos as the Neanderthals to the Chimpanzee?

Traits for systemizing lead to a propensity for problem solving and innovation which can be selected for in a population. Autistic traits are associated with years of schooling, childhood intelligence and openness to new experiences. People with Autism Spectrum Conditions are overrepresented in the fields of mathematics and engineering. Parents of Autistic children are twice as likely than average to work in engineering. Traits that make someone a strong systemizer may have led to innovations in technology in the past. People with a strong propensity towards systemizing tend to seek out like minded individuals which further perpetuates Autistic traits in a population. People are constantly relying on technology, and new innovations in the industrialized world of the 21st century. New innovations and ideas in the worlds of sciences, technology, engineering, and mathematics are constantly being developed and explored. People with a genetic propensity for systemizing pose an advantage in this world that they may not have in a past that relied more on socialization and social connections.

Autism is a brain specialized towards systemizing and pattern recognition. Its prominence within a given population is likely frequency dependent. People with the condition take up a niche of understanding and investigation but are selected for up to a threshold within a population. Beyond this threshold, expression of the trait is no longer beneficial, and leads to competition. The competition for niche space keeps the frequency below a threshold and encourages variability and specialization in a population. In the 21st century where new niches in the fields of sciences, technology, engineering, and mathematics are constantly opening for specialized minds: we will likely see an increase in the prominence of Autistic traits. Shifting the threshold.

When it comes to Human Self Domestication, individuals lie on a spectrum of domestication with Autism exhibiting attenuated features of domestication. Autistic people share many traits with individuals who were raised without or with limited Human contact (feralization). Autism Spectrum Conditions may represent a state that is closer to the ancestral Human condition; wherein, conditions like Allism evolved as a means of cooperating with and anticipating the behaviour of other individuals. Domestication involved a decrease in brain size as humans began to rely on the combined intellect of one another rather than individual knowledge. Brain size also likely relaxed as we were not constantly fighting for our survival.

Deficits in Theory of Mind constrain belief in a God. To wonder about a God we must first be able to grasp the mental states of others, and extrapolate that to unseen minds. The literal brain of the Autistic may have trouble comprehending the concept of a mind absent of a physical body. The Autistic person is less inclined to assign agency to unknown phenomena, leading to a naturally more Atheistic view of the world. The parts of the brain that are affected by Autism are the same parts that are activated by religious thoughts. The lack of activity in this region likely contributes to the Autistic perception of religion and Gods. This difference in thinking about Gods and religion likely only leaves Autistic people more isolated from their peers because they feel that they just don't understand them. What kind of ramifications might this have had on people of the past who found the concepts of a God confusing. Were they further isolated by the people around them and would have found it difficult to pursue relationships and have led them to being less evolutionarily successful?

My own apathy regarding a God comes from a disconnection with unseen agents. Asking who created the universe implies that there is a who to begin with. How could consciousness exist without a physical brain? I would search for systematic causal answers rather than appealing to agency. The world seemed to make more sense as a system governed by scientific principles without a mind behind it than a mind controlling the system. If a mind requires a physical body, then God cannot exist within the laws of nature, and therefore must exist outside of nature. If that is the case, then its existence and non-existence is indiscernible.

Autism is a multifaceted condition, in which Theory of Mind deficits do not fully explain the wide range of religious experiences of Autistic people. Autistic people do not grow up in a vacuum; they would incorporate concepts of a God from the people around them into their understanding of the world. They would adapt God concepts to their unique thinking styles and world understanding. Religion serves as a tool to make Autistic people— as well as Allistic people—feel less isolated. Just as Autism and a predisposition towards Atheism has a genetic underpinning, a predisposition towards religious thinking is heritable and selected for under certain conditions.

Chapter 6

Disability, Neurodiversity, Religion, and Modern Society

What does it mean to be different? Is Autism a disability? What is the connection between Autism and other mental conditions? What is the connection between religion and other neurological conditions? What are some unique challenges that Autistic people face today and what can society do to help them flourish?

The Story of the Average

Leibniz and Newton came up with Calculus. What is on the mind of that cashier at the grocery store? Or the guy who cleans the school hallways? The vast majority of the world's story will be left untold. Lost to the sea of the many. Lost to time. The stories that we do hear, the ones that rise above the masses are by the people who stand out. The ones that want their story to be told. Those who do not imitate, for imitation is the behaviour of a busied mind. The stories that we hear are of a different race, the one percent, those who want their story to be heard. This one percent is not like the whole. It sequesters certain traits. We put the two-headed calf on display while we slaughter countless each day. Traits of an inclining to stand out rather than blend into the crowd. You are safe in a crowd. You hear stories of the oddities and not of the mundane, for that is what pulls us out of reality. Nature selects these stories because they stand out from the mundane. The people whose stories we hear are those that want to be heard, want a predator to hear them, rather than to simply blend into society. Neurodiversity is the ultimate black dot in the sea of blue. The stories that we hear are of a moved average of people. This is a world where disability becomes an ability, the ability to stand out in the sea of the many. We see the freaks rather than just the normal people.

The Real Problem with Autism and Communication

We do not do what you expect us to do. And this messes with the model in your head. People have these set scripts in their heads of what people say and how certain social situations ought to play out.

Hi, how are you?

I am good, how are you?

I am well, thank you for asking

How was your day, did you do anything interesting?

Often when I am tired, anxious or simply just stuck on something, I am not going to play along with this script. *Hi, how are you? Do you have chocolate?* They look at me strangely. I remember one day I had a bad throat infection and had nearly lost my voice. I knew that I was not going to get to a clinic until Monday. I was waiting for a bus outside of the grocery store on a Saturday afternoon on what I guess was a warm day in December. An older man walked by me and said, *"Is it summer again?"* I, in my extremely raspy voice said, "who are you?" I guess he did not hear me the first time because he asked me the same question again. Now I did not know this person, nor why they were asking me such a question, and me just wanting to get on the bus and rest said again in the same raspy voice, "who are you?" He scoffed at me and walked away. Much of Autism communication therapy for children is getting them to pick up social cues from adults and learn how to engage with them to get our needs met. It is to allow us to interact with others like we were anyone else. But this severely discounts our experience and how we navigate the world. When I am buying vitamins at a health-food store, I do not want to strike up a conversation about how warm my winter coat is. It's winter, it's Canada; it's cold. I just want to buy my stuff and go! Most people just fall in line, and are happy, and we are expected too. But maybe we should question why these scripts matter so much to us. Am I really going to strike up a meaningful conversation with every Joe-Blow on the dating website who messages me "Hi" and only has a shirtless picture of himself? Is that realistic? More recently someone asked me the classic, "Hi how are you?" I responded with a compliment and a question about them. They did not seem to like that and responded with, "I asked: how are you?"

As if the latter would produce a more meaningful conversation than the former method I proposed. He unmatched me.

Here is a real kicker! My supervisor and I had stopped at a gas station/sandwich shack on our way out to a field site. Prior to getting out, she asked me if I wanted a bottle of water. This was an environmental consulting company, and I was working as an environmental scientist; I had brought with me my own reusable water bottle as I always do. I told her no thanks. I had mentioned to her that I make it a point to not buy bottled water and that I found the concept of bottled water ridiculous. I went to the sandwich stand while she put gas in the truck and went into the store. She came out and offered me a bottle of water. I, in front of the cashier at the sandwich stand told her, I didn't ask for that. She looked at me crossly and asked me if I was going to take it. I said I wouldn't. She sneered at me as if I had mortally wounded her and walked off. It was a long car ride to the field site. Was I just supposed to accept the bottle of water? If you were really thinking about me and caring about me, you would have remembered our conversation and not bought me the bottle of water; perhaps you would have asked me if I wanted you to buy me something to drink. But instead, you decided to buy the bottle of water and attempt to impose your will and values onto me and then get upset when I turned down your "*gesture of kindness.*"

While waiting in line at a Dollarama in Ottawa Ontario there was a mother and a young child (no more than 2 years) two spots ahead of me and an older woman (I would have put her in her fifties) right in front of me. She had a whole shopping cart full of miscellaneous items. The toddler would pick up lollipops and other candies in the aisle while waiting in the line and give them to the mother. When the mother refused to buy them and put them back where they came from the child inevitably started crying and wailing. I took in a deep breath and let out a sigh. The woman in front of me chuckled and said quietly to me, "just needs a few smacks on the ass you know!" I gave her a disgusted look from my face and said, "Sorry, I don't support child abuse." "I don't think it's child abuse, do you have kids?" she said. "No, but that's beside the point." "Who the hell are you?" she sneered at me and turned around. Was I supposed to just blindly agree with this person and laugh? Was I supposed to be happy that this woman was thinking of hitting a crying child and judging the mother because the toddler was doing what toddlers do? What an absolute nightmare, I was shamed and made to feel bad because I did not think that a woman spanking her kid was the answer. Not only do I personally not agree with this sentiment, but current psychology has concluded that spanking kids and other forms of corporal punishment are not effective means of parenting happy and healthy children!

My dog is in a better place. He is looking down upon us. Your dog is dead, there is no better place, just gone. I'm sorry but I just don't see it and that is often framed as my problem rather than theirs.

The double empathy problem refers to a disjuncture in reciprocity between two differently disposed social actors which becomes more marked the wider the disjuncture in perception becomes (Milton 2012). The empathizing mind is hard wired to anticipate and predict the actions of other empathizing minds. It has a hard time predicting the actions of the systemizing mind that is adapted to viewing the world in a different manner. Rather than think of Autism as a disorder in communication, it is better thought of as people using different communication styles to communicate information. This is demonstrated well in the study by Crompton and colleagues (2020) wherein Autistic people were able to communicate information to one another as effectively as Non-Autistics but that communication broke down between Autistics and non-Autistics. Communication with non-Autistic people involves the understanding of social cues and nuances that Autistic people may not readily pick up on and are either different or absent when communicating with other Autistics. From my own experience, I have a much easier time communicating with and conversing with other Autistic people compared to non-Autistics. I am better able to predict their thoughts and behaviours due to our similar cognitive styles. The systemizing mind may look to optimize communication and is less concerned with emotion compared to the empathizing mind, which looks more to communicate on an emotional level. I, for example, am interested more in brute facts and am not good at getting across my emotions. For the empathizing mind, connecting with people on an emotional level is vital in sharing information in a way that the Autistic brain is not. This frames Autism as a difference in communication style rather than a deficit in communication. Rather than teach Autistic people how to communicate with non-Autistic people by picking up on their social cues and teaching us scripts to memorize, we could each learn something about communication from each other.

Is Autism a Disability?

This question is hard for me to answer. If you had asked me as a teenager or young adult, "Am I disabled?" I would have said, "no." I was considered bright and advanced for my age growing up. I was taught that if you work hard, you can achieve anything. You can be whoever and whatever you want to be. I will never be Prime Minister, and there was likely nothing I could have done to make that happen. I had to accept that and move on. I worked hard, I got the good grades, I got the credentials, but I still ended up on disability and with a lack of job prospects and security. I fought my way through school, not taking any extra help because I thought it showed weakness. I thought that I had to be just as good as everyone else. If I could contend with my peers, then I would be good enough. I saw disability as something to overcome, rather than a part of me. My Autism is what allowed me to memorize large amounts of information to take tests. It is my Autism that allowed me to be good with numbers. Yet it is also the reason I have been let go from so many jobs. It is the reason people would not give me a job. It is the reason I missed the experiences that other people my age were having. I was taught to be normal, to look normal, and blend into society. That meant being able to do everything anyone else could do, and do it on my own. I was told things like, "Don't let your diagnosis limit you." It was that kind of language that led me to not get diagnosed until I was twenty-four. It was that kind of language that led me to keeping my diagnosis hidden, even from medical professionals. It was that language that led me to not accept the help that was offered to me because I would have been seen as less able. It was not until I was in my 30s and applying for government disability support that I finally accepted that I was somehow disabled.

Accepting that I needed to be on disability felt like a slap in the face; I spent my entire life trying to prove I was competent only to end up arguing that I was not. I thought that I did everything right, but I ended up on the bottom anyway. Despite getting an education, my practical skills and interaction difficulties just seemed to lead me into poor situations. I would float from job to job barely staying above the poverty line. I continuously found myself taking jobs I was overqualified for and had little to nothing to do with my educational background. I became slowly detached from my field and from the academic community at large. It became harder and harder to find work in my field. Without a solid career I felt depressed and lacked a sense of place in this world. I often feel like this condition robbed me of a normal life.

Autistic people on average are more unemployed and underemployed than the general population (Canada Survey on Disability 2012; Burgess and Cimera 2014; Hayatullah 2023). The median annual income for Autistic people that year was $2900 (Canada Survey on Disability 2012). That is just over the amount for working 40 hrs a week at $20 dollars an hour for one month.

Like most labels, disability can be viewed as a spectrum from more disabled to less disabled. Disability is not stagnant; it can vary throughout a person's life. A person who is unable to articulate themselves, has difficulty interacting with people and has trouble understanding the minds and thoughts of others would have difficulty functioning in society. A person who has trouble understanding causal systems, navigating in space, and difficulty in processing numbers may seem disabled in certain situations, but we may not label this person as disabled compared to the former (Baron-Cohen 2002). Impairments in empathizing are seen as more disabling in our world than impairments in systemizing (Baron-Cohen 2002), because society relies heavily on social interactions. Disability has been traditionally viewed as something to overcome, and something to be eliminated from the person (Oliver 1983; Abberley 1987; Bampi et al. 2010; Oliver 2013); rather than as a part of the person. In the case of Autism, Autistic people are born into, and expected to navigate, a world that was not made for them. This model places the onus on the Autistic person to constantly work on fitting into a non-Autistic mould (Beardon 2008; 2017; Woods 2017). It teaches Autistic people that they are only as good as their ability to appear as non-Autistic as possible, and to fit into the predominant neurotype at any cost (Beardon 2008; 2017; Woods 2017). This approach places undue stress on the Autistic person, often leading to mental health complications, physical exhaustion, and in more serious cases suicide (Woods 2017).

The social model of disability frames society as the disabling agent upon disabled people rather than the condition or lesion as the disabling factor (Oliver 1983; 2013; Abberly 1987). It sees disability as part of someone. Rather than seeing disability as something to be fixed, the onus is on society to make accommodations to better integrate people with impairments into it. Not all disabilities can readily be fixed, nor is "fixing" them really the solution in all cases. Rather than fix the person, we should work to allow disabled people to live the best lives possible. As society becomes more accessible, people become less disabled.

Autism may be seen as a disability in communication, for an Autistic person's inability to understand the thoughts and emotions of others. This stems from deficits in Theory of Mind (Baron-Cohen 1997). Do communication difficulties stem from the Autistic tendency to focus on objects over people or is this focus a result of a failure to communicate with the people around them (Baron-Cohen 2002)? Weak Central Coherence (a tendency to focus on small details rather than big picture thinking) can be viewed as both a weakness and a strength under different conditions (Happe and Frith 1996).

Classifying Autism as a disability allows Autistic people to access resources to help them to better integrate into society. Computer technology can be used to bridge communication barriers. As we continue to advance technologically more niches will open to better integrate Autism into society, Autism will be seen as less of a disability, and more of as a way of being. It is my hope that Autistic people of all abilities get the resources they deserve to live happy and successful lives.

Is Religion a Mental Illness?

Schizophrenia Spectrum Disorder (SSD) is a condition characterized by a loss of contact with reality (Tamminga et al. 2020) and a difficulty discerning reality from non-reality (Tamminga et al. 2020; DSM-V). Symptoms include delusions, hallucinations, paranoia, and disorganized thinking (DSM-V). Delusions tend to be bizarre, implausible, and not derived from ordinary life experiences (Tamminga et al. 2020). A man spends long stretches of time in a cave and comes out claiming he was speaking to an Angel (Sura 96, The Quran). Each time after he claims to have heard an Angel, he becomes disoriented, his heart is racing, and he finds it hard to breath; he reports he had been squeezed (Hussain 2020). If a person claimed to have had this experience today without the religious context, what would we think of them? From the outset, a person who is communicating with disembodied minds may appear delusional. What is the difference between a religious experience in which a person recounts communicating with God or ghosts and the delusions described in Schizophrenia? Delusion-like beliefs are held widely by the general population (Cook 2015). Religious content is a common theme in the hallucinations and delusions experienced by those with SSD (Cook 2015). Religious themes in hallucinations and delusions are more common in Saudi Arabia than in the United Kingdom (Kent and Wahass 1996). Religious delusions are becoming less common in the western world as religion declines in popularity (Stompe et al. 2003). The difference between everyday religious experiences and delusions is their grounding in the larger culture, and their impact on the lives of people experiencing them (APA 2018; McKay and Ross 2021; Krzystank et al. 2012; Cook 2015). The word *spectrum* indicates that people with the condition can range from being severely impacted to mildly impacted. The severity of the condition can change throughout a person's life, and depending on the situation (DSM-V). The experiences of the condition bleeds into what is considered normal behaviour. The experiences of people with SSD disrupt their ability to live a normal life and properly integrate into society (Cook 2015; McKay and Ross 2021).

Patients with Schizophrenia experience dysfunction in the left Temporal lobe (Bruder et al. 1999; John 2009). This is the same part of the brain that is affected in Autism, and is activated during the experiencing of religious experiences and the performance of religious ritual (Persinger 1984; Comings 2010). Patients with SSD typically have smaller left Temporal lobes and experience decreased activity in this area (Bruder et al. 1999).

Religion and spirituality play a significant role in the lives of people with SSD (Grover et al. 2014). People with Schizophrenia tend to be more involved in the religious community and participate in religious activities compared to the general population (Huguelet et al. 1997; Grover et al. 2014). People experiencing delusions of religious content are less likely to seek treatment than those who experience delusions of a nonreligious nature (Siddle et al. 2002); rather they seek help from the religious community (Grover et al. 2014). Religiousness and participation in religious activities is associated with increased social integration, decreased risk of suicide, and overall better quality of life in people with SSD (Mohr et al. 2006; Huguelet et al. 2009). Involvement in religious communities gives patients an outlet to explore their delusions and allows them to better integrate them into their daily lives (Grover et al. 2014). The affirmation of these experiences within the wider culture was associated with better well being; while the disaffirmation of these experiences was associated with lesser well being and greater personal loss from mental illness (Tepper et al. 2001). Most patients with Schizophrenia attribute the condition to supernatural means, while less religious patients attribute the condition to medical causes (Napo and Auckenthaler 2012; Johnson et al. 2012; Saravanan et al. 2007; Unal and Yalvac 2007; Kate et al. 2012). Religiosity and spirituality tend to play a significant role in the lives of people with Schizophrenia. The positive impact of religion and spirituality on the quality-of-life outcomes for people with Schizophrenia should be considered in the treatment of the condition (Shah et al. 2011). Comparing religious experiences to Schizophrenia is not to say that all people who adhere to a religion are mentally ill, but that religion is a symptom of the wider human condition; wherein too much or too little can result in maladjustment to society. The over attribution of agency can leave a person disconnected from both physical reality and the people around them (Huguelet et al. 1997; Grover et al. 2014). Religion helps these people to reintegrate into the community. If Autism is a condition of a lack of recognition of agency, then Schizophrenia is an over attribution of agency around you.

Autism and Mental Health

Autistic people have higher rates of psychiatric conditions compared to the general population (Kessler et al. 2003; Joshi et al. 2013). The most common psychiatric conditions being Attention Deficit Hyperactivity Disorders, Anxiety, and Depressive Disorders (Underwood et al. 2010; Crane et al. 2019). Lifetime prevalence of depression in the ASD population may be as high as 76% (Billstedt et al. 2005; Joshi et al. 2013). Increased rates of depression often lead to increased risk of suicide (Bennett 2016; Mayes et al. 2013) and poorer quality of life in Autistic people (Ghazuiddin et al. 2002; White et al. 2021).

Autistic people often feel socially isolated from their peers and lack strong support systems compared to the general population. The inability to intuitively connect with people through the Theory of Mind leaves Autistic people with reduced social networks. Their difference in how they see the world can lead to an inability to create social connections (Maiano et al. 2016). They tend to miss others' points of view and feelings (Baron-Cohen 1997). Autistic people often feel like they must force themselves to fit into society (Hull et al. 2017); this creates feelings of rejection and disconnection from the world. Their disconnect from the world leads to increased solitary behaviour which only serves to further separate them (Humphrey and Hebron 2015; Humphrey and Symes 2011). Their difficulty with religious concepts only serves to further isolate them from well established structures in society (Norenzayan 2013).

Autistic people face bullying at higher rates than other groups (Casssidy et al. 2014; Cappadocia et al. 2012). This social othering exacerbates feelings of difference in Autistic individuals. This disconnect leads to social withdrawal which further exacerbates loneliness and disconnect (Ghazuiddin et al. 2002). Social withdrawal is often seen as a symptom of Autism and can be overlooked in a clinical setting as a sign of depression (Van Heijst 2019). Autistic people are often made to feel like they are the problem, that they caused family issues, and are the source of distress in their families (Hudson et al. 2019). Autistic people with greater cognitive abilities face higher incidences of depression (Buck et al. 2014; Sterling et al. 2008; Greenlee et al. 2016; Wing 1981), likely because they are more aware of their differences. Reduced social skills and a resistance to change leave Autistic people with fewer coping mechanisms (White et al. 2021; Van Heijst 2019). Their reduced ability to understand and relate to others combined with their unique understanding of the world leaves them feeling out of place with society.

Autistics face challenges with education, employment, and general self direction (White et al. 2021). Autistic people often struggle to achieve and maintain appropriate employment due to communication differences (White et al. 2021). This inability to secure employment and achieve goals in life leads to a lack of self direction and feelings of mastery which can make them feel like life is meaningless (White et al. 2021; Van Heijst et al. 2019). Reduced opportunities can leave Autistic people without a sense of direction; they may accept jobs that are beneath their skill level because they feel that it's all they can get (White et al. 2021). Autistic people also tend to stay in these jobs longer rather than go out there and find a job that better fits their skill set out of a resistance to change and feelings of inadequacy (White et al. 2019; Van Heijst et al. 2019). A history of failure leads them to believe that it is the best that they can do. Increasing opportunities and social networks for Autistic people leads to a better sense of control in their lives and increased self direction (White et al. 2019). Being able to achieve goals gives a sense of belonging and reduces depressive symptoms (White et al. 2019).

Autistic people face higher rates of depression and suicidality because of poorer outcomes in education and employment. It is important to create resources to give Autistic people the tools to live happy and fulfilling lives that give them a sense of mastery and self direction. The ability to form social networks leads to a greater sense of belonging in the community and increased overall mental health (Maiano et al. 2016; Kim et al. 2000; White et al. 2019). For me what has helped is creating a community of Autistic people who are able to give each other a sense of belonging and foster lifelong friendships. Screening for depressive symptoms in Autism can lead to early detection and a better ability to provide resources. Increasing a sense of community and self direction in Autistic people leads to better outcomes, and reduces depressive feelings and feelings of suicidality.

Autism and Borderline Personality Disorder

Borderline Personality Disorder (BPD) is a neurological condition characterized by pervasive patterns of instability in relationships, emotional instability, impulsivity, and fear of abandonment (DSM-V). People with the condition experience unstable relationships that oscillate between idealization and devaluation, intense anger, emotional extremes, chronic feelings of emptiness, and an unstable sense of self (DSM-V). Their fear of abandonment can often lead to frantic efforts to avoid abandonment and emotional dysregulation surrounding abandonment (DSM-V). They often feel insecure and anxious in relationships, constantly on the lookout for indications of rupture and abandonment (DSM-V).

There is a large degree of overlap in the symptomatology of Borderline Personality Disorder (BPD) and ASD (Dell'Osso et al. 2023; Dudas et al. 2018). Autistic people tend to display more traits of BPD and are diagnosed with the condition at higher rates than the general population (Dell'Osso et al. 2023; Anckarsater et al. 2006; Hofvander et al. 2009; Nanchen et al. 2016; May et al. 2021). Likewise, people with BPD exhibit higher rates of ASD and ASD traits (Del'Osso et al. 2018; Nanchen et al. 2016). Due to their similarity in etiology, and the unique characteristics of people on the Autism Spectrum, Autistic people may be at a heightened risk of developing the condition. Key features of both conditions are dichotomous thinking tendencies, emotional dysregulation, and trouble forming and maintaining relationships (Bemmouna et al. 2023).

People with BPD tend to display more Autistic traits than controls, particularly enhanced systemizing abilities (Dell'Osso et al. 2018), and a reduced ability to empathize (Jeung and Herpertz 2014). Both conditions experience trouble in reading emotions, interpersonal functioning and relationships (Jeung and Herpertz 2014). They tend to score higher on the AQ and the SQ than the general population (Dudas et al. 2018; Richards et al. 2023; Bemmouna et al. 2023). Results of these tests were closer to that of Autistic people than the general population (Dudas et a;. 2018). Similarly, Autistic people tend to score higher for BPD traits than the general population (Richards et al. 2023; May et al. 2021; Bemmouna et al. 2023).

People with Borderline Personality Disorder are prone to viewing situations and people in black and white terms; people are either all bad or they are all good (Napolitano and McKay 2007). They may oscillate from one extreme to the other very quickly which can impact their perceptions and relations with other people (DSM-V). Viewing things in black and white is a discrete form of thinking that is very systematic: either A or not A (Suzuki and Hirai 2023). The Autistic propensity to read situations in black and white terms can lead to seeing people in binary ways (Suzuki and Hirai 2023). If people are either one way or another, then their actions are easier to analyze and predict. They may have been exposed to people who would turn their emotions on a dime, appearing happy and inviting one minute and cold and angry the next. Which would prime them to thinking that all people are that way. They miss the nuances of human behaviour and communication in favour of being able to place people into neat categories. The propensity for systemization and dichotomous thinking in Autistic people can lead to development of Borderline Personality traits.

People with Borderline Personality Disorder experience a disruption in a sense of agency of their own actions due to a pattern in which impulses are rapidly acted upon (Bradely and Westen 2005). They are acted upon at such a rate that the author of the action does not recognize their own agency in the act (Bradely and Westen 2005). This distorted sense of agency often leads to conflicts in relationships (Bradely and Westen 2005). Because Autistic people do not readily recognize external agency, they also experience difficulty in recognizing their own agency in their behaviours and how they affect others (Williams and Happe 2010; Zalla and Sperduti 2015).

Common experiences of people with BPD include frequent changes in life plans; failure to achieve goals; remaining in abusive relationships; and financial difficulties (Dyer 2020). Continuous failure in jobs leads to frequent changes in life plans. Autistic people have trouble in the workforce and may frequently lose jobs for getting into conflicts with their boss or for doing things differently. Insecurity in jobs often leads to financial difficulties and impedes Autistic people from reaching their full potential.

Emotional Dysregulation (ED) is a core part of both ASD and BPD (Daros and Williams 2019; Conner et al. 2021; Cai et al. 2018; Samson et al. 2014; Swain et al; 2015; Moseley et al. 2020; Oumaya et al. 2008). Emotional dysregulation is defined as a pattern of emotional expression or experience that interferes with goal-oriented behaviour (Beauchaine 2015). In both Autistic people and in people with BPD, emotional dysregulation leads to self harming, suicidal behaviour (Moseley et al. 2020; Maddox et al. 2017; Conner et al. 2020; Moseley et al. 2022), and generally poor outcomes in life (Beck et al. 2020). Autistic people are biologically vulnerable to ED by virtue of emotional sensitivity, inflexibility in thinking, and differences in social cognition (Conner et al. 2021; Mazefsky and White 2014). A smaller Corpus callosum means reduced connectivity from the right to the left side of the brain, and less communication between your emotions and the logical side of the brain; it is easier to let yourself get carried away by your emotions or by rationality.

People with BPD are more likely to have grown up in an invalidating environment, experiencing abuse and neglect as children (Bemmouna et al.

2023; Linehan 1993; Brambilla et al. 2004). It is this abuse as a child which primes them to think of relationships as negative and to view themselves in a negative light (DSM-V). Experiencing abuse and abandonment as a child makes them hypersensitive to signs of abandonment as adults (DSM-V). Autistic people are more likely to have suffered abuse and to have been invalidated at the hands of parents and other caregivers (Dell'Osso et al. 2023; McDonnell et al. 2019). Their atypical functioning and differences in communication styles often lead to misunderstanding and rejection from peers (Warrier and Baron-Cohen 2021; Hellstrom 2019; Fuld 2018). They are more often bullied by their peers. Due to delays in Theory of Mind, Autistic people may not properly recognize the intentions of people around them and thus, fail to recognize bullying behaviours (Baron-Cohen 1985; Warrier and Baron-Cohen 2021; Rai et al. 2018a; 2018b). They may have trouble understanding the intentions of people around them. Differences in Theory of Mind lead to trouble understanding others and understanding relationships (Conner et al. 2021; Warrier and Baron-Cohen 2021; Hellstrom 2019; Fuld 2018). Communication challenges may lead to unstable relationships in Autistic people (Conner et al. 2021; Mazefsky and White 2014; Bemmouna and Weiner 2023). Their inability to read emotions and predict behaviours can lead to conflict, antagonism, and trouble forming relationships (Warrier and Baron-Cohen 2021; Hellstrom 2019; Fuld 2018). They grow up not knowing who their friend or foe is and have a hard time trusting the people around them. People around them appear to be their friend one minute and cause them pain the next, leading to difficulty with trust and understanding relationships as adults (Ghazuiddin et al. 2002). A history of unstable and unsuccessful relationships can lead Autistic people to be hypersensitive to signs of real and perceived abandonment (Dyer 2020; Bemmouna et al. 2023; Bemmouna and Linehan 2023; Linehan 1993). It is important to note that people with BPD tend to have trouble forming and maintaining relationships due to mistrust, antagonism, and frequently shifting emotions rather than a difference in Theory of Mind (Minzenberg et al. 2006; Palihawadana et al. 2019). Heightened sensitivity to abandonment and rejection, combined with poor relationship skills and emotional dysregulation can lead to frantic efforts to avoid relationship rupture (Bemmouna et al. 2023; Bemmouna and Linehan 2023; Linehan 1993). Autistic people tend to grow up feeling invalidated and othered by the people around them (Gates 2019; Bemmouna et al. 2023). They may feel unloved and as if they do not fit into this world. This pattern of rejection and othering can lead to self harm and suicidal behaviour (Ryden et al. 2008). They grow up believing that they are the cause of problems around them, and that people would be better off if they did not exist. Autistic people engage in self harming and suicidal behaviours at rates higher than the general population (Maddox et al. 2017; Cassidy et al. 2014; Bemmouna et al. 2023). Patients with both ASD and BPD attempt suicide more frequently and show the highest rates of substance abuse and negative self-image (Ryden et al. 2008) compared to controls or patients with only one of the conditions (Oumaya et al. 2008). Emotional dysregulation is a strong predictor of self harm and suicidal behaviour in both groups (Wolff et al. 2019; Gratz et al. 2022). This unique history can lead to Autistic people growing up feeling unloved and having a negative self image (Dell'Osso et al. 2023; McDonnell et al. 2019). Autistic people are prone to having fixated and obsessive interests (Baron-Cohen 1990). If Autistic people commit suicide at higher rates than the baseline, it is foreseeable that an Autistic person could obsess and fixate on suicide and suicidal thoughts as an escape mechanism. Take an emotionally dysregulated child who struggles to form and maintain friendships, raise them in an invalidating environment exposed to abuse and a lack of support and they grow up to be emotionally dysregulated adults with a heightened risk of developing mental health issues (Cazalis et al. 2022; Hailes et al. 2019) and relationship difficulties (Bemmouna et al. 2023). The next step would be to see if there is a genetic correlation between the two conditions indicating a higher likelihood of development.

The compromising environment that some people on the Autism Spectrum tend to grow up in because of difficulty reading social situations, and communication differences, combined with their propensity to read situations in black and white would seem to be the perfect recipe for developing Borderline Personality traits (Linehan 1993). The overlap in symptomatology of these two conditions emphasizes the need to screen for signs of each condition in corresponding groups—particularly in adult females diagnosed with BPD—as a means to form a better understanding of those affected and to provide better tools for success (Richards et al. 2023). It is important to recognize signs of abuse early to intervene and prevent lifelong trauma. The connection between Borderline Personality Disorder (and potentially other psychological conditions) and Autism gives a cautionary tale of how society treats people and how Autistic people grow to view themselves and others around them. The way that we treat people who see the world differently from the rest of us, and who face greater challenges in connecting, can set them up for further psychological and social issues in their future. Giving young Autistic people the skills to better navigate relationships and handle intense emotions can lead to better outcomes in life (Bemmouna et al. 2023).

My experience with doctors and clinicians who are in the mental health field is that they are often not properly trained to recognize Autism in adults. They come across a young person who presents as struggling with relationships. They may not have a lot of friends or a strong support system. They have a hard time holding down a job. They are quick to anger. They feel depressed in life. They have meltdowns. They are feeling fed up with society and feel like they don't belong. They have a history of drug use. There may be some run-ins with the law. There is self harming behaviour and a risk of suicide. Clinicians in the mental health field will look at this list and conclude that they have someone presenting with BPD. The doctors and clinicians then prescribe them Dialectical Behavioural Therapy and they sell it like this amazing therapy that is going to fix you and take all your troubles away. But they fail to recognize the underlying issues in these individuals. Has this person grown up in an othering environment where they constantly did not feel like they were accepted by people around them? Do you notice that this person may not be looking up at you as they talk? Do they have a hard time taking care of themselves, especially when stressed? Do they seem to have a strong aversion to change, and handling change in their lives? The biggest change in someone's life is often the transition period from being a child and having things taken care of for you and having to take care of yourself and navigate this world. That is roughly the time that most adults start to develop mental health issues, and they have found themselves in the mental health system. A system that is often underfunded and tends to throw pills at people. Many people in the mental health field trained to pick up on mental health conditions like bipolar or BPD are often not trained to recognize signs of Autism in adults. They are not trained to recognize Autism. They are not trained in how to properly diagnose Autism in adults. They are unfamiliar with the criteria of Autism, and how it presents in people who grew up without this crucial diagnosis. But they may be able to diagnose BPD. The clinicians in question may be right in picking up on signs of Borderline in these young adults. But they are failing to see the total picture. They need to recognize, and properly address the Autism first in these people. Before they can work on the BPD aspects

Summary

Millions of people are born and die every minute, and most of them will not be remembered for generations to come. The ones that do get remembered, the ones that make history are those that stand out; those that have something to say. Being loud and going against the grain gets you caught. We evolved to conform and not to stand out. Those that do are often seen as disorderly and aberrations.

The Double Empathy problem frames Autism less as a deficit in communication and more as a difference in communicating. When neurotype is controlled for, the difference in correct information transfer was mostly eliminated. The differences in communication styles are what cause communication to break down between neurotypes. Rather than view Autism as solely a deficit, we could each learn how to communicate better by working together.

The differences that people with Autism Spectrum Conditions experience are often disabling in our current society. Rather than see disability as something to be overcome or fixed in order to better fit into society the Social Model of Disability posits that society should adapt to accommodate people with disabilities to allow more people to participate and lead fuller happier lives.

By offering a sense of community and purpose, religion has a positive impact on the mental health of those who adhere to it. The symptoms of mental health conditions can affect a person's perception and experience with religion. Many parallels have been drawn between the religious experiences people have and the experiences of delusions. Indeed many people who claim to have had a religious experience may have been under the influence of mental health conditions. Religion gets a free pass on delusional thinking for its prevalence and integration into modern society. The delusions and disorganized thinking of people with Schizophrenia Spectrum disorder are often religious in nature. People with Schizophrenia Spectrum Disorder tend to be more religious and are involved in their religious communities more than the average person in modern society. In the past, the experiences of people with Schizophrenia and similar conditions may have been thought of as experiences with God or other religious figures.

Schizophrenia and Autism are opposite ends of the same spectrum wherein one is they are the over and under attribution of agency to experiences.

Autistic people experience more mental health and psychiatric conditions than average: particularly depression, anxiety and Attention Deficit Disorder. Autistic people often struggle to form strong intimate relationships, they more frequently experience difficulties in education and employment which leaves them without a sense of purpose and direction in life. Autistic people are more likely to have suffered from bullying and other forms of abuse. Autistic people as a result have higher rates of suicide on average. It is important to provide people with the support that they need to live happier, fuller lives. Increasing social bonds and a sense of community for Autistic people can reduce depressive feelings and feelings of suicidality.

Borderline Personality Disorder is characterized by instability in relationships and strong emotional dysregulation. People on the Autism Spectrum tend to meet more of the criteria of and have higher rates of Borderline Personality Disorder. People with Borderline Personality disorder score higher on tests for Autistic traits than the general population. The genetic makeup combined with the etiology and unique experiences of those on the Autism Spectrum may put them at a higher risk of developing Borderline Personality Disorder and similar conditions. Autism and Borderline Personality Disorder may be so deeply intertwined because the original cohort that the diagnostic criteria of Borderline Personality Disorder is based on likely included a higher than baseline percentage of people that would have also met criteria for Autism today. It may be impossible to disentangle these two conditions.

Discussion and Conclusions

The Theory of Mind refers to the ability to recognize the thoughts, feelings, and beliefs of others as separate from our own. The Theory of Mind allows us to attribute beliefs that are different from our own to others. It is the ability to understand the mental states of others that mediates interactions between individuals, and allows us to predict their behaviours. Autism refers to differences in the Theory of Mind. Autistic people have trouble representing others' representations of the world in their own minds. For the Autistic person, the development of the Theory of Mind is delayed and less intuitive. It requires Autistic people to use reflective thinking to determine that people have knowledge, thoughts, and beliefs separate from their own; and that they would behave differently according to those beliefs.

A key component in the development of Theory of Mind is imitation. Imitation is a form of tinkering with the minds of others to better understand how both theirs and our own operate. Imitation allows one to engage with the world around them by seeing how others respond to their behaviours and seeing their behaviours in others. When the infant's actions are imitated, the infant learns that the other person in the room is paying attention to them and is "like me". The recognition of self-other equivalences is the starting point for social cognition. Children who lack the *aboriginal* capacity for perceiving self-other equivalences in such imitation games might enjoy them less. If they do not have the aboriginal inclination towards imitation, they will be less successful at making predictions concerning the behaviours of other people. Autistic children lack the extended attention to faces and voices in typically developing children. Autistic children do not readily make eye contact like typically developing children and are thus less likely to engage in imitation. Without imitation, Autistic children are unable to develop the common-sense psychology necessary for early Theory of Mind development. The absence of imitation leads to delays in social understanding and communicative functioning. Autistic adults can grasp Theory of Mind concepts through intelligence and cognitive reasoning. Baron-Cohen and Colleagues (1986) concluded that Autistic children have a deficit in understanding of the social world while having an intact understanding of the physical world. It is this deficit in the understanding of the social world that leads to a difficulty in representing and understanding the mind of a God.

The Temporal Parietal Junction is the part of the brain where Theory of Mind and false belief reasoning takes place. The right TPJ becomes activated during the attribution of mental states to others. This part of the brain also houses mirror neurons which become active during imitation and perspective taking. Autistic people demonstrated decreased connectivity between the Temporal and Parietal regions of the brain. The Autistic brain also experiences less activation in the RTPJ in response to exposure to Theory of Mind stimuli and the completion of Theory of Mind tasks. The decrease in functional connectivity, primarily between the Parietal regions and the frontal regions, and inter-hemispheric connections implies that there is a distinct deficit in the processing of information that would require multiple brain regions: particularly in social tasks. The disruption of connectivity in the Theory of Mind regions of the brain in Autism leads to Theory of Mind deficits. Autism is a difference in brain organization that leads to differences in Theory of Mind development.

Theory of Mind deficits do not fully encompass the profile of Autism Spectrum Disorder. Simon Baron-Cohen described two different ways of thinking and understanding the world: Systemizing and Empathizing. Systemizing refers to observing how the input of a system changes its output in a lawful cause and effect manner. It is taking these inputs and outputs and trying to make predictions from them. Systemizing is a powerful tool at predicting changes in the physical world. The process of systemizing has been formalized into the scientific method. The scientific method is a process of gathering information in nature to test hypotheses and form conclusions based on the world around us. Systemizing works extremely well when there is a low degree of variance in the behaviour of the system. Problems in systemizing start to arise when the changes of the system are governed by a mind or an agent and can be changed at will. When it comes to understanding the behaviours of people, the same input does not render the predicted output depending on the person, other people around them, and the situation. This makes the behaviours of people harder to predict using systemizing. To properly understand systems with high degrees of variability or systems in which the change is governed by a mind, empathizing is often required.

Empathizing refers to the drive to identify another person's emotions and thoughts and respond to them with the appropriate behaviours. It allows us to connect with the emotions of others and predict change in agentive systems. Empathizing uses the Theory of Mind to connect the mental states of others with that of our own and to predict appropriate outcomes. It allows us to infer intent, whereas systemizing cannot. It is our ability to empathize that allows us to connect with other people and form meaningful relationships.

Some people are strong empathizers while others are strong systemizers. The abilities to systemize and empathize are measured using the Systemizing and Empathizing Quotients respectively. There is a moderately strong and significant anticorrelation between systemizing and empathizing abilities. Strong systemizing abilities translate to strengths in pattern recognition, map navigation, and other skills that require awareness of the physical world. Empathizing translates to reading and understanding emotions, and connecting to the emotions of others. Humans as a species tend to lean towards empathizing over systemizing. This makes evolutionary sense for a species that evolved living and cooperating in large groups. Autistic people tend to score lower on measures of empathizing and lack the innate framework for tuning into the emotions of others.

The human brain can be divided into two separate halves laterally. The right-side of the brain governs tasks related to systemizing while the left governs empathizing. In Autism there is less connectivity between the right and left sides of the brain. This makes it more difficult to switch between these two processes and integrate information from each half. Males tend to have a stronger affinity for systemizing over females, and *we would say* are right-brain dominant. The Autistic brain possesses atypical lateralization. Each side of the brain works more independently compared to controls. The Autistic brain contains a greater prevalence of longitudinal and short range connections (within hemisphere) over interhemispheric and long range connections in controls. Since short range connections are more typical of the right side of the brain, there is a strong disposition towards thinking and processing strategies typically associated with right-brain responses to stimuli. The strengths associated with Autism include skills in spatial processing, attention to detail, intuitive physics, and intuitive mathematics. These strengths can be attributed to differences in brain lateralization and connectivity which begins in early development. Autistic people have an increased understanding of number theory and mathematical sense from a young age. Autism Spectrum Disorders are characterized by a deficit in Theory of Mind and a disposition towards systemizing over empathizing. This deficit can be made up for using reflective thinking and systemizing to understand the minds of others through trial and error, and the understanding of their own minds. If Autism represents the extreme systemizing brain, then there must exist a condition of the extreme empathizing brain, we call this brain Allism.

Religious beliefs are found in nearly all human cultures. Religion revolves around the beliefs and behaviours regarding the notion that some part of the human experience survives the act of physical death. Religions postulate the existence of minds without bodies (or at least bodies that can be seen). In most religions a God refers to an agent who created the universe and who plays an active role in our lives and in shaping the forces of nature. Religion comes from the Greek: Re-legos meaning to re-connect. It is the force that binds people together through a common belief in a shared reality. It allows people who share little to no relation to know something about and cooperate with one another.

Religions begin with the postulation of the existence of supernatural, counter-intuitive, psychological, intentional, and creative entities. These entities are known to somehow defy the known laws of nature. These entities possess agency, wants, desires, and emotions. The existence of these entities is spawned from a desire for meaning and control in a seemingly meaningless and random existence. Religion encompasses the set of behaviours and values that are centered on a belief in immaterial unseen agents whose stories contribute to a shared history, lifestyle, and set of moral systems.

For us to understand these agents we must conceptualize beings that defy typically recognized criteria of existence. To envision a thinking, creating, and agentive God requires us to conceive of a mind and thoughts that exist separate from our own and separate from a body. Once envisioned, we seek to understand their thoughts, feelings, and motives much as we would another person. We connect with a God using the Theory of Mind.

Religions involve us assigning agency to physical and natural processes to understand cause and effect. The Existential Theory of Mind refers to attributing mental states to objects, physical phenomena, and other entities that do not typically possess human thoughts. Introducing the concept of the soul as immaterial and separate from the human body opens the possibility for minds to exist without bodies. If religion is an extension of the Theory of Mind, then people with a weak Theory of Mind (or who lack an intuitive Theory of Mind) would necessarily present challenges when it comes to believing in supernatural phenomena, and connecting with a God. Stimulation of the Temporal lobe produces religious experiences. We see that the part of the brain connected to the Theory of Mind is also responsible for religious thought.

Human beings have a natural tendency to attribute agency to unexplained phenomena, this is known as the Hyperactive Agency Detection Device. This tendency gets passed down from generation to generation and disseminated throughout the group. Once humans have posited the presence of an agent, they must then determine the desires of said agent. This process makes religious thinking extremely intuitive and impulsive. People more prone to intuitive thinking are more likely to believe in a God. The fact that religion is integrated into so many distinct mental processes makes it so hard to come out of; however, for those who it is not so well integrated into their minds, may have an easier time.

When people are primed to think analytically, they are less likely to express belief in the supernatural. People who are more inclined to think analytically are less likely to express religious belief, and to see agency behind certain phenomena. Autistic people are less likely to attribute agency to unexplained phenomena, or even in cases where agency is involved. While the non-Autistic people could readily pick upon the presence of agency. The movement of the figures activated the TOM networks in their brains to recognize agency. For the Autistic, the idea that the mind could exist without a physical body leaves no physical body for the mind to exist within. In them, the concept of a God becomes harder to grasp. Rather than the Hyperactive Agency Detection Device, Autistic people have a Hyperactive Pattern Detection Device.

People on the Autism Spectrum may still participate in religious practices to achieve community and a sense of belonging. They would form they're own concepts of a God from people around them, and their experiences.

How is religion useful to society? We operate based on the shared belief that everyone will act in accordance with prescribed laws. The more beliefs that people share, the closer their goals align, and the closer their mental states are to one another. The more they will benefit from cooperation. To determine that two or more people share the same beliefs, these beliefs must be communicated to one another in a manner that is unmistakable. Religions often involve a set of visual features that communicate one's adherence to them. Religions build upon what cultures have already created to communicate a shared history and a shared system of beliefs and values. Those who correctly determined the intentions of others were more likely to survive. To prevent deception, these signals often require a large amount of commitment to make them harder to fake. In religion, the set of rules, rituals and other behaviours are directly tied to the existence of a supernatural watchful deity, and an afterlife. These sets of behaviours help signify that you believe in the same God. These rules require commitment which discourages deception and free riding. This shared set of belief in a supernatural watcher helped reduce interpersonal anxieties and insured cooperation within communities. This insurance of cooperation allowed humans to live in larger groups, and accomplish greater things. Larger group sizes allow people to specialize and gain new skills. We no longer had to remember individual peoples; we could just remember symbols that represented groups of people. We begin to see people as groups rather than as individuals. Religion facilitates us in predicting the shared beliefs of others, and thus who to cooperate with.

If you are unable to communicate these shared beliefs, you are less likely to be trusted. Atheists are often the least trusted group of people. People with different mindsets may not readily pick up on what someone is trying to communicate with them through outward signals. These people will not know who to trust and are less likely to be trusted.

Human beings possess many traits in common with domesticated animals. Religion domesticated humans by encouraging friendliness and cooperation while discouraging aggression. The lowering of aggression increased the tolerance of one another in larger groups. Under domestication, prosociality was selected as a requirement for cooperating with others. Those who cooperated the best would be more likely to pass on their genes.

Religion has allowed us to reduce our anxieties surrounding death and uncertainty. It gives people the illusion of control, or that someone is in control. Religion gives us answers in the face of uncertainty. Religion, and being part of a large group, made our lives more predictable. Religion gives us clear direction in how to live our lives within a community.

Information is passed on through memes. A meme refers to a piece of information that moves through a population through non-genetic means. Memes can travel both vertically and horizontally through space to disseminate information much more efficiently than genes. Memes compete with other memes to reach the most people in the shortest amount of time. Memes change behaviour much faster and more flexibly than genes. People follow memes to reinforce group cohesion, memes can affect the genetics of a population. Writing and computer technology has given memes the ability to travel faster and persist longer.

The hallmark of civilization is the ability to live in large groups of unrelated and anonymous people. The construction of large monuments like Gobekli Teppe required the cooperation of large groups of people over a large amount of time. Watchful eyes reinforce cooperation, religion provides the foundation for high levels of human organization. Once built, the monument becomes a meeting place for the exchange of goods and information. Civilization requires the coming together of large groups of people with a common goal and a common belief. But with a strong foundation of social services, cooperation and accountability, religion becomes less and less necessary. The state largely replaces it. Modernism replaces the promise of punishment and reward in an afterlife with the here and now.

Autism is by no means a new phenomenon; it has been here throughout human evolution and even before humans. Our closest cousins in the animal kingdom are opposites when it comes to social structure, and social behaviour. Their strengths, group dynamics, and social behaviour exemplify the differences between Autism and Allism and how differences in the environment can shape the behaviours of organisms.

Autistic traits have persisted in the human population and do not seem to be going anywhere. Genes involved in the typical development of the brain are also involved in the genesis of conditions like Autism. A subset of rare and uncommon Neanderthal-derived alleles play an active role in Autism susceptibility. Neanderthals had much lower population densities than modern humans did at the time they arrived in Eurasia (Bocquet-Appel and Degioanni 2013). This would have made them more susceptible to extinction and the overtaking by modern human populations (Sørensen 2011). Perhaps Neanderthals never evolved the capacity to live in large groups as we did at the same time in history. It is curious to ponder the kinds of cultures and group dynamics of Neanderthals. Did they possess what we would recognize as religion?

Autism is the summation of selection for genes that lead to a propensity for systemizing. Genes implicated in the expression of Autistic traits are associated with years in schooling, childhood intelligence, lifelong learning, and openness to new experiences. Traits that make someone a strong systemizer have led to innovations in technology throughout the past. Lifelong learning allows for the accumulation of knowledge and the honing of new skills. The investigation of natural systems leads to better predictions of the natural world and innovations. These factors are what allow Autistic traits to persist in a population. In a population, you need followers, and you need disruptors. Systemizers are selected for their ability to harness new information, identify patterns, and investigate new phenomena; while empathizers are selected for being able to communicate this new information throughout the population. For new information to survive you need a higher frequency of people who can spread it over people who create it. This makes the available niche space for systemizers limited but never zero. Too many systemizers would create an excess of competition. As environmental circumstances change, the frequency of systemizers and empathizers will change. Genes for Autism would tend to concentrate in certain areas of specialization. In the Industrial world where people are increasingly reliant on technology and innovation, more niches for Autism open up and we see an increase in prevalence.

Domestication refers to the process of habituating animals to humans; Human self domestication refers to habituating humans to the constant presence of other humans. Within a population, certain individuals would be more or less susceptible to the process of domestication. Autistic people tend to not fare as well in large group settings compare of. Autistic people tend to exhibit larger brain sizes, higher levels of reactive aggression, and reduced communicative language abilities. Altered states of candidate genes for the domestication process are overrepresented in Autism. Autism impacts a person's ability to communicate, and form social bonds with others; the Autistic phenotype is resistant to the process of human self domestication.

Autism refers to the impairment in attributing mental states and agency to others. The Autistic person is less inclined to assign agency to unknown phenomena and are more likely to seek out non-agentive explanations. The natural inclination away from assigning agency would lead to a disconnect between them and the agents other people saw; and from the people experiencing these agents. The decreased activity in the part of the brain that is connected to religion in Autistic people leads to difficulty in the understanding of unseen agents and religion. Developmental deficits in mentalization disrupt the intuitive understanding of religious representations regarding intentional agents. The disconnect that Autistic people experience between the emotional states of other people leads to deficits in the understanding of the mind of a God. Autistic people learn about concepts of God and religion from their peers and incorporate it into their understanding of the world. They may be more prone to see God as an impersonal force rather than a personal God.

We live in an extremely group-centric world where individuals do not tend to stand out. Those who write history and shift the world are aberrations in the system. If we think about things this way, it is easy to ascribe neurological and biological differences that we have only identified in recent history to those of the past.

Autism is not necessarily a disorder of communication but a mismatch in the styles of communication between different types of brains. When neurotype is controlled for, communication of information is less affected in both cases. Treating Autism as a disorder in communication severely discounts the Autistic experience. The disconnect in communication is often pinned on the Autistic person over the Non-Autistic person, and Autistic people are simply expected to correct themselves. The systemizing brain is wired differently; thus the empathizing brain has a harder time predicting its thought patterns and actions. If we look at communication from both sides, we could learn something about each other.

We live in a world that largely does not cater to people with disabilities. People who do not fit the norm are simply expected to overcompensate to get by. Disability is often seen as a bad word; something to be overcome rather than something to be accommodated, and accounted for. Autistic people tend to have a harder time in the education system, and in the working environment. With a lack of social support, fewer strong relationships, and poorer career prospects, Autistic people often feel out of place and without a sense of direction in this world. This leads to overall poorer mental health outcomes and higher rates of suicide. Forcing Autistic people into an Allistic mold teaches them that they are only as good as their ability to not appear Autistic. This places undue stress on the Autistic person. The social model of disability places society as the disabling force upon disabled people. Rather than seeing disability as something to be fixed, it places the onus on society to accommodate and better integrate these people into it. Utilizing technology can help to bridge communication barriers. Classifying Autism as a disability allows Autistic people the resources to better integrate themselves into society. Increasing social networks and opportunities for Autistic people leads to a better sense of self direction, integration into society, and reduces depressive symptoms.

Symptoms of Schizophrenia Spectrum Disorder include delusions, hallucinations, paranoia, and disorganized thinking. Religious experiences and practices can be seen as hallucinations and delusions, and may produce what looks like disorganized thinking. Religious experiences get a pass because they are widely accepted and grounded in the larger culture, and largely do not negatively affect a person's ability to participate in society. In fact, it is the absence of religious experiences that impedes the ability of a person to participate in society. Religion and spirituality tend to play a significant role in the lives of people affected by SSD. People with SSD tend to be more involved in the religious community and participate in more religious activities than the general population. Religion helps them to have a connection to the wider society and leads to better outcomes. Autism is an under-attribution of agency to the natural world; Schizophrenia is the over-attribution of agency. Humanity is skewed towards Schizophrenia over Autism.

Borderline Personality Disorder is a condition characterized by pervasive instability in relationships, emotional instability, impulsivity, and a fear of abandonment. Autistic people tend to display more Borderline Personality traits, and people with BPD tend to experience more Autistic traits. Both conditions experience a high degree of emotional dysregulation, lack of impulse control, and self-harming tendencies. People with Borderline Personality Disorder have enhanced systemizing abilities, a reduced ability to empathize, and a propensity towards black and white thinking. The neurological structure and etiology of Autism combined with the environment that Autistic people are often raised in predisposes them to developing Borderline Personality traits. Borderline Personality Traits should be considered as part of the wider Autistic phenotype and a part of the diagnostic process for adults. The way we treat people who experience the world differently can set them up for further psychological issues later in life.

For Autistic people, Theory of Mind is less automatic, it requires the use of reflective vs reflexive thinking to determine that people have knowledge, thoughts, and beliefs separate from their own. Autistic children gravitate towards objects over faces early in life, and thus do not develop the skills that come from imitation as infants. Autistic children tend to have a deficit in the understanding of the social world while having an intact understanding of the physical world. The Autistic brain leans more towards systemizing over empathizing, and the Allistic brain towards empathizing over systemizing. Humanity is skewed towards empathizing. Systemizing works extremely well when there is a low degree of variance in the behaviour of the system. The behaviours of people in response to various forms of input makes for a poor system.

Early in our evolution, humans would attribute agency to unknown phenomena. If there is agency, then they would be better able to understand and connect with what is happening to them. Assuming the presence of agency is adaptive over not assuming the presence of an agent in most cases;

assuming the presence of an agent signals you to respond, while not assuming the presence of an agent can get you killed. This would have selected for the hyperactive detection of agency in humans. We began to attribute agency to natural phenomena such as weather patterns, natural disasters, and eventually to how we got here in the first place. Overtime, the assumption of agency would become intuitive. Which eventually led to an over-reliance on intuition and the assumption of agency.

This eventually led to the assumption of the existence of unseen, disembodied agents that exerted control over the world around us. We would attribute thoughts, feelings, and beliefs to these agents as we would to humans. We would begin to predict that acting in a certain way over others would change the behaviours of these agents in our favour, and thus change our environment. We began to develop systems of actions and morality to appease these agents, and change their behaviours for our favour. If our mind was mapping these agents, then religion gave us the manual of what to do to please these agents and to please other people. It allowed us to cooperate based on shared beliefs and answer questions revolving around life and death.

Within a population, some individuals would be more likely to assume agency over others. Those who did not assume agency were more likely to seek out naturalistic explanations for certain phenomena. Rather than be agency detectors, they became pattern detectors. They honed their skills in predicting outcomes through the analysis of patterns over connecting to thought processes that may have seemed foreign to them. These traits would be selected against but would remain in the population in small numbers. Over time, traits for the recognition of patterns proved useful in the population. Different environmental and sociological circumstances would select for higher and lower frequencies of each type throughout our history. This would bring the two types of people in conflict with one another; where one would see the presence of a mind behind natural phenomena, the other would see mindless processes as explanations. One may conclude that the agents around them do not like these people, and that is why they cannot see them. The other may conclude that they simply do not understand. People would begin to attribute thoughts and intentions similar yet separate from their own to these unseen agents. From there they would wonder how they would feel if someone could not see, or obey them, and project these feelings onto the unseen agents. Ultimately working together, with both viewpoints in different situations, to better make sense of the world would have been the best solution.

Autistic people have a propensity towards systemizing and pattern recognition, over empathizing and mentalization. Autistic people tend to not recognise agency, when in the presence of agent-controlled events, more often than the norm. Their accuracy for detecting agency is less adept, or the threshold of agency detection is much higher—which would make it more precise. They need a lot more to be convinced of the presence of an agent over the lack thereof. Autistic people are less likely to attribute agency to various phenomena. Even when an agent is present behind a given process or phenomena, Autistic people tend to not recognize its presence and will incorrectly assume its absence. This deficit in the recognition of agency conflicts with the recognition and assumption of the presence of the unseen, disembodied minds in religion. The counterintuitive nature of disembodied minds would seem too foreign to the Autistic mind. Most people would want to believe that there is a way to change natural phenomena so that they are less at the mercy of the world around them. If there is a mind behind natural phenomena, then the mind can be changed. Autistic people would not see the utility in behaving in a certain way to affect the thoughts and feelings of these agents. Rather than follow rules ascribed by a God to help them get to paradise, they would see the utility of cooperation to achieve greater goals. They would see natural phenomena as something they had no control over. Rather than seek to control natural phenomena, they would seek to better understand and predict it to better plan for disasters and exert some kind of control over their lives. Rather than seek control via empathizing, they would seek control using knowledge and innovation to create new technology that would eventually change the environment. It was this process of observation and making predictions that led to the scientific method.

Religion refers to the process of bringing people together in cooperation based on a set of shared beliefs. These beliefs become reinforced within a population to further support cooperation in a positive feedback loop. By selecting for cooperation and against conflict and aggression, religion slowly domesticated humanity. This would serve to further other the people who did not possess these beliefs. A subset of humans less inclined towards prosociality would be resistant to the domestication process. They may feel less need to associate with religion as a force that brings people together socially. These people would be seen as aberrations, outcasts, and people to not be trusted. By selecting for prosociality, cooperation, and the ability to infer agency: religion selected for Allistic traits over Autistic ones.

Atheism refers to the lack of belief in Gods, and other supernatural entities of religion. There is an overrepresentation of Atheism in the fields of the natural sciences, technology, and mathematics. Both Atheists and people in these fields score higher on measures of Autistic traits than the general population. Caldwell-Harris showed that Autistic people tended to ascribe more to Atheism or less mainstream concepts of a God over mainstream religious practices. An object-focussed worldview, and a natural propensity to understand the world around them led to an inclination towards the sciences and away from assigning agency to natural phenomena. A strong tendency towards systemizing, combined with a non-intuitive Theory of Mind constrained the ability to see agency in the world, and thus connect to a God. Autistic people are less inclined towards a religious worldview. This does not mean the Autistic person cannot believe in a God or subscribe to a religion. Their differences in mentalization, Theory of Mind, and a propensity towards systemization make the belief in unseen disembodied agents that exert control over the natural world less intuitive. At the same time, it makes an understanding of the natural world through observation of systems and laws more intuitive.

Religion is the result of selection for the recognition of agency in a sentient species. It has allowed humanity to cooperate and build civilizations. Religion has shaped humanity as much as we have shaped it. Religion selected for traits that would help to spread it. It selected for people to spread its ideas to other people who would subsequently follow its teachings. It selected for prosociality, for empathy, and the recognition of agency. Religion selects for traits on the other side of the spectrum from Autism. With the rise of Autism, and systemizing becoming more and more selected for in our modern technological age we see that religion and its adherents decline. With the advent of laws and moral systems to hold civilization together, religion is becoming less and less necessary. The advancement of science allowed us to better understand and exert control over the natural world in ways appealing to unseen agents never could. We no longer need to assume someone is lurking in the bushes to survive. As society advances, we will continue to select for minds adept for the scientific world. Those people will be more likely to adopt an Atheistic worldview and give rise to more Autistic children. What are the consequences of that on humanity? Humanity is changing and society must change with it. Some people will be able to keep their belief in a God, and their ties to religion through this transition; while others will finally feel gratified in this new world order.

To religious parents of Autistic children, teach them about religion and its utility in the current world. Teach them about other religions. Tell them why you believe and let them ask you questions. Science should not be taboo; no subject should be taboo. Let them come to their understanding of the world through innate exploration, and do not seek to punish them for seeing the world differently. Religion is not for everyone.

I Could See What Others Could Not.

"What do you mean you don't believe in God?" They would ask me.

"I see no reason to believe that such a being exists," I would say.

"How did you get here then?"

"I don't know, but rather than assign a God to it, let's figure that out together."

"You are going to Hell!"

"I see no reason to believe that such a place exists, nor that it is even possible for such a place to exist. I also would not revere any being who created the place that you described." It is disturbing to me that children are raised to accept and support the existence of such a place.

"Why are you here? Why is anything here?"

"I don't know, but I want to find out for myself rather than have someone assign me my life."

For the Autistic person, the understanding of nature, abstract symbols and the physical world is intuitive; while the understanding of human emotions and spirituality is a process.

Sometimes I wonder if people grasp the concept that sometimes things happen, and someone did not make it happen to you. Here is an idea, if someone did not do this to you, then there is no one to get angry at when something happens to you that was out of your control. There is no question of, "what did I do to deserve this?" No one is testing you. No one is pulling your strings.

I have often been called closed minded for calling myself an Atheist; but my mind is just different from yours. Your brain would rather believe that someone is there when they are not. My brain needs to know that someone is there, or it more often assumes they are not. Your brain would rather believe that you are being watched. In my brain, I am the watcher. Your brain likes to imitate, and follow the crowd; I just get lost in it. Where you see intent, I need to be convinced of it. Where there was no intent, I may incorrectly assume intent. When someone says there must be a reason and this reason must be a thinking agent; I say, what if there was not an agent? My brain would rather think I got cancer, or that my baby died, or that I was born blind due to non-agentive causes; rather than someone willed these things to happen. There is some solace in not believing in a grandiose plan, that someone is testing you or that someone is punishing you.

The Autistic Borderline

Here are some behaviours I have exhibited that get labelled as Borderline Personality traits as an adult that had their origins in my Autism. Following people around, trying to be friends with, and interact with them manifested into stalking behaviours. My first clear incidence of stalking behaviour that I can recognize was around eleven years old. I would wander the hallways of schools, wander around favourite hang out places to try to make friends, and go so far as to change classes, project groups, or sign up for extra curricular activities just to be around, and potentially interact with a person or people. It seems innocent at ten or eleven years; it becomes concerning at sixteen. I have often seen an Autistic person (usually a young adult male) following people around trying to have an interaction with them, and missing social cues that the person wants to be left alone. Becoming obsessed with a person as a love interest. Getting upset to the point of screaming at people because one too many things in my day did not go right, and I lost all my spoons. Getting very upset when plans change, and things don't follow through. Not learning good emotional coping mechanisms, and bottling up my emotions until I explode. Becoming engulfed in an activity, and acting out when someone tells me we need to go. Seeing people as either all good or all bad. Obsessions, and idealizations of people; followed by loathing when the idealization period ends. Desiring people to feel the pain that I feel was inflicted upon me by them as a means of obtaining justice. Intense and rapid mood swings and emotional surges. An easily agitated nature. A poor sense of my own and others' boundaries. Becoming disproportionately upset and argumentative over a friend's mistake or miscommunication. Feeling as though the world does not want or has rejected me. Lingering in a person's life long after the relationship dissolves. Self harm as a means of regulating and expressing intense emotions. Are these Autistic or Borderline behaviours? Did my unchecked and undiagnosed Autism manifest into behaviours considered anti-social as an adult? Was I more likely to develop Borderline traits because I am Autistic? Was I more prone to developing antisocial behaviours because of the environment I was raised in? I often must make a concerted effort to not veer into antisocial behaviours. I have social anxiety; of course I do, I'm Autistic!

References

2018. APA Dictionary of Psychology: Delusion. American Psychological Association. https://dictionary.apa.org/delusion

Abberley P. 1987. The Concept of Oppression and the Development of a Social Theory of Disability. Disability Handicap and Society 2(1): 5-19

Acharya S., and Shukla S. 2012. Mirror neurons: Enigma of the metaphysical modular brain. Journal of Natural Sciences: Biology and Medicine 3(2): 118-124

Agnati L.F., Barlow P., Ghidoni R., Borroto-Escuela D.O., Guidolin D., and Fuxe K., 2012. Possible Genetic and Epigenetic Links Between Human inner Speech, Schizophrenia and Altruism. Brain Research 1476: 38-57

Agnvall B., Bélteky J., and Jensen P. 2017. Brain Size is Reduced by Selection for Tameness in Red Junglefowl–Correlated Effects in Vital Organs. Scientific Reports 7(1): 3306

Agnvall B., Katajamaa R., Altimiras J., and Jensen P. 2015. Is Domestication Driven by Reduced Fear of Humans? Boldness, Metabolism and Serotonin Levels in Divergently Selected Red Junglefowl (Gallus gallus). Biology Letters 11(9): 20150509

Aichhorn M, Perner J, Weiss B, Kronbichler M, Staffen W, Ladurner G. Temporo-Parietal junction activity in theory-of-mind tasks: falseness, beliefs, or attention. J Cogn Neurosci. 2009 Jun;21(6):1179-1192

Aichhorn M., Perner J., Kronbichler M., Staffen W., and Ladurner G. 2006. Do visual perspective tasks need Theory of Mind? NeuroImage 3: 1059-1068

Alwan S., Reefhuis J., Rasmussen S.A., Olney R.S., and Friedman J.M. 2007. Use of Selective Serotonin-Reuptake Inhibitors in

Pregnancy and The Risk of Birth Defects. Obstetrical & Gynecological Survey 62(11): 702-703

Ameis S.H., Fan J., Rockel C., Voineskos A.N., Lobaugh N.J., Soorya L. TingWang A., Hollander E., and Anagnostou. 2011. Impaired Structural Connectivity of Socio-Emotional Circuits in Autism Spectrum Disorders: A Diffusion Tensor Imaging Study. PLoSONE 6(11): 28044

American Psychiatric Association. 2013. Diagnostic and statistical manual of mental disorders (5th ed.).

Anckarsäter H., Stahlberg O., Larson T., Hakansson C., Jutblad S.B., Niklasson L., Nydén A., Wentz E., Westergren S., Cloninger C.R., and Gillberg C. 2006. The Impact of ADHD and Autism Spectrum Disorders on Temperament, Character, and Personality Development. American Journal of Psychiatry 163(7): 1239-1244

Annett, M. 1999. Handedness and lexical skills in undergraduates. Cortex: A Journal Devoted to the Study of the Nervous System and Behavior 35(3): 357–372

Arnold A.P. 2009. The organizational–activational hypothesis as the foundation for a unified theory of sexual differentiation of all mammalian tissues. Hormones and behavior 55(5): 570-578

Arumugam, K., 2015. Neural Correlates of Religious and Spiritual Experiences (Master's thesis)

Asperger H. 1944. Autistic Psychopathy in Childhood

Atkinson A.R. 2020. HIDD'n HADD in Intelligent Design. Journal of Cognition and Culture 20(3-4): 304-316

Atran S. 2002. The Neuropsychology of Religion. Neurotheology: Brain, Science, Spirituality and Religious Experience: ch-10

Atran S., and Norenzayan A. 2004a. Religion's evolutionary landscape: Counterintuition, commitment, compassion, communion. Behavioral and brain sciences 27(6): 713-730

Atran S., and Norenzayan A. 2004b. Why minds create gods: Devotion, deception, death, and rational decision making. Behavioral and Brain Sciences 27(6): 754-770

Auyeung B., Baron-Cohen S., Chapman E., Knickmeyer R., Taylor K., and Hackett G., 2006. Foetal testosterone and the child systemizing quotient. European Journal of Endocrinology 55(suppl_1): 123-130.

Azari N.P., Nickel J., Wunderlich G., Niedeggen M., Hefter H., Tellmann L., Herzog H., Stoerig P., Birnbacher D., and Seitz R.J. 2001. Neural Correlates of Religious Experience. European Journal of Neuroscience 13(8): 1649-1652.

Badahdah, A.M. and Tiemann, K.A. 2009. Religion and mate selection through cyberspace: a case study of preferences among Muslims. *Journal of Muslim Minority Affairs 29(1):* 83-90.

Baddeley A.D. 2001. Is working memory still working? American Psychology 56(11): 851-864

Badner J.A., and Gershon E.S. 2002. Regional meta-analysis of published data supports linkage of autism with markers on chromosome 7. Molecular Psychiatry 7(1): 56-66

Bampi L., Guilhem D., and Alves E. 2010. Social Model: A New Approach of The Disability Theme. Revista Latino-Americana De Enfermagem 18: 816-823

Bar-Yosef O. 2002. The Upper Paleolithic Revolution. Annual Review of Anthropology 31(1): 363-393

Baranek G.T. 2002. Efficacy of sensory and motor interventions for children with autism. Journal of autism and developmental disorders 32: 397-422

Barnea-Goraly N., Kwon H., Menon V., Eliez S., Lotspeich L., and Reiss A.L. 2004. White matter structure in autism: preliminary evidence from diffusion tensor imaging. Biological Psychiatry 55(3): 323-326

Baron-Cohen S. 1990. Autism: A Specific Cognitive Disorder of and lsquo; Mind-Blindness'. International Review of Psychiatry 2(1): 81-90

Baron-Cohen S. 1995. Mindblindness: An essay on autism and Theory of Mind. The MIT Press.

Baron-Cohen S. 1997. Mindblindness: An Essay on Autism and Theory of Mind. MIT press

Baron-Cohen S. 1998. Does Autism Occur More often in Families of Physicists, Engineers, and Mathematicians? Autism 2(3): 296-301

Baron-Cohen S. 2002. The extreme male brain theory of autism. Trends in Cognitive Sciences 6(6): 248-254

Baron-Cohen S. 2006. The hyper-systemizing, assortative mating theory of autism. Progress in Neuropsychopharmacology and Biological Psychiatry 30(5): 865-872

Baron-Cohen S. 2008. Autism, hypersystemizing, and truth. Quarterly Journal of Experimental Psychology 61(1): 64-75

Baron-Cohen S. 2009. Autism: the empathizing-systemizing (E-S) theory. Annals of the New York Academy of Science 1156: 68-80

Baron-Cohen S. 2010. Empathizing, systemizing, and the extreme male brain theory of autism. Progress in Brain Research 186: 167-175

Baron-Cohen S. and Hammer J. 1997. Parents of Children with Asperger Syndrome: What is the Cognitive Phenotype? Journal of Cognitive Neuroscience 9(4): 548-554

Baron-Cohen S., and Belmonte M.K. 2005. Autism: a window onto the development of the social and the analytic brain. Annual Review of Neuroscience 28: 109-126

Baron-Cohen S., and Swettenham. 1997. Theory of mind in autism: its relationship to executive function and central coherence. D. Cohen & F. Volkmar (eds). Handbook of Autism and Pervasive Developmental Disorders. 2nd Edition. John Wiley and Sons.

Baron-Cohen S., and Wheelwright S. 2004. The empathy quotient: an investigation of adults with Asperger syndrome or high functioning autism, and normal sex differences. Journal of Autism and Developmental Disorders 34(2):163-75

Baron-Cohen S., Ashwin E., Ashwin C., Tavassoli T., and Chakrabarti B. 2009. Talent in autism: hyper-systemizing, hyper-attention to detail and sensory hypersensitivity. Philosophical Transactions of the Royal Society B: Biological Sciences 364(1522): 1377-1383

Baron-Cohen S., Auyeung B., Nørgaard-Pedersen B., Hougaard D.M., Abdallah M.W., Melgaard L., Cohen A.S., Chakrabarti B., Ruta L., and Lombardo M.V. 2015. Elevated Fetal Steroidogenic Activity in Autism. Molecular Psychiatry 20(3): 369-376

Baron-Cohen S., Golan O., Wheelwright S., Granader Y., and Hill J. 2010. Emotion word comprehension from 4 to 16 years old: A developmental survey. Frontiers in Evolutionary Neuroscience 2: 109

Baron-Cohen S., Knickmeyer R.C., and Belmonte M.K. 2005. Sex differences in the brain: implications for explaining autism. Science 310(5749): 819-823

Baron-Cohen S., Leslie A. M., and Frith U. 1986. Mechanical, behavioural, and Intentional understanding of picture stories in autistic children. British Journal of Developmental Psychology 4(2): 113–125.

Baron-Cohen S., Leslie A. M., and Frith. U. 1985. Does the autistic child have a "Theory of Mind"? Cognition 21: 37-46

Baron-Cohen S., O'Riordan M., Stone V., Jones R., and Plaisted K. 1999. Recognition of faux pas by normally developing children and children with Asperger syndrome or high-functioning autism. Journal of Autism and Developmental Disorders 29(5): 407-418

Baron-Cohen S., Richler J., Bisarya D., Gurunathan N., and Wheelwright S. 2003. The systemizing quotient: an investigation of adults with Asperger syndrome or high-functioning autism, and normal sex differences. Philosophical Transactions of the Royal Society of London Britain Biological Sciences 358(1430): 361-374

Baron-Cohen S., Wheelwright S., Burtenshaw A., and Hobson E., 2007. Mathematical Talent is Linked to Autism. Human Nature 18: 125-131.

Baron-Cohen S., Wheelwright S., Skinner R., Martin J., and Clubley E., 2001. The autism-spectrum quotient (AQ): Evidence from asperger syndrome/high-functioning autism, males and females, scientists, and mathematicians. Journal of autism and developmental disorders 31: 5-17

Barrett J.L. 2000. Exploring the Natural Foundations of Religion. Trends in Cognitive Sciences 4(1): 29-34

Barrett J.L. 2004. Why Would Anyone Believe in God? Lanham: Alta Mira Press

Barrett J.L., and Church I.M. 2013. Should CSR Give Atheists Epistemic Assurance? On Beer-Goggles, Bffs, and Skepticism Regarding Religious Beliefs. The Monist 96(3): 311-324

Bartlett A.A., Singh R., and Hunter R.G. 2017. Anxiety and Epigenetics. Neuroepigenomics in Aging and Disease: 145-166

Basabose A.K., 2005. Ranging Patterns of Chimpanzees in a Montane Forest of Kahuzi, Democratic Republic of Congo. International Journal of Primatology 26: 33-54

Bauer J. 2005. Why I Feel What you Feel. Communication and the Mystery of Mirror Neurons. Hamburg, Germany: Hoffmann und Campe.

Bayer U., and Hausmann M. 2010. Hormone therapy in postmenopausal women affects hemispheric asymmetries in fine motor coordination. Hormonal Behavior 58(3): 450-456

Beardon L. 2008. Asperger Syndrome and Perceived Offending Conduct: A Qualitative Study (Online). Ed.D Thesis, Sheffield Hallam University

Beardon L. 2017. Luke Beardon: Perspectives on Autism (Online Blog). https://blogs.shu.ac.uk/autism/?doing_wp_cron=1490259625. 4494929313 659667968750

Beauchaine T.P. 2015. Future Directions in Emotion Dysregulation and Youth Psychopathology. Journal of Clinical Child & Adolescent Psychology 44(5): 875-896.

Beauregard M., and Paquette V. 2006. Neural Correlates of a Mystical Experience in Carmelite Nuns. Neuroscience Letters 405(3): 186-190

Beck K.B., Greco C.M., Terhorst L.A., Skidmore E.R., Kulzer J.L., and McCue M.P., 2020. Mindfulness-Based Stress Reduction for Adults with Autism Spectrum Disorder: Feasibility and Estimated Effects. Mindfulness 11: 1286-1297.

Becker E. and Karnath, H.O. 2007. Incidence of visual extinction after left versus right hemisphere stroke. Stroke 38(12): 3172-3174

Beking T., Geuze R.H., Van Faassen M., Kema I.P., Kreukels, B.P. and Groothuis T.G.G. 2018. Prenatal and pubertal testosterone affect brain lateralization. Psychoneuroendocrinology, 88: 78-91

Bellugi U., Wang P. P., and Jernigan T. L. 1994. Williams syndrome: An unusual neuropsychological profile. In Atypical cognitive deficits in developmental disorders: Implications for brain function. S. H. Broman & J. Grafman (Eds.). Lawrence Erlbaum Associates Inc: 23–56

Belmonte M.K. 2008. Human, but more so: what the autistic brain tells us about the process of narrative. In: Autism and Representation. Ed: Mark Osteen. New York: Routledge: 166-179

Belyaev D.K. 1979. Destabilizing Selection as a Factor in Domestication. Journal of Heredity 70(5): 301–308

Belyaev D.K., Plyusnina I.Z., and Trut L.N. 1985. Domestication in the silver fox (Vulpes fulvus Desm.): Changes in Physiological Boundaries of The Sensitive Period of Primary Socialization. Applied Animal Behaviour Science 13(4): 359-370

Bemmouna D., Lagzouli A. and Weiner L., 2023. The Biosocial Correlates and Predictors of Emotion Dysregulation in Autistic Adults Compared to Borderline Personality Disorder and Nonclinical Controls. Molecular Autism 14(1): 47

Bemmouna D., Lagzouli A., and Weiner L. 2023. The Biosocial Correlates and Predictors of Emotion Dysregulation in Autistic Adults Compared to Borderline Personality Disorder and Nonclinical Controls. Molecular Autism 14(1): 47

Benítez-Burraco A. 2018. Differences in the Neanderthal BRCA2 Gene Might be Related to Their Distinctive Cognitive Profile. Hereditas 155(1): 38

Benítez-Burraco A., Lattanzi W., and Murphy E. 2016. Language Impairments in ASD Resulting from a Failed Domestication of The Human Brain. Frontiers in Neuroscience 10: 203026

Benítez-Burraco A., Progovac L. 2020. Language Evolution: Examining the Link Between Cross-Modality and Aggression Through the Lens of Disorders. Philosophical Transactions of the Royal Society of London British Biological Sciences 376(1824): 20200188

Benítez-Burraco A., Ferretti F., and Progovac L. 2021. Human Self-Domestication and The Evolution of Pragmatics. Cognitive Science 45(6): e12987

Bennett, M. 2016. The Importance of Interviewing Adults on the Autism Spectrum About Their Depression and Suicidal Ideation Experiences. Journal of Autism and Developmental Disorders 46: 1492-1493.

Benson J.E., and Sabbagh M.A. 2009. Theory of Mind and Executive Functioning. Developmental Social Cognitive Neuroscience

Bering J. 2001 Religion explained: The evolutionary origins of religious thought. Basic Books.

Bering J. M. 2002. The Existential Theory of Mind. Review of General Psychology 6(1): 3-24

Bering J. M., and Bjorklund D. F. 2004. The Natural Emergence of Reasoning About the Afterlife as a Developmental Regularity. Developmental Psychology 40(2): 217–233

Bering J.M. 2003. Towards a cognitive theory of existential meaning. New Ideas in Psychology 21(2): 101-120

Bering J.M. 2006a. The folk psychology of souls. Behavioral and Brain Sciences 29(5): 453-462

Bering J.M. 2006b. The Cognitive Psychology of Belief in the Supernatural: Belief in a deity or an afterlife could be an evolutionarily advantageous by-product of people's ability to reason about the minds of others. American Scientist 94(2): 142-149

Berlucchi G. 1972. Anatomical and physiological aspects of visual functions of Corpus Callosum. Brain Research 37(2): 371-392

Berlucchi, G. 1965. Callosal activity in unrestrained, unanesthetized cats. Archives Italiennes de Biologie 103(4): 623–634

Bihrle A.M. 1990. Visuospatial processing in Williams syndrome and Down syndrome. University of California, San Diego, and San Diego State University

Bihrle A.M., Bellugi U., Delis D., and Marks S. 1989. Seeing either the forest or the trees: Dissociation in visuospatial processing. Brain and Cognition 11(1): 37-49

Billstedt E., Gillberg C., and Gillberg C. 2005. Autism After Adolescence: Population-Based 13-To 22-Year Follow-Up Study of 120 Individuals with Autism Diagnosed in Childhood. Journal Of Autism and Developmental Disorders 35: 351-360

Binder J.R., Desai R.H., Graves W.W., and Conant L.L. 2009. Where is the semantic system? A critical review and meta-analysis of 120 functional neuroimaging studies. Cerebral Cortex 19(12): 2767-96

Binnie L. and Williams J. 2003. Intuitive psychology and physics among children with autism and typically developing children. Autism 7(2): 173-193

Bisazza A., Facchin L., Pignatti R., and Vallortigara G. 1998. Lateralization of detour behaviour in poeciliid fish: the effect of species, gender, and sexual motivation. Behavior Brain Research 91(1-2): 157-164

Bishop D.V. 2013. Cerebral asymmetry and language development: cause, correlate, or consequence?. Science, Bishop D.V., 2013. Cerebral asymmetry and language development: cause, correlate, or consequence? Science 340(6138): 1230531: 1230531.

Blackmore S. 2010. Dangerous Memes, or What the Pandorans let Loose. In Library of Congress Cataloging-in-Publication Data: 297

Blackstock E.G. 1978. Cerebral asymmetry and the development of early infantile autism. Journal of autism and childhood schizophrenia 8(3): 339-353

Blanke O., Mohr C., Michel C.M., Pascual-Leone A., Brugger P., Seeck M., Landis T., and Thut G., 2005. Linking Out-Of-Body Experience and Self Processing to Mental Own-Body Imagery at The TemporoParietal Junction. Journal of Neuroscience 25(3): 550-557

Bless J.J., Westerhausen R., Torkildsen J.V.K., Gudmundsen M., Kompus K., and Hugdahl K. 2015. Laterality across languages: Results from a global dichotic listening study using a smartphone application. Laterality: Asymmetries of Body, Brain, and Cognition 20(4): 434-452

Bloemen O.J.N., de Koning M.B., Schmitz N., Nieman D. H., Becker H.E., de Haan L., Dingemans P., and Linszen D. H. 2010. White-matter markers for psychosis in a prospective ultra-high-risk cohort. Psychological Medicine 40(8):1297-1304

Bloom P. 2005. Is God an Accident? Atlantic Monthly 296(5): 105.

Bloom P. 2007. Religion is Natural. Developmental Science 10(1): 147-151

Boddaert N., Chabane N., Gervais H., Good C.D., Bourgeois M., Plumet M.H., Barthélémy C., Mouren M.C., Artiges E., Samson Y., Brunelle F., Frackowiak R.S., and Zilbovicius M. 2004. Superior Temporal sulcus anatomical abnormalities in childhood autism: a voxel-based morphometry MRI study. Neuroimage 23(1): 364-369

Boersma M., Kemner C., de Reus M.A., Collin G., Snijders T.M., Hofman D., Buitelaar J.K., Stam C.J. and Van Den Heuvel, M.P. 2013.

Disrupted functional brain networks in autistic toddlers. Brain Connectivity 3(1): 41-49

Botvinick M.M., Cohen J.D., and Carter C.S. 2004. Conflict monitoring and anterior cingulate cortex: an update. Trends in Cognitive Science 8(12): 539-46

Boyer P. 1994. The naturalness of religious ideas: A cognitive theory of religion. University of California Press.

Boyer P. 2000. Functional origins of religious concepts: Ontological and strategic selection in evolved minds. Journal of the Royal Anthropological Institute 6(2): 195-214

Boyer P. 2001. Religion Explained: The Evolutionary Origins of Religious Thought. Basic Books

Boyer P. 2003. Religious Thought and Behaviour as By-Products of Brain Function. Trends In Cognitive Sciences 7(3): 119-124

Boyer P. 2008. Being human: Religion: Bound to Believe? Nature 455(7216): 1038-1039

Bradley R., and Westen D. 2005. The Psychodynamics of Borderline Personality Disorder: A View from Developmental Psychopathology. Development and Psychopathology 17(4): 927-957

Bradshaw J. L., and Rogers L. J. 1993. The evolution of lateral asymmetries, language, tool use, and intellect. Academic Press

Brambilla P., Soloff P.H., Sala M., Nicoletti M.A., Keshavan M.S., and Soares J.C. 2004. Anatomical MRI Study of Borderline Personality Disorder Patients. Psychiatry Research. Neuroimaging 131(2): 125-133

Breier J.I., Fletcher J.M., Foorman B.R, Klaas P., and Gray L.C. 2003. Auditory Temporal Processing in Children with Specific Reading Disability with and Without Attention

Deficit/Hyperactivity Disorder. Journal of Speech, Language, and Hearing Research 46(1): 31-42

Broca P.P. 1861. Loss of Speech, Chronic Softening and Partial Destruction of the Anterior Left Lobe of the Brain. Classics in the History of Psychology. York University, Toronto, Ontario

Brock J., Einav S., and Riby D.M. 2008. The other end of the spectrum? Social cognition in Williams syndrome. Social cognition: Development, Neuroscience, and Autism: 281-300

Brubaker A., and Cross R. 2015. Evolutionary Constraints on Equid Domestication: Comparison of Flight Initiation Distances of Wild Horses (Equus Caballus Ferus) and Plains Zebras (Equus Quagga). Journal Of Comparative Psychology 129: a0039677

Bruder G., Kayser J., Tenke C., Amador X., Friedman M., Sharif Z., and Gorman J. 1999. Left Temporal Lobe Dysfunction in Schizophrenia: Event-Related Potential and Behavioral Evidence from Phonetic and Tonal Dichotic Listening Tasks. Archives of General Psychiatry 56(3): 267-276

Brunet E., Sarfati Y., Hardy-Baylé M.C., Decety J. 2003. Abnormalities of brain function during a nonverbal Theory of Mind task in schizophrenia. Neuropsychologia 41(12): 1574-1582

Buck T.R., Viskochil J., Farley M., Coon H., McMahon W.M., Morgan J., and Bilder, D.A. 2014. Psychiatric Comorbidity and Medication use in Adults with Autism Spectrum Disorder. Journal of Autism and Developmental Disorders 44: 3063-3071

Bulbulia J. 2004. The cognitive and evolutionary psychology of religion. Biology and philosophy 19: 655-686.

Burgess S., and Cimera R.E. 2014. Employment Outcomes of Transition-Aged Adults with Autism Spectrum Disorders: A State of The States Report. American Journal of Intellectual and Development Disabilities 119(1): 64-83

Buunk, A.P., Pollet, T.V. and Dubbs, S., 2012. Parental control over mate choice to prevent marriages with out-group members: A study among Mestizos, Mixtecs, and blacks in Mexico. Human Nature, 23(3), pp.360-374.

Bzdok D., Laird A., Zilles K., Fox P. and Eickhoff S. 2012a. An Investigation of the Structural, Connectional, and Functional Subspecialization in the Human Amygdala. Human Brain Mapping 34(12): 3247-3266

Bzdok D., Laird A.R., Zilles K., Fox P.T., and Eickhoff S.B. 2013. An investigation of the structural, connectional, and functional subspecialization in the human amygdala. Human Brain Mapping 34(12): 3247-3266

Bzdok D., Schilbach L., Vogeley K., Schneider K., Laird A.R., Langner R., and Eickhoff S.B. 2012b. Parsing the neural correlates of moral cognition: ALE meta-analysis on morality, Theory of Mind, and empathy. Brain Structure and Function 217(4): 783-796

Cagan A., and Blass T. 2016. Identification of Genomic Variants Putatively Targeted by Selection During Dog Domestication. BMC Evolutionary Biology 16: 1-13

Cai R.Y., Richdale A.L., Uljarević M., Dissanayake C., and Samson A.C., 2018. Emotion Regulation in Autism Spectrum Disorder: Where we are and Where we Need to go. Autism Research 11(7): 962-978.

Caldwell-Harris C., Murphy C., Velazquez T., and McNamara P. 2011. Religious Belief Systems of Persons with High Functioning Autism. Annual Meeting of the Cognitive Science Society 33

Cappadocia M.C., Weiss J.A., and Pepler D. 2012. Bullying Experiences Among Children and Youth with Autism Spectrum Disorders. Journal of Autism and Developmental Disorders 42: 266-277

Cardinale R.C., Shih P., Fishman I., Ford L.M. and Müller R.A. 2013. Pervasive rightward asymmetry shifts of functional networks in autism spectrum disorder. JAMA Psychiatry 70(9): 975-982

Carlson S.M., and Moses L.J. 2001. Individual differences in inhibitory control and children's Theory of Mind. Child Development 72(4):1032-53

Carlson. S. M., Moses L. J. and Breton C. 2002. How specific is the relation between executive function and Theory of Mind? Contributions of inhibitory control and working memory. Executive Functions and Development: Studies of Typical and Atypical Children 11(2): 73-92

Carter C.S., Braver T.S., Barch D.M., Botvinick M.M., Noll D., and Cohen J.D. 1998. Anterior Cingulate Cortex, Error Detection, and the Online Monitoring of Performance. Science 280(5364): 747-749

Casanova M.F., Buxhoeveden D.P., Switala A.E., and Roy E. 2002. Minicolumnar pathology in autism. Neurology 58(3): 428-432

Cassidy S., Bradley P., Robinson J., Allison C., McHugh M., and Baron-Cohen S. 2014. Suicidal Ideation and Suicide Plans or Attempts in Adults With Asperger's Syndrome Attending A Specialist Diagnostic Clinic: A Clinical Cohort Study. The Lancet Psychiatry 1(2): 142-147

Cavanna A.E. and Trimble M.R. 2006. The Precuneus: A Review of Its Functional Anatomy and Behavioural Correlates. Brain 129(3): 564-583

Cazalis F., Reyes E., Leduc S., and Gourion D. 2022. Evidence That Nine Autistic Women out of Ten Have Been Victims of Sexual Violence. Frontiers in Behavioral Neuroscience 16: 852203

Chakrabarti B., and Baron-Cohen S. 2006. Empathizing: neurocognitive developmental mechanisms and individual differences. Progress in Brain Research 156: 403-417

Chou K.H., Cheng Y., Chen I.Y., Lin C.P. and Chu W.C. 2011. Sex-linked white matter microstructure of the social and analytic brain. Neuroimage 54(1): 725-733

Cieri R.L., Churchill S.E., Franciscus R.G., Tan J., and Hare B. 2014. Craniofacial Feminization, Social Tolerance, and the Origins of Behavioral Modernity. Current Anthropology 55(4): 419-443

Clark K., and Visuri I. 2019. Autism and the Panoply of religious belief, disbelief, and experience. Neurology and Religion: 139-148

Clements W. A., and Perner J. 1994. Implicit understanding of belief. Cognitive Development 9(4): 377–395

Cohen. A., Fair D., Dosenbach, N., Miezin F., Dierker D., van Essen D., Schlaggar B., and Petersen S. 2008. Defining functional areas in individual human brains using resting functional connectivity MRI. Neuroimage 41(1): 45-57

Coleman T.J., Hood R.W., and Shook J.R. 2015. An Introduction to Atheism, Secularity, and Science. Science, Religion and Culture 2(3): 1-14

Comings D.E. 2010. The Neurobiology, Genetics and Evolution of Human Spirituality: The Central Role of The Temporal Lobes. NeuroQuantology 8(4): 478-494

Connellan J., Baron-Cohen S., Wheelwright S., Batki A. and Ahluwalia J., 2000. Sex differences in human neonatal social perception. Infant behavior and Development 23(1): 113-118

Connellan J., Baron-Cohen S., Wheelwright S., Batki, A., and Ahluwalia J. 2000. Sex differences in human neonatal social perception. Infant Behavior and Development 23(1):113–118

Conner C.M., Golt J., Shaffer R., Righi G., Siegel M., and Mazefsky C.A. 2021. Emotion Dysregulation is Substantially Elevated in

Autism Compared to the General Population: Impact on Psychiatric Services. Autism Research 14(1): 169-181

Conner C.M., White S.W., Scahill L., and Mazefsky C.A. 2020. The Role of Emotion Regulation and Core Autism Symptoms in the Experience of Anxiety in Autism. Autism 24(4): 931-940

Coolidge Jr, H.J., 1933. Pan paniscus, Pygmy Chimpanzee from South of The Congo River. American Journal of Physical Anthropology 18(1): 1-59

Corsi, P. 1972. Memory and the Medial Temporal Region of the Brain. Doctoral Thesis in Philosophy. McGill University, Montreal

Courchesne E., Mouton P.R., Calhoun M.E., Semendeferi K., Ahrens-Barbeau C., Hallet M.J., Barnes C.C., and Pierce K. 2011. Neuron number and size in Prefrontal cortex of children with autism. JAMA. 306(18): 2001-2010

Crane L., Adams F., Harper G., Welch J., and Pellicano E. 2019. 'Something Needs to Change': Mental Health Experiences of Young Autistic Adults in England. Autism 23(2): 477-493

Crespi B., and Summers K., 2014. Inclusive Fitness Theory for The Evolution of Religion. Animal Behaviour 92: 313-323

Crespi B.J. 2016. Autism as a Disorder of High Intelligence. Frontiers in Neuroscience 10: 206417

Crompton C. J., Ropar D., Evans-Williams C. V., Flynn E. G., and Fletcher-Watson S. 2020. Autistic Peer-To-Peer Information Transfer is Highly Effective. Autism 24(7): 1704-1712

Curtis C. E., and D'Esposito M. 2003. Persistent activity in the prefrontal cortex during working memory. Trends Cognitive Science 7(9): 415-423

D'Argembeau A., Xue G., Lu Z.L., Van der Linden M., and Bechara A., 2008. Neural Correlates of Envisioning Emotional Events in The Near and Far Future. Neuroimage 40(1): 398-407

Damasio A. 1994. Decartes' Error: Emotion, Reason, and the Human Brain. New York: Grosset

Dapretto M., Davies M.S., Pfeifer J.H., Scott A.A., Sigman M., Bookheimer S.Y., and Iacoboni M. 2006. Understanding Emotions in Others: Mirror Neuron Dysfunction in Children with Autism Spectrum Disorders. Nature Neuroscience 9(1): 28-30

Daros A.R. and Williams G.E. 2019. A Meta-Analysis and Systematic Review of Emotion-Regulation Strategies in Borderline Personality Disorder. Harvard Review of Psychiatry 27(4): 217-232

Davachi L., Mitchell J.P., and Wagner A.D. 2003. Multiple routes to memory: distinct medial Temporal lobe processes build item and source memories. Proceedings of the National Academy of Sciences 100(4): 2157-2162

David D., Szentagotai A., Lupu V., Cosman D. 2008. Rational emotive behavior therapy, cognitive therapy, and medication in the treatment of major depressive disorder: a randomized clinical trial, posttreatment outcomes, and six-month follow-up. Journal of Clinical Psychology 64(6): 728-746

David N., Newen A., and Vogeley, K. 2008. The ''sense of agency'' and its underlying cognitive and neural mechanisms. Consciousness and Cognition 17: 523–534

Davis, M. H. 1994. Empathy: A social psychological approach. Westview Press.

Dawkins R. 1976. The Selfish Gene. Oxford University Press

De Fossé L., Hodge S.M., Makris N., Kennedy D.N., Caviness V.S. Jr., McGrath L., Steele S., Ziegler D.A., Herbert M.R., Frazier J.A., Tager-Flusberg H., and Harris G.J. 2004. Language-association cortex asymmetry in autism and specific language impairment. Annals of Neurology 56(6): 757-766

De Waal F.B. 1986. The Integration of Dominance and Social Bonding in Primates. The Quarterly Review of Biology 61(4): 459-479

De Waal F.B. 1995. Sex as an Alternative to Aggression in the Bonobo. Sexual Nature, Sexual Culture 37

Deacon T. 2010. A Role for Relaxed Selection in the Evolution of the Language Capacity. Proceedings of the National Academy of Sciences of the United States of America 107 (Suppl 2): 9000-9006

Dell'Osso L., Cremone I.M., Nardi B., Tognini V., Castellani L., Perrone P., Amatori G. and Carpita, B. 2023. Comorbidity and Overlaps between Autism Spectrum and Borderline Personality Disorder: State of the Art. Brain Sciences 13(6): 862

Dennett D. C. 1987. The Intentional Stance. The MIT Press

Dennett. D. 1978. Beliefs About Beliefs. Behavioral and Brain Sciences 1(04): 568-570

Desco M., Navas-Sanchez F.J., Sanchez-González J., Reig S., Robles O., Franco C., Guzmán-De-Villoria J.A., García-Barreno P. and Arango C. 2011. Mathematically gifted adolescents use more extensive and more bilateral areas of the fronto-Parietal network than controls during executive functioning and fluid reasoning tasks. Neuroimage 57(1): 281-292

Desmedt J.E., and Robertson D. 1977. Differential Enhancement of Early and Late Components of the Cerebral Somatosensory Evoked Potentials During Forced-Paced Cognitive Tasks in Man. The Journal of Physiology 271(3): 761-782

Diamond J. 2012. The Local Origins of Domestication. Biodiversity in Agriculture: Domestication, Evolution and Sustainability: 9-18

Diamond M.C. 1976. Anatomical Brain Changes Induced by Environment. In: Petrinovich, L., McGaugh, J.L. (eds). Knowing, Thinking, and Believing. Springer, Boston, MA.

Diana R.A., Yonelinas A.P., and Ranganath C. 2007. Imaging Recollection and Familiarity in the Medial Temporal Lobe: A Three-Component Model. Trends In Cognitive Sciences 11(9): 379-386

Dinstein I., Pierce K., Eyler L., Solso S., Malach R., Behrmann M., and Courchesne E., 2011. Disrupted Neural Synchronization in Toddlers with Autism. Neuron 70(6): 1218-1225

Doran D.M., McNeilage A., Greer D., Bocian C., Mehlman P., and Shah N., 2002. Western Lowland Gorilla Diet and Resource Availability: New Evidence, Cross-Site Comparisons, and Reflections on Indirect Sampling Methods. American Journal of Primatology: Official Journal of the American Society of Primatologists 58(3): 91-116

Duncan J., and Owen A.M. 2000. Common regions of the human frontal lobe recruited by diverse cognitive demands. Trends in Neurosciences 23(10): 475-483

Dunn W., Myles B.S., and Orr S. 2002. Sensory processing issues associated with Asperger syndrome: A preliminary investigation. The American Journal of Occupational Therapy 56(1): 97-102

Durkheim E. 1912. Les formes élémentaires de la vie religieuse. Le système totémique en Australie. Bibliothèque de Philosophie Contemporaine. Paris

Dyer J. 2020. Borderline Personality Disorder: A Complete BPD Guide for Managing Your Emotions and Improving Your Relationships. Independently Published

Eggleton P., and Vane-Wright R.I. 1994. Phylogenetics and Ecology. Academic Press

El-Baz F., Hamza R.T., Ayad M.S., Mahmoud N.H. 2014. Hyperandrogenemia in Male Autistic Children and Adolescents: Relation to Disease Severity. International Journal of Adolescent Medical Health 26:79–84

Eller D. 2010. You Atheists Just Aren't Natural - an essay on Barrett's "Why Would Anyone Believe in God?" Academia.edu. https://www.academia.edu/3614358/You_Atheists_Just_Arent _Natural_an_essay_on_Barretts_Why_Would_Anyone_Belie ve_in_God_

Epley N., Converse B.A., Delbosc A., Monteleone G.A., and Cacioppo J.T. 2009. Believers' Estimates of God's Beliefs are more Egocentric than Estimates of Other People's Beliefs. Proceedings of the National Academy of Sciences 106(51): 21533-21538

Escalante-Mead P.R., Minshew N.J., and Sweeney J.A. 2003. Abnormal brain lateralization in high-functioning autism. Journal of Autism and Developmental Disorders 33: 539-543

Etkin A., Egner T., and Kalisch R. 2011. Emotional processing in anterior cingulate and medial prefrontal cortex. Trends in Cognitive Science 15(2): 85-93

Ewart A.K., Morris C.A., Atkinson D., Jin W., Sternes K., Spallone P., Stock A.D., Leppert M., and Keating M.T. 1993. Hemizygosity at the elastin locus in a developmental disorder, Williams syndrome. Nature Genetics 5(1): 11-16

Eyler L.T., Pierce K., and Courchesne, E. 2012. A failure of the left Temporal cortex to specialize for language is an early emerging and fundamental property of autism. Brain 135(3): 949-960

Eyre H.A., Siddarth P., Acevedo B., Van Dyk K., Paholpak P., Ercoli L., Cyr N.S., Yang H., Khalsa D.S., and Lavretsky H. 2017. A Randomized Controlled Trial of Kundalini Yoga in Mild Cognitive Impairment. International Psychogeriatrics 29(4): 557-567

Farmer C., Butter E., Mazurek M.O., Cowan C., Lainhart J., Cook E.H., DeWitt M.B., and Aman M. 2015. Aggression In Children with Autism Spectrum Disorders and a Clinic-Referred Comparison Group. Autism 19(3): 281-291

Farran E.K. and Jarrold C. 2003. Visuospatial cognition in Williams syndrome: reviewing and accounting for the strengths and weaknesses in performance. Developmental Neuropsychology 23(1-2): 173-200

Fatemi S.H., Snow A.V., Stary J.M., Araghi-Niknam M., Reutiman T.J., Lee S., Brooks A.I. and Pearce D.A. 2005. Reelin Signaling is Impaired in Autism. Biological Psychiatry 57(7): 777-787

Fernandez-Duque D. and Baird J. 2005. Is there a 'social brain'? Lessons from eye-gaze following, joint attention, and autism. In Malle B. and Hodges S. (Eds). Other Minds

Feuerbach L. 2004. The Essence of Christianity. Barnes & Noble Publishing

Filippova E.B. 1996. The effect of the phases of the estrous cycle on functional interhemispheric asymmetry in rats. Zhurnal Vysshei Nervnoi Deiatelnosti Imeni I P Pavlova 46(4): 753-761

Flynn, J. R. 2007. What is intelligence? Beyond the Flynn effect. Cambridge University Press.

Focquaert F., Steven M., Woldford G., Colden, A., and Gazzaniga M. 2007. Empathizing and systemizing cognitive traits in the sciences and humanities. Personality and Individual Differences 43(3): 619–625

Fogassi L., Ferrari P.F., Gesierich B., Rozzi S., Chersi F., Rizzolatti G. 2005. Parietal lobe: from action organization to intention understanding. Science 308(5722): 662-667

Francis L.J. 1997. The psychology of gender differences in religion: A review of empirical research. Religion 27(1): 81-96

Freud S. 1930. Civilization and its Discontents. James Strachey (Trans.). Norton Publishing

Friston E.Q.K. 2004. Autism, Oxytocin and Interoception. Psychology 60: 693-716

Frith C.D., and Frith U. 1999. Interacting minds--a biological basis. Science 286(5445): 1692-1695

Frith C.D., and Frith U. 2006. The neural basis of mentalizing. Neuron 50(4): 531-534

Frye D., Zelazo P., Palfai, T. 1995. Theory of mind and rule-based reasoning. Cognitive Development 10(4): 483-527

Fukuda A., and Watanabe M. 2019. Pathogenic Potential of Human SLC12A5 Variants Causing KCC2 Dysfunction. Brain Research 1710: 1-7

Furuichi T. 2009. Factors Underlying Party Size Differences Between Chimpanzees and Bonobos: A Review and Hypotheses for Future Study. Primates 50: 197-209

Furuichi T. 2011. Female Contributions to The Peaceful Nature of Bonobo Society. Evolutionary Anthropology: Issues, News, and Reviews 20(4): 131-142

Furuichi T., Sanz C., Koops K., Sakamaki T., Ryu H., Tokuyama N., and Morgan D., 2015. Why do wild bonobos not use tools like chimpanzees do? In Bonobo Cognition and Behaviour. Brill: 179-214

Fuster J. M., Bauer, R.H., and Jervey, J.P. 1985. Functional interactions between inferoTemporal and prefrontal cortex in a cognitive task. Brain Research 330: 299–307.

Fuster J.M. 2002. Frontal lobe and cognitive development. Journal of Neurocytology 31(3-5): 373-85

Gabriel M.G., Curtiss J., Hofmann S.G., Khalsa S.B.S. 2018. Kundalini Yoga for Generalized Anxiety Disorder: An Exploration of Treatment Efficacy and Possible Mechanisms. International Journal of Yoga Therapy 28(1): 97-105

Gallagher H.L, and Frith C.D. 2003. Functional imaging of 'Theory of Mind'. Trends in Cognitive Science 7(2): 77-83

Gallagher H.L. and Frith C.D. 2003. Functional Imaging of 'Theory of Mind'. Trends in Cognitive Sciences 7(2): 77-83

Gallese V., Fadiga L., Fogassi L., and Rizzolatti G. 1996. Action recognition in the premotor cortex. Brain 119 (Pt 2): 593-609

García-Sesnich, J.N., Flores M.G., Ríos, M.H. and Aravena, J.G. 2017. Longitudinal and Immediate Effect of Kundalini Yoga on Salivary Levels of Cortisol and Activity of Alpha-Amylase and its Effect on Perceived Stress. International Journal of Yoga 10(2): 73-80.

Gazzaniga M. 2000. Cerebral specialization and interhemispheric communication: Does the Corpus Callosum enable the human condition? Brain 123 (7): 1293–1326

Gazzaniga, M. 2005. Forty-five years of split-brain research and still going strong. Nature Reviews Neuroscience 6: 653–659

Geertz A.W. 2010. Brain, Body, and Culture: A Biocultural Theory of Religion. Method & Theory in the Study of Religion 22(4): 304-321

Gervais W.M. and Norenzayan, A., 2013. Religion and the Origins of Anti-Atheist Prejudice. Intolerance and Conflict: A Scientific and Conceptual Investigation: 126-145

Gervais, W. M., and Norenzayan, A. 2012. Analytic thinking promotes religious disbelief. Science 336(6080): 493–496

Ghaziuddin M., Ghaziuddin N., and Greden J. 2002. Depression In Persons with Autism: Implications for Research and Clinical Care. Journal Of Autism and Developmental Disorders 32: 299-306

Ghetti S., DeMaster D.M., Yonelinas A.P., and Bunge S.A. 2010. Developmental differences in medial Temporal lobe function during memory encoding. Journal of Neuroscience 30(28): 9548-9556

Gibbons A. 2012. Bonobos Join Chimps as Closest Human Relatives. Science| AAAS

Gitelman D.R., Alpert N.M., Kosslyn S., Daffner K., Scinto L., Thompson W. and Mesulam M.M. 1996. Functional Imaging of Human Right Hemispheric Activation for Exploratory Movements. Annals of Neurology 39(2): 174-179

Gogoleva S.S., Volodin J.A., Volodina E.V. and Trut L.N. 2008. To Bark or Not to Bark: Vocalizations by Red Foxes Selected for Tameness or Aggressiveness Toward Humans. Bioacoustics 18(2): 99-132

Golan, O., and Baron-Cohen S. 2006. Systemizing empathy: Teaching adults with Asperger syndrome or high-functioning autism to recognize complex emotions using interactive multimedia. Development and Psychopathology 18(2): 591–617

Goldenfeld N., Baron-Cohen S., and Wheelwright S. 2005. Empathizing and systemizing in males, females and autism. Clinical Neuropsychiatry 2: 338-345

Gong G., He Y., and Evans A.C. 2011. Brain connectivity: gender makes a difference. Neuroscientist 17(5): 575-591

Gong G., Rosa-Neto P., Carbonell F., Chen, Z.J. He, Y., and Evans, A.C. 2009. Age-and gender-related differences in the cortical anatomical network. Journal of Neuroscience 29(50): 15684-15693

Goodall J. 1986. Social Rejection, Exclusion, and Shunning Among the Gombe Chimpanzees. Ethology and Sociobiology 7(3-4): 227-236

Gopnik A., and Astington, J. 1988. Children's understanding of representational change and its relation to the understanding of false belief and the appearance-reality distinction. Child Development, 59(1): 26–37

Gray K., Knobe J., Sheskin M., Bloom P., and Barrett, L.F. 2011. More than a body: mind perception and the nature of objectification. Journal of personality and social psychology 101(6): 1207-1220

Green R.E., Krause J., Briggs A.W., Maricic T., Stenzel U., Kircher M., Patterson N., Li H., Zhai W., Fritz M.H.Y., And Hansen N.F., 2010. A Draft Sequence of The Neandertal Genome. Science 328(5979): 710-722

Greenbaum G., Friesem D.E., Hovers E., Feldman M.W., and Kolodny O. 2019. Was inter-Population Connectivity of Neanderthals and Modern Humans the Driver of the Upper Paleolithic Transition Rather than its Product? Quaternary Science Reviews 217: 316-329

Greenberg D.M., Warrier V., Allison C., and Baron-Cohen S. 2018. Testing the empathizing–systemizing theory of sex differences and the extreme male brain theory of autism in half a million people. Proceedings of the National Academy of Sciences 115(48): 12152-12157

Greenlee J.L., Mosley A.S., Shui A.M., Veenstra-VanderWeele J., and Gotham K.O. 2016. Medical and Behavioral Correlates of Depression History in Children and Adolescents with Autism Spectrum Disorder. Pediatrics 137(Supplement_2): 105-114

Grill-Spector K., Kushnir T., Hendler T., Edelman S., Itzchak Y., 1998. Malach R. A sequence of object-processing stages revealed by fMRI in the human occipital lobe. Human Brain Mapping 6(4): 316-328

Grill-Spectora K., Kourtzia Z., and Kanwisher N. 2001. The lateral occipital complex and its role in object recognition. Vision Research 41: 1409-1422

Grimshaw J., Freemantle N., Wallace S., Russell I., Hurwitz B., Watt I., and Long A, Sheldon T. 1995. Developing and implementing clinical practice guidelines. Qualitative Health Care 4(1): 55-64

Grover S., Chakrabarti S., Ghormode D., Dutt A., Kate N., and Kulhara P. 2014. Clinicians' Versus Caregivers' Ratings of Burden in Patients with Schizophrenia and Bipolar Disorder. International Journal of Social Psychiatry 60(4): 330-336

Gruber T., Potts K. B., Krupenye C., Byrne M.-R., Mackworth-Young C., McGrew, W. C., Reynolds V., and Zuberbühler K. 2012. The Influence of Ecology on Chimpanzee (Pan Troglodytes) Cultural Behavior: A Case Study of Five Ugandan Chimpanzee Communities. Journal of Comparative Psychology 126(4): 446-457

Gunz S., Rozen-Knisbacher I., Blumenfeld A., Hendler K., and Yahalom C. 2023. The Prevalence of Autism Among Children with Albinism. European Journal of Ophthalmology: 11206721231206091

Guthrie S. 1993. Faces in the Clouds: A New Theory of Religion. New York and Oxford: Oup Usa

Hadjikhani N., Joseph R.M., Snyder J., and Tager-Flusberg H. 2006. Anatomical differences in the mirror neuron system and social cognition network in autism. Cerebral Cortex 16(9): 1276-82

Haidt J. 2007. The New Synthesis in Moral Psychology. Science 316(5827): 998-1002

Hailes H.P., Yu R., Danese A., and Fazel, S. 2019. Long-term Outcomes of Childhood Sexual Abuse: an Umbrella Review. The Lancet Psychiatry 6(10): 830-839

Hall, J. A. 1978. Gender effects in decoding nonverbal cues. Psychological Bulletin 85(4): 845–857

Hampson E., Rovet J.F. and Altmann D. 1998. Spatial reasoning in children with congenital adrenal hyperplasia due to 21-hydroxylase deficiency. Developmental Neuropsychology 14(2-3): 299-320

Hamza R.T., Hewedi D.H., and Ismail M.A. 2010. Basal and Adrenocorticotropic Hormone Stimulated Plasma Cortisol Levels Among Egyptian Autistic Children: Relation to Disease Severity. Italian Journal of Pediatrics 36(71): 1-6

Happé F. and Frith U. 2006. The weak coherence account: detail-focused cognitive style in autism spectrum disorders. Journal of Autism and Developmental Disorders 36(1): 5-25

Happe F., and Frith U. 1996. The Neuropsychology of Autism. Brain 119(4): 1377-1400

Harari Y.N. 2014. Sapiens: A Brief History of Humankind. Random House

Harari Y.N. 2017. Homo Deus: A Brief History of Tomorrow. Harper Collins

Hare B. 2017. Survival of the Friendliest: Homo sapiens Evolved via Selection for Prosociality. Annual Review of Psychology 68(1): 155-186

Hare B., and Tomasello M. 2005. Human-Like Social Skills in Dogs? Trends in Cognitive Science 9(9) : 439-444

Hare B., Brown M., Williamson C., and Tomasello M. 2002. The Domestication of Social Cognition in Dogs. Science 22(5598): 1634-1636

Hare B., Melis A.P., Woods V., Hastings S., and Wrangham R. 2007. Tolerance Allows Bonobos to Outperform Chimpanzees on a Cooperative Task. Current Biology 17(7): 619-623

Hare B., Wobber V., and Wrangham R. 2012. The Self-Domestication Hypothesis: Evolution of Bonobo Psychology is Due to Selection Against Aggression. Animal Behaviour 83(3): 573-585

Harris I., Egan G., Sonkkila C., Tochon-Danguy H., Paxinos G., Watson J. 2000. Selective right Parietal lobe activation during mental rotation: A parametric PET study. Brain 123 (1): 65–73

Harris S., Kaplan J.T., Curiel A., Bookheimer S.Y., Iacoboni M., and Cohen M.S. 2009. The Neural Correlates of Religious and Nonreligious Belief. Plos One 4(10): 7272

Harshman R.A., Crawford H.J., Hecht, E 1976. Marihuana, Cognitive Style, and Lateralized Hemispheric Functions

Hashimoto R. and Sakai K. 2002. Specialization in the Left Prefrontal Cortex for Sentence Comprehension. Neuron 35(3): 589-597

Hausmann M., and Güntürkün O. 2000. Steroid fluctuations modify functional cerebral asymmetries: the hypothesis of progesterone-mediated interhemispheric decoupling. Neuropsychologia, 38(10): 1362-1374

Hausmann M., Becker C., Gather U. and Güntürkün O., 2002. Functional cerebral asymmetries during the menstrual cycle: a cross-sectional and longitudinal analysis. Neuropsychologia 40(7): 808-816

Hausmann, M. 2017. Why sex hormones matter for neuroscience: A very short review on sex, sex hormones, and functional brain asymmetries. Journal of Neuroscience Research 95(1-2): 40-49

Hauth I., de Bruijn Y.G., Staal W., Buitelaar J.K., and Rommelse N.N. 2014. Testing the Extreme Male Brain Theory of Autism

Spectrum Disorder in a Familial Design. Autism Research 7(4): 491-500

Hauth J.C., Ewell M.G., Levine R.J., Esterlitz J.R., Sibai B., Curet L.B., Catalano P.M., Morris C.D., and Calcium for Preeclampsia Prevention Study Group. 2000. Pregnancy Outcomes in Healthy Nulliparas Who Developed Hypertension. Obstetrics and Gynecology 95(1): 24-28

Hayatullah A. 2023. Most Canadian Adults with Autism are Unemployed: Survey. CTV News. https://www.ctvnews.ca/lifestyle/most-canadian-adults-with-autism-are-unemployed-survey-1.6343138

Heaton, R. K. 1981. Wisconsin card sorting test manual. Psychological Assessment Resources. Odessa, FL

Hegarty M., and Waller D. 2004. A dissociation between mental rotation and perspective-taking spatial abilities. Intelligence 32(2): 175–191

Heilman M. E. 1983. Sex bias in work settings: The Lack of Fit model. Research in Organizational Behavior 5: 269–298

Hendrickx S. 2015. Women and girls with autism spectrum disorder: Understanding life experiences from early childhood to old age. Jessica Kingsley Publishers

Henrich J. 2009. The evolution of costly displays, Cooperation and Religion: Credibility Enhancing Displays and Their Implications for Cultural Evolution. Evolution and Human Behavior 30(4): 244-260.

Henrich J., 2015. Culture and Social Behavior. Current Opinion in Behavioral Sciences 3: 84-89

Henrich N. and Henrich J.P. 2007. Why humans cooperate: A cultural and evolutionary explanation. Oxford University Press

Herbert M.R., Harris G.J., Adrien K.T., Ziegler D.A., Makris N., Kennedy D.N., Lange N.T., Chabris C.F., Bakardjiev A., Hodgson J. and Takeoka M. 2002. Abnormal asymmetry in language association cortex in autism. Annals of Neurology: Official Journal of the American Neurological Association and the Child Neurology Society 52(5): 588-596

Herrmann E., Hare B., Call J., and Tomasello, M. 2010a. Differences in the Cognitive Skills of Bonobos and Chimpanzees. PloS One 5(8): e12438

Herrmann E., Hernández-Lloreda M.V., Call J., Hare B., and Tomasello M. 2010b. The Structure of Individual Differences in The Cognitive Abilities of Children and Chimpanzees. Psychological Science 21(1): 102-110

Herrmann E., Hernández-Lloreda M.V., Call J., Hare B., and Tomasello M., 2010. The Structure of Individual Differences in the Cognitive Abilities of Children and Chimpanzees. Psychological Science 21(1): 102-110

Herzog H., Lele V.R., Kuwert T., Langen K.J., Kops E.R. and Feinendegen L.E., 1990. Changed Pattern of Regional Glucose Metabolism During Yoga Meditative Relaxation. Neuropsychobiology 23(4): 182-187

Hines M., 2010. Sex-related variation in human behavior and the brain. Trends in Cognitive Sciences 14(10): 448-456

Hines M., Brook C., and Conway G.S., 2004. Androgen and psychosexual development: Core gender identity, sexual orientation, and recalled childhood gender role behavior in women and men with congenital adrenal hyperplasia (CAH). Journal of Sex Research 41(1): 75-81

Hines M., Fane B.A., Pasterski V.L., Mathews G.A., Conway G.S. and Brook C., 2003. Spatial abilities following prenatal androgen abnormality: Targeting and mental rotations performance in individuals with congenital adrenal hyperplasia. Psychoneuroendocrinology 28(8): 1010-1026

Hines M., Golombok S., Rust J., Johnston K.J., Golding, J. and Parents and Children Study Team, A.L.S.O., 2002. Testosterone during pregnancy and gender role behavior of preschool children: A longitudinal, population study. Child Development 73(6): 1678-1687

Hiscock M., Perachio N., and Inch R. 2001. Is there a sex difference in human laterality? IV. An exhaustive survey of dual-task interference studies from six neuropsychology journals. Journal of Clinical and Experimental Neuropsychology 23(2): 137-148

Hobson N.M., Schroeder J., Risen J.L., Xygalatas D., and Inzlicht M. 2018. The Psychology of Rituals: An Integrative Review and Process-Based Framework. Personality and Social Psychology Review 22(3): 260-284

Hobson P. R. 1991. Against the theory of "Theory of Mind." Developmental Psychology 9(1): 33-51

Hobson R. P. 1990. On acquiring knowledge about people and the capacity to pretend: Response to Leslie (1987). Psychological Review 97(1): 114–121

Hofvander B., Delorme R., Chaste P., Nydén A., Wentz E., Ståhlberg O., Herbrecht E., Stopin A., Anckarsäter H., Gillberg C., and Råstam M. 2009. Psychiatric and Psychosocial Problems in Adults with Normal-Intelligence Autism Spectrum Disorders. BMC Psychiatry 9: 1-9

Holdstock J.S., Mayes A.R., Roberts N., Cezayirli E., Isaac C.L., O'Reilly R.C., and Norman K.A. 2002. Under what conditions is recognition spared relative to recall after selective hippocampal damage in humans? Hippocampus 12(3): 341-51

Homae F., Yahata N., and Sakai K.L. 2003. Selective enhancement of functional connectivity in the left prefrontal cortex during sentence processing. NeuroImage 20(1): 578-586

Hudson C.C., Hall L., and Harkness K.L. 2019. Prevalence of Depressive Disorders in Individuals with Autism Spectrum Disorder: A Meta-Analysis. Journal Of Abnormal Child Psychology 47: 165-175

Huguelet P., Binyet-Vogel S., Gonzalez C., Favre S., and McQuillan A. 1997. Follow-Up Study of 67 First Episode Schizophrenic Patients and Their Involvement in Religious Activities. European Psychiatry 12(6): 279-283

Hull L., Petrides K.V., Allison C., Smith P., Baron-Cohen S., Lai M.C., and Mandy W. 2017. "Putting on My Best Normal": Social Camouflaging in Adults with Autism Spectrum Conditions. Journal of Autism and Developmental Disorders 47(8):2519-2534

Hume D. 1793. The Natural History of Religion (Vol. 4). Printed and told by JJ Tourneisen

Humphrey N. and Hebron, J. 2015. Bullying of Children and Adolescents with Autism Spectrum Conditions: A 'State of The Field' Review. International Journal of Inclusive Education 19(8): 845-862

Humphrey N. and Symes W. 2011. Peer Interaction Patterns Among Adolescents with Autistic Spectrum Disorders (ASD) In Mainstream School Settings. Autism 15(4): 397-419

Hunt A.D., and Jaeggi A.V. 2022. Specialised Minds: Extending Adaptive Explanations of Personality to the Evolution of Psychopathology. Evolutionary Human Sciences 4: e26

Hussain M. A. 2020. Why did Angel Jibreel Squeeze the Prophet Mohammed PBUH? Islam QA. Short Link: https://islamqa.org/?p=136607. Accessed: Jan 4, 2024

Hvilsom C., Frandsen P., Børsting C., Carlsen F., Sallé B., Simonsen B.T., and Siegismund H.R. 2013. Understanding Geographic Origins and History of Admixture Among Chimpanzees in European Zoos, with Implications for Future Breeding Programmes. Heredity 110(6): 586-593

Hwang Y.S., Evans D., and Mackenzie J. 2007. Theory-Of-Mind Continuum Model: Why Mind Matters in Philosophy, Psychology and Education. International Journal of Interdisciplinary Social Sciences 2(3): 249-258

Igelström K.M., Webb T.W., Kelly Y.T., Graziano M.S. 2016. Topographical Organization of Attentional, Social, and Memory Processes in the Human TemporoParietal Cortex. eNeuro 3(2)

Inzlicht M., McGregor I., Hirsh J.B., and Nash K. 2009. Neural Markers of Religious Conviction. Psychological Science 20(3): 385-392

Irons W. 2001. Religion as a Hard-To-Fake Sign of Commitment. Evolution and the Capacity for Commitment: 292-309

Irons W. 2008. Why People Believe (What Other People See as) Crazy Ideas. The Evolution of Religion: Studies, Theories, and Critiques. J. Bulbulia, R. Sosis, C. Genet, R. Genet & K. Wyman (Eds.): 51-57

Itahashi T., Yamada T., Watanabe H., Nakamura M., Jimbo D., Shioda S., Toriizuka K., Kato N., and Hashimoto R. 2014. Altered network topologies and hub organization in adults with autism: a resting-state fMRI study. PLoS One 9(4): 9411

Iuculano, T. and Kadosh, R.C., 2013. The mental cost of cognitive enhancement. Journal of Neuroscience 33(10): 4482-4486

Jeung H. and Herpertz S.C. 2014. Impairments of Interpersonal Functioning: Empathy and Intimacy in Borderline Personality Disorder. Psychopathology 47(4): 220-234

John J.P. 2009. Fronto-Temporal Dysfunction in Schizophrenia: a Selective Review. Indian Journal of Psychiatry 51(3): 180-190

Johnson S., Sathyaseelan M., Charles H., Jeyaseelan V., and Jacob K.S. 2012. Insight, Psychopathology, Explanatory Models and Outcome of Schizophrenia in India: A Prospective 5-Year Cohort Study. BMC Psychiatry 12: 1-12

Jolliffe T., Lansdown R., Robinson C. 1992. Autism: a Personal Account. Communication 26: 12-19

Jones W., Bellugi U., Lai Z., Chiles M., Reilly J., Lincoln A., and Adolphs R. 2000. II. Hypersociability in Williams syndrome. Journal of Cognitive Neuroscience 12(Supplement 1): 30-46

Joshi G., Wozniak J., Petty C., Martelon M.K., Fried R., Bolfek A., Kotte A., Stevens J., Furtak S.L., Bourgeois M., and Caruso J. 2013. Psychiatric Comorbidity and Functioning in a Clinically Referred Population of Adults with Autism Spectrum Disorders: A Comparative Study. Journal Of Autism and Developmental Disorders 43: 1314-1325

Just M.A., Cherkassky V.L., Keller T.A., and Minshew N.J. 2004. Cortical activation and synchronization during sentence comprehension in high-functioning autism: evidence of underconnectivity. Brain 127(8): 1811-21

Just M.A., Cherkassky V.L., Keller T.A., Kana R.K., and Minshew N.J. 2007. Functional and anatomical cortical underconnectivity in autism: evidence from an FMRI study of an executive function task and Corpus Callosum morphometry. Cerebral Cortex 17(4): 951-961

Kanner, L. 1943. Autistic disturbances of affective contact. Nervous Child 2: 217–250

Kano F., Hirata S., and Call J. 2015. Social Attention in The Two Species of Pan: Bonobos Make More Eye Contact Than Chimpanzees. Plos One 10(6): e0129684

Kanold P. 2009. Subplate neurons: crucial regulators of cortical development and plasticity. Frontiers in Neuroanatomy 3 (16): 1-9

Kapoor D.S. 1973. Socialization and Feral Children. Revista Internacional de Sociologia 31(5): 195

Karmiloff-Smith A., Tyler L.K., Voice K., Sims K., Udwin O., Howlin P. and Davies M., 1998. Linguistic dissociations in Williams syndrome: Evaluating receptive syntax in on-line and off-line tasks. Neuropsychologia 36(4): 343-351

Karnath H.O., Ferber S., Himmelbach M. 2001. Spatial awareness is a function of the Temporal not the posterior Parietal lobe. Nature 411(6840): 950-953

Karnath H.O., Fruhmann Berger M., Küker W., and Rorden C. 2004. The Anatomy of Spatial Neglect based on Voxelwise Statistical Analysis: A Study of 140 Patients. Cerebral Cortex 14(10): 1164–1172

Karnath H.O., Rennig J., Johannsen L., and Rorden C. 2011. The anatomy underlying acute versus chronic spatial neglect: a longitudinal study. Brain 134 (3): 903–912

Karnath, H.O. 2009. A right perisylvian neural network for human spatial orienting. The cognitive neurosciences 4: 259-268

Kate N., Grover S., Kulhara P., and Nehra R. 2012. Supernatural Beliefs, Aetiological Models and Help Seeking Behaviour in Patients with Schizophrenia. Industrial Psychiatry Journal 21(1): 49-54

Keehn B., Muller R.A., and Townsend J. 2013. Atypical Attentional Networks and the Emergence of Autism. Neuroscience and Biobehavioral Reviews 37: 164-183

Kelemen D. 2004. Are Children "Intuitive Theists"? Reasoning About Purpose and Design in Nature. Psychological Science 15(5): 295-301

Kelly E.W. 1995. Spirituality And Religion in Counseling and Psychotherapy: Diversity in Theory and Practice. American Counseling Association

Kelly M.E., Loughrey D., Lawlor B.A., Robertson I.H., Walsh C., and Brennan S. 2014. The impact of cognitive training and mental stimulation on cognitive and everyday functioning of healthy older adults: a systematic review and meta-analysis. Ageing Research Review 15: 28-43

Kent G., and Wahass S. 1996. The Content and Characteristics of Auditory Hallucinations in Saudi Arabia and the UK: A Cross-Cultural Comparison. Acta Psychiatrica Scandinavica 94(6): 433–437

Kéri S. 2023. Autism and Religion. Children 10(8): 1417

Kertesz A., Polk M., Howell J., and Black S.E. 1987. Cerebral dominance, sex, and callosal size inMRI. Neurology 37(8): 1385-1385

Kessler R.C., Ormel J., Demler O., and Stang P.E. 2003. Comorbid Mental Disorders Account for The Role Impairment of Commonly Occurring Chronic Physical Disorders: Results from the National Comorbidity Survey. Journal of Occupational and Environmental Medicine 45(12):1257-66

Kim J.A., Szatmari P., Bryson S.E., Streiner D.L. and Wilson F.J. 2000. The Prevalence of Anxiety and Mood Problems Among Children with Autism and Asperger Syndrome. Autism 4(2): 117-132

Kim. C. 2013. I Think I Might Be Autistic: A Guide to Autism Spectrum Disorder Diagnosis and Self-Discovery for Adults. Narrow Gauge

Kim. C. 2014. Nerdy, Shy, and Socially Inappropriate: A User Guide to an Asperger Life. Jessica Kingsley Publishers

Kimura, D. 1999. Sex and cognition. The MIT Press

Klass P.E., Needleman R., and Zuckerman. 2003. The developing brain and early learning. Archives of Disease in Childhood 88: 651-654

Klein R.G. 2009. The Human Career: Human Biological and Cultural Origins. University of Chicago Press

Knaus T.A., Silver A.M., Kennedy M., Lindgren K.A., Dominick K.C., Siegel J. and Tager-Flusberg H. 2010. Language laterality in autism spectrum disorder and typical controls: a functional, volumetric, and diffusion tensor MRI study. Brain and Language 112(2): 113-120

Knickmeyer R., Baron-Cohen S., Raggatt P., and Taylor K., 2005. Foetal testosterone, social relationships, and restricted interests in children. Journal of Child Psychology and Psychiatry 46(2): 198-210

Kohler K. 1918. Jewish theology: Systematically and Historically Considered. Macmillan. New York

Koops K., Furuichi T., and Hashimoto C. 2015. Chimpanzees and Bonobos Differ in Intrinsic Motivation for Tool Use. Scientific Reports 5(1): 1-7

Korenberg J.R. Chen X.N. Hirota H., Lai Z., Bellugi U., Burian D., Roe B., and Matsuoka R. 2000. VI. Genome structure and cognitive map of Williams syndrome. Journal of Cognitive Neuroscience 12(Supplement 1): 89-107

Korenberg J.R., Aaltonen J., Brahe C., and Cabin D. 1997. Report of the sixth international workshop on human chromosome 21 mapping 1996. Cytogenetic and Genome Research 79(1/2): 22

Kostovic I., and Judas M. 2010. The development of the subplate and thalamocortical connections in the human foetal brain. Acta Paediatrica 99(8): 119-1127

Kozhevnikov M., and Hegarty M. 2001. A dissociation between object manipulation spatial ability and spatial orientation ability. Memory and Cognition 29(5): 745–756

Kreuter C., Kinsbourne M., and Trevarthen C. 1972. Are deconnected cerebral hemispheres independent channels? A preliminary study of the effect of unilateral loading on bilateral finger tapping. Neuropsychologia 10(4): 453-461

Krzystanek M., Krysta K., Klasik A., and Krupka-Matuszczyk I. 2012. Religious Content of Hallucinations in Paranoid Schizophrenia. Psychiatria Danubia 24(1): 65-69

Kumar A., Sundaram S.K., Sivaswamy L., Behen M.E., Makki M.I., Ager J., Janisse J., Chugani H.T. and Chugani D.C. 2010. Alterations in frontal lobe tracts and Corpus Callosum in young children with autism spectrum disorder. Cerebral Cortex 20(9): 2103-2113

Labonne J.D., Driessen T.M., Harris M.E., Kong I.K., Brakta S., Theisen J., Sangare,M., Layman L.C., Kim C.H., Lim J., and Kim H.G., 2020. Comparative Genomic Mapping Implicates LRRK2 for Intellectual Disability and Autism At 12q12, And HDHD1, as Well As PNPLA4, for X-Linked Intellectual Disability at Xp22. 31. Journal of Clinical Medicine 9(1): 274

Lai M.C., Lombardo M.V., Ruigrok A.N., Chakrabarti B., Wheelwright S.J., Auyeung B., Allison C. MRC AIMS Consortium and Baron-Cohen S. 2012. Cognition in males and females with autism: similarities and differences. PLOS One 7(10): e47198

Laing E., Butterworth G., Ansari D., Gsödl M., Longhi E., Panagiotaki G., Paterson S., and Karmiloff-Smith A. 2002. Atypical development of language and social communication in toddlers with Williams syndrome. Developmental Science 5(2): 233-246

Langergraber K.E., Prüfer K., Rowney C., Boesch C., Crockford C., Fawcett K., Inoue E., Inoue-Muruyama M., Mitani J.C., Muller

M.N. and Robbins M.M. 2012. Generation Times in Wild Chimpanzees and Gorillas Suggest Earlier Divergence Times in Great Ape and Human Evolution. Proceedings of the National Academy of Sciences 109(39): 15716-15721

Lasley B.L., Loskutoff N.M., and Anderson G.B. 1994. The Limitation of Conventional Breeding Programs and the Need and Promise of Assisted Reproduction in Nondomestic Species. Theriogenology 41(1): 119-132.

Lazar S.W., Bush G., Gollub R.L., Fricchione G.L., Khalsa G., and Benson H. 2000. Functional Brain Mapping of The Relaxation Response and Meditation. Neuroreport 11(7): 1581-1585

Leach H.M. 2003. Human Domestication Reconsidered. Current Anthropology 44(3): 349-368

Lebowitz E.R., Leckman J.F., Silverman W.K., and Feldman R. 2016. Cross-Generational Influences on Childhood Anxiety Disorders: Pathways and Mechanisms. Journal of Neural Transmission 123: 1053-1067

Lee P.S., Foss-Feig J., Henderson J.G., Kenworthy L.E., Gilotty L., Gaillard W.D., and Vaidya C.J. 2007. Atypical neural substrates of Embedded Figures Task performance in children with Autism Spectrum Disorder. Neuroimage 38(1): 184-193

Lehman A. J. D. 2010. Evolution, Autism and Social Change: A New Feminine Theory of Evolution That Explains Autism. Neoteny.org.
https://www.academia.edu/60625843/Evolution_Autism_and_Social_Change_A_New_Feminine_Theory_of_Evolution_That_Explains_Autism

Leisman G., Melillo R., Melillo T., Machado C., Machado-Ferrer Y., Chinchilla M. and Carmeli E. 2022. Taking Sides: Asymmetries in the Evolution of Human Brain Development in Better Understanding Autism Spectrum Disorder. Symmetry 14(12): 2689

Leisman G., Melillo R., Melillo T., Machado C., Machado-Ferrer Y., Chinchilla M., and Carmeli E., 2022. Taking Sides: Asymmetries in the Evolution of Human Brain Development in Better Understanding Autism Spectrum Disorder. Symmetry 14(12): 2689

Leonard C.M., Towler S., Welcome S., Halderman L., Otto R., Eckert M., and Chiarello C. 2008. Size Matters: Cerebral Volume Influences Sex Differences in Neuroanatomy. Cerebral Cortex 18(12): 2920–2931

Leslie A. M. 1991. The Theory of Mind impairment in autism: Evidence for a modular mechanism of development? In A. Whiten (Ed.), Natural theories of mind: Evolution, development, and simulation of everyday mindreading: 63–78. Basil Blackwell

Leslie A. M., and Frith, U. 1988. Autistic children's understanding of seeing, knowing, and believing. British Journal of Developmental Psychology 6(4): 315–324

Leslie A.M., Friedman O., and German T.P. 2004. Core mechanisms in "Theory of Mind". Trends Cognitive Science 8(12): 528-33

Leslie, A. M. 1987. Pretense and representation: The origins of "Theory of Mind." Psychological Review 94(4): 412–426

Lillard A. S., and Flavell J. H. 1990. Young children's preference for mental state versus behavioral descriptions of human action. Child Development 61(3): 731–741

Lillard, A., and Flavell, J. 1990. Young Children's Preference for Mental State versus Behavioral Descriptions of Human Action. Child Development 61(3): 731-741

Lindeman M., Svedholm-Häkkinen, A.M., and Lipsanen J. 2015. Ontological Confusions but not Mentalizing Abilities Predict Religious Belief, Paranormal Belief, and Belief in Supernatural Purpose. Cognition 134: 63-76

Linehan M.M. 1993. Dialectical Behavior Therapy for Treatment of Borderline Personality Disorder: Implications for the Treatment of Substance Abuse. NIDA Research Monograph 137: 201-201

Linnaeus, Carl von. 1735. Systema Naturae. Tomus II: Vegetabilia. Facsimile. Weinheim : New York :J. Cramer; Stechert-Hafner Service Agency

Lomelin D.E. 2010. An Examination of Autism Spectrum Disorders in Relation to Human Evolution and Life History Theory. University of Nebraska Lincoln. https://digitalcommons.unl.edu/nebanthro/57/

Lutchmaya S., Baron-Cohen S., and Raggatt, P. 2002. Foetal testosterone and eye contact in 12-month-old human infants. Infant Behavior and Development 25(3): 327-335

Maddox B.B., Trubanova A., and White S.W. 2017. Untended Wounds: Non-suicidal Self-injury in Adults with Autism Spectrum Disorder. Autism 21(4): 412-422.

Magat M., and Brown C. 2009. Laterality enhances cognition in Australian parrots. Proceedings of Biological Sciences 276(1676): 4155-62

Maïano C., Normand C.L., Salvas M.C., Moullec G., and Aimé A. 2016. Prevalence of School Bullying Among Youth with Autism Spectrum Disorders: A Systematic Review and Meta-Analysis. Autism Research 9(6): 601-615

Maij D.L., van Harreveld, F., Gervais W., Schrag Y., Mohr C., and van Elk M. 2017. Mentalizing skills do not differentiate believers from non-believers, but credibility enhancing displays do. PloS One 12(8): e0182764

Mailund T., Halager A.E., Westergaard M., Dutheil J.Y., Munch K., Andersen L.N., Lunter G., Prüfer K., Scally A., Hobolth A., and Schierup, M.H. 2012. A New Isolation with Migration

Model Along Complete Genomes Infers Very Different Divergence Processes Among Closely Related Great Ape Species. PLoS Genetics 8(12): e1003125

Malenky R.K., and Stiles E.W. 1991. Distribution of Terrestrial Herbaceous Vegetation and its Consumption by Pan Paniscus in the Lomako Forest, Zaire. American Journal of Primatology 23(3): 153-169

Malenky, R.K. and Wrangham, R.W., 1994. A Quantitative Comparison of Terrestrial Herbaceous Food Consumption by Pan Paniscus in the Lomako Forest, Zaire, and Pan Troglodytes in The Kibale Forest, Uganda. American Journal of Primatology 32(1): 1-12

Marks I.M., and Nesse R.M. 2013. Fear and Fitness: An Evolutionary Analysis of Anxiety Disorders. Fear and Anxiety: 155-169

Marshall T. 2014. I Am AspienGirl: The Unique Characteristics, Traits and Gifts of Females on the Autism Spectrum

May T., Pilkington P.D., Younan R., and Williams K. 2021. Overlap of Autism Spectrum Disorder and Borderline Personality Disorder: A Systematic Review and Meta-Analysis. Autism Research 14(12): 2688-2710

Mayes S.D., Gorman A.A., Hillwig-Garcia J., and Syed E. 2013. Suicide Ideation and Attempts in Children with Autism. Research In Autism Spectrum Disorders 7(1): 109-119

Mazefsky C.A., and White S.W., 2014. Emotion Regulation: Concepts and Practice in Autism Spectrum Disorder. Child and Adolescent Psychiatric Clinics 23(1): 15-24

McCauley R.N. 2011. Why Religion is Natural and Science is Not. Oxford University Press

McDonnell C.G., Boan A.D., Bradley C.C., Seay K.D., Charles J.M., and Carpenter L.A. 2019. Child Maltreatment in Autism Spectrum Disorder and Intellectual Disability: Results from a Population-

Based Sample. Journal of Child Psychology and Psychiatry 60(5): 576-584.

McEwen B.S. 2001. Plasticity of the hippocampus: adaptation to chronic stress and allostatic load. Annals of the New York Academy of Sciences 933: 265-277

McGilchrist I. 2009. A Problem of Symmetries. Philosophy, Psychiatry, and Psychology 16(2): 161-169

McGilchrist I. 2019. Cerebral lateralization and religion: a phenomenological approach. Religion, Brain, and Behavior 9(4): 319-339

McGilchrist I. 2019. The Master and His Emissary: The Divided Brain and The Making of the Western World. Yale University Press

McGilchrist, I. 2009. A Problem of Symmetries. Philosophy, Psychiatry, & Psychology 16(2) : 161-169

McKay R. T., and Ross R. M. 2021. Religion and Delusion. Current Opinion in Psychology 40: 160-166

McKay R., Efferson C., Whitehouse H., and Fehr E. 2011. Wrath of God: Religious Primes and Punishment. Proceedings of the Royal Society B: Biological Sciences 278(1713): 1858-1863

Mckenzie, R., Andrew R.J., and Jones R.B. 1998. Lateralization in chicks and hens: new evidence for control of response by the right eye system. Neuropsychologia 36(1): 51-58

Meltzer A., and Van de Water J. 2017. The Role of The Immune System in Autism Spectrum Disorder. Neuropsychopharmacology 42(1): 284-298

Meltzoff A. N. 1995. Understanding the intentions of others: Re-enactment of intended acts by 18-month-old children. Developmental Psychology 31(5): 838–850

Meltzoff A. N. 2002. Elements of a developmental theory of imitation. In A. N. Meltzoff & W. Prinz (Eds.), The imitative mind: Development, evolution, and brain bases: 19–41). Cambridge University Press

Meltzoff A. N., and Gopnik, A. 1993. The role of imitation in understanding persons and developing a Theory of Mind. *In* S. Baron- Cohen, H. Tager-Flusberg, & D. J. Cohen (Eds.). Understanding other minds: 335-366. New York: Oxford University Press

Meltzoff A. N., and Moore M. K. 1992. Early Imitation Within a Functional Framework: The Importance of Person Identity, Movement, and Development. Infant Behavioral Development 15(4): 479-505

Meltzoff A. N., Kuhl P. K., and Moore M. K. 1991. Perception, representation, and the control of action in newborns and young infants: Toward a new synthesis. In M. J. S. Weiss & P. R. Zelazo (Eds.), Newborn attention: Biological constraints and the influence of experience: 377–411. Ablex Publishing

Meltzoff N. 1985. Immediate and deferred imitation in fourteen- and twenty-four-month-old infants. Child Development 56(1): 62–72

Merner N.D., Chandler M.R., Bourassa C., Liang B., Khanna A.R., Dion P., Rouleau G.A., and Kahle K.T. 2015. Regulatory Domain of Cpg Site Variation in SLC12A5, Encoding the Chloride Transporter KCC2, in Human Autism and Schizophrenia. Frontiers in Cellular Neuroscience 9: 386

Merriam Webster. https://www.merriam-webster.com/dictionary/religion

Mervis C.B., and Bertrand J. 1997. Developmental Relations Between Cognition and Language: Evidence from Williams Syndrome. In: Communication and Language Acquisition: Discoveries from atypical development. Adamson, LB.; Romski, MA. (Eds). New York: Brookes: 75-106

Mikita N., Hollocks M.J., Papadopoulos A.S., Aslani A., Harrison S., Leibenluft E., Simonoff E., and Stringaris A. 2015. Irritability in Boys with Autism Spectrum Disorders: An Investigation of Physiological Reactivity. Journal of Child Psychology and Psychiatry 56(10): 1118-1126

Milner, B. 1954. Intellectual function of the Temporal lobes. Psychological Bulletin 51(1): 42–62

Milton D.E. 2012. On The Ontological Status of Autism: The 'Double Empathy Problem'. Disability & Society 27(6): 883-887

Minshew N.J., and Williams D.L. 2007. The new neurobiology of autism: cortex, connectivity, and neuronal organization. Archives of Neurology 64(7): 945-50

Miyake A., Friedman N.P., Emerson M.J., Witzki A.H., Howerter A., and Wager T.D. 2000. The unity and diversity of executive functions and their contributions to complex "Frontal Lobe" tasks: a latent variable analysis. Cognitive Psychology 41(1): 49-100

Moerkerke M., Peeters M., de Vries L., Daniels N., Steyaert J., Alaerts K., and Boets B. 2021. Endogenous Oxytocin Levels in Autism-A Meta-Analysis. Brain Science 11(11):1545

Mohr S., Brandt P.Y., Borras L., Gilliéron C., and Huguelet P. 2006. Toward an Integration of Spirituality and Religiousness into The Psychosocial Dimension of Schizophrenia. American Journal of Psychiatry 163(11): 1952-1959

Moseley R.L., Druce T., and Turner-Cobb J.M., 2020. 'When my Autism Broke': A Qualitative Study Spotlighting Autistic Voices on Menopause. Autism 24(6): 1423-1437

Moseley, R.L., Gregory, N.J., Smith, P., Allison, C., Cassidy, S. and Baron-Cohen, S., 2022. Non-Suicidal Self-Injury and its Relation to Suicide Through Acquired Capability: Investigating this

Causal Mechanism in a Mainly Late-Diagnosed Autistic Sample. Molecular Autism 13(1): 45

Moses L.J., and Tahiroglu D. 2010. Clarifying the Relation Between Executive Function and Children's Theory of Mind. In: Self and Social Regulation: Social Interactions and The Development of Social Understanding and Executive Functions. Eds: Sokol B., Muller, U., Carpendale, J., Young A., and Iarocci G. Oxford University Press

Muller. H. F. 2007. Brain in Mind: The Mind–Brain Relation with the Mind at the Center. Constructive Foundations 3(1): 30-37

Murray M. and Moore L. 2009. Costly Signaling and The Origin of Religion. Journal of Cognition and Culture 9(3-4): 225-245

Muth A., Hönekopp J., Falter-Wagner C. 2014. Visuo-Spatial Performance in Autism: A Meta-analysis. Journal of Autism and Developmental Disorder 44(12): 3245-3263

Myles B.S. 2003. Behavioral forms of stress management for individuals with Asperger syndrome. Child and Adolescent Psychiatric Clinics 12(1): 123-141

Myles B.S. and Southwick J. 2005. Asperger syndrome and difficult moments: Practical solutions for tantrums, rage, and meltdowns. AAPC Publishing

Nair A., Jolliffe M., Lograsso Y. S., Bearden C. E. 2020. A Review of Default Mode Network Connectivity and its Association with Social Cognition in Adolescents with Autism Spectrum Disorder and Early-Onset Psychosis. Frontiers In Psychiatry 11: 548922

Nanchen K., Brodfuehrer A., Heinrichs M., Philipsen A., van Elst L.T., and Matthies S. 2016. Autistic Traits in Patients with Borderline Personality Disorder. Zeitschrift Fur Psychiatrie, Psychologie Und Psychotherapie 64(4): 247-255

Napo F., Heinz A., and Auckenthaler A. 2012. Explanatory Models and Concepts of West African Malian Patients with Psychotic Symptoms. European Psychiatry 27(S2): 44-49

Napolitano L.A., and McKay D. 2007. Dichotomous Thinking in Borderline Personality Disorder. Cognitive Therapy and Research 31: 717-726

Nettle D. 2012. Social Scale and Structural Complexity in Human Languages. Philosophical Transactions of the Royal Society of London B Biological Sciences 367(1597):1829-1836

Nettle D., and Bateson M. 2012. The Evolutionary Origins of Mood and its Disorders. Current Biology 22(17): R712-R721

Nettle, D. 2006. The evolution of personality variation in humans and other animals. American Psychologist 61(6): 622–631

Nettle, D. 2007. Personality: What makes you the way you are. Oxford University Press

New M.I. 1998. Diagnosis and management of congenital adrenal hyperplasia. Annual Review of Medicine 49(1): 311-328

Newton-Fisher N.E. 2007. Chimpanzee Hunting Behavior. Academia.edu. https://www.academia.edu/574109/Chimpanzee_Hunting_Behavior

Nguyen L., and Frye D. 1999. Children's Theory of Mind: Understanding of Desire, Belief and Emotion with Social Referents. Social Development 8(1): 70-92

Niego A., and Benítez-Burraco A. 2021. Autism and Williams Syndrome: Dissimilar Socio-Cognitive Profiles with Similar Patterns of Abnormal Gene Expression in the Blood. Autism 25(2): 464-489

Niego, A. and Benítez-Burraco, A., 2019. Williams syndrome, human self-domestication, and language evolution. Frontiers in Psychology 10: 420868.

Nielsen J.A., Zielinski B.A., Fletcher P.T., Alexander A.L., Lange N., Bigler E.D., Lainhart J.E. and Anderson J.S., 2014. Abnormal lateralization of functional connectivity between language and default mode regions in autism. Molecular Autism 5(1): 1-11

Nordenström A., Servin A., Bohlin G., Larsson A., and Wedell A., 2002. Sex-typed toy play behavior correlates with the degree of prenatal androgen exposure assessed by CYP21 genotype in girls with congenital adrenal hyperplasia. The Journal of Clinical Endocrinology and Metabolism 87(11): 5119-5124

Nordsletten A.E., Larsson H., Crowley J.J., Almqvist C., Lichtenstein P., and Mataix-Cols D. 2016. Patterns of Nonrandom Mating within and Across 11 Major Psychiatric Disorders. JAMA Psychiatry 73(4): 354-361

Norenzayan A. 2013. Big gods: How religion transformed cooperation and conflict. Princeton University Press

Norenzayan A. 2016. Theodiversity. Annual Review of Psychology 67: 465-488

Norenzayan A. and Gervais W.M. 2013. The Origins of Religious Disbelief. Trends in Cognitive Sciences 17(1): 20-25

Norenzayan A., Gervais W.M., and Trzesniewski K.H. 2012. Mentalizing Deficits Constrain Belief in a Personal God. PLoS ONE 7(5)

Norenzayan A., Shariff A.F. 2008. The origin and evolution of Religious Prosociality. Science 322(5898): 58-62

Norenzayan A., Shariff A.F., Gervais W.M., Willard A.K., McNamara R.A., Slingerland E., and Henrich, J. 2016. The cultural evolution of prosocial religions. Behavioral and Brain Sciences 39: e1.

Norenzayan, A. 2014. Does Religion make People Moral? Behaviour 151(2-3): 365-384

Norris P. and Inglehart R. 2004. Public Opinion Among Muslims and the West. In Framing Terrorism. Routledge: 203-228

Norris P. and Inglehart R., 2011. Sacred and Secular: Religion and Politics Worldwide. Cambridge University Press

Northoff G., Heinzel A., De Greck M., Bermpohl F., Dobrowolny H., and Panksepp J., 2006. Self-Referential Processing in Our Brain— A Meta-Analysis of Imaging Studies on the Self. Neuroimage 31(1): 440-457

O'Boyle M.W., Cunnington R., Silk T.J., Vaughan D., Jackson G., Syngeniotis A. and Egan G.F. 2005. Mathematically gifted male adolescents activate a unique brain network during mental rotation. Cognitive Brain Research 25(2): 583-587

O'Neill D.K., and Chong S. 2001. Preschool Children's Difficulty Understanding the Types of Information Obtained Through the Five Senses. Child Development 72(3): 803-815

Ochs E., Kremer-Sadlik T., Sirota K.G. and Solomon O. 2004. Autism and the social world: An anthropological perspective. Discourse Studies 6(2): 147-183

Ogden, T. H. 1997. Reverie and interpretation: Sensing something human. Jason Aronson.

Okanoya K. 2017. Sexual Communication and Domestication May Give Rise to The Signal Complexity Necessary for the Emergence of Language: An Indication From Songbird Studies. Psychonomic. Bulletin Review 24: 106–110

Oliver M. 1983. Social Work with Disabled People. British Association of Social Workers. Macmillan

Oliver M. 2013. The Social Model of Disability: Thirty Years On. Disability & Society 28(7): 1024-1026

Onishi K. H., and Baillargeon R. 2005. Do 15-month-old infants understand false beliefs? Science 308(5719): 255–258

Oumaya M., Friedman S., Pham A., Abou Abdallah T., Guelfi J.D. and Rouillon F. 2008. Borderline Personality Disorder, Self-mutilation and Suicide: Literature Review. L'encephale 34(5): 452-458

Ozonoff S., and Miller J. N. 1995. Teaching Theory of Mind: A new approach to social skills training for individuals with autism. Journal of Autism and Developmental Disorders 25(4): 415–433

Ozonoff S., Strayer D.L., McMahon W.M., and Filloux F. 1994. Executive function abilities in autism and Tourette syndrome: an information processing approach. Journal of Child Psychology and Psychiatry 35(6): 1015-1032

Ozonoff, S., Pennington B. F., and Rogers S. J. 1991. Executive function deficits in high-functioning autistic individuals: relationship to Theory of Mind. Journal of Child Psychology and Psychiatry 32(7): 1081-1105

Park H.J., and Friston K. 2013. Structural and functional brain networks: from connections to cognition. Science 342(6158): 123841

Park H.R., Lee J.M., Moon H.E., Lee D.S., Kim B.N., Kim J., Kim D.G., and Paek S.H. 2016. A Short Review on the Current Understanding of Autism Spectrum Disorders. Experimental Neurobiology 25(1): 1

Pasterski V.L., Geffner M.E., Brain C., Hindmarsh P., Brook C., and Hines M. 2005. Prenatal hormones and postnatal socialization by parents as determinants of male-typical toy play in girls with congenital adrenal hyperplasia. Child development 76(1): 264-278

Pennycook G., Cheyne J.A., Seli P., Koehler D.J., and Fugelsang J.A. 2012. Analytic cognitive style predicts religious and paranormal belief. Cognition 123(3): 335-346

Persinger M.A. 1983. Religious and Mystical Experiences as Artifacts of Temporal Lobe Function: A General Hypothesis. Perceptual and Motor Skills 57(3_suppl): 1255-1262

Persinger M.A. 1983. Religious and Mystical Experiences as Artifacts of Temporal Lobe Function: A General Hypothesis. Perceptual and Motor Skills 57(3): 1255-1262

Persinger M.A. 2001. The Neuropsychiatry of Paranormal Experiences. The Journal of Neuropsychiatry and Clinical Neurosciences 13(4): 515-524

Persinger M.A., and Makarec K. 1987. Temporal Lobe Epileptic Signs and Correlative Behaviors Displayed by Normal Populations. The Journal of General Psychology 114(2): 179-195

Petersen R.C., Smith G.E., Waring S.C., Ivnik R.J., Tangalos E.G., and Kokmen E. 1999 Mild cognitive impairment: clinical characterization and outcome. Archives of Neurology 56(3): 303-308

Petersen S.E., Fox P.T., Posner M.I., Mintun M., and Raichle M.E. 1989. Positron emission tomographic studies of the processing of singe words. Journal of Cognitive Neuroscience 1(2): 153-170.

Piaget, J. (1954). The construction of reality in the child. Basic Books.

Piazza J., Bering J.M. and Ingram G. 2011. "Princess Alice is Watching You": Children's Belief in an Invisible Person Inhibits Cheating. Journal of Experimental Child Psychology 109(3): 311-320

Pichon I., Boccato G., and Saroglou V. 2007. Nonconscious Influences of Religion on Prosociality: A Priming Study. European Journal of Social Psychology 37(5): 1032-1045

Plyusnina I.Z., Oskina I.N., and Trut L.N. 1991. An Analysis of Fear and Aggression During Early Development of Behaviour in

Silver Foxes (Vulpes vulpes). Applied Animal Behaviour Science 32(2-3): 253-268

Polimanti R., and Gelernter J., 2017. Widespread Signatures of Positive Selection in Common Risk Alleles Associated to Autism Spectrum Disorder. PLoS Genetics 13(2): e1006618

Pollard C.A., Barry C.M., Freedman B.H., and Kotchick B.A. 2013. Relationship Quality as a Moderator of Anxiety in Siblings of Children Diagnosed with Autism Spectrum Disorders or Down Syndrome. Journal of Child and Family Studies 22: 647-657

Ponce de León M.S., Golovanova L., Doronichev V., Romanova G., Akazawa T., Kondo O., Ishida H. and Zollikofer C.P. 2008. Neanderthal Brain Size at Birth Provides Insights into the Evolution of Human Life History. Proceedings of the National Academy of Sciences 105(37): 13764-13768

Povinelli D.J., and Bering J.M. 2002. The mentality of apes revisited. Current Directions in Psychological Science 11(4): 115-119

Powell A. 2009. Divination, Royalty, and Insecurity in Classical Sparta. Kernos. Revue Internationale et Pluridisciplinaire de Religion Grecque Antique (22): 35-82

Prabhakar S., Noonan J.P., Paabo S., and Rubin E.M. 2006. Accelerated Evolution of Conserved Noncoding Sequences in Humans. Science 314(5800): 786-786

Prado-Martinez J., Sudmant P.H., Kidd J.M., Li H., Kelley J.L., Lorente-Galdos B., Veeramah K.R., Woerner A.E., O'Connor T.D., Santpere G. and Cagan A., 2013. Great Ape Genetic Diversity and Population History. Nature 499(7459): 471-475

Priewasser B., Roessler J., and Perner J. 2013. Competition as rational action: Why young children cannot appreciate competitive games. Journal of Experimental Child Psychology 116(2): 545–559

Prince-Hughes D. ed. 2002. Aquamarine Blue 5: Personal Stories of College Students with Autism. Ohio University Press

Prior M.R., and Bradshaw J.L. 1979. Hemisphere functioning in autistic children Cortex 15(1): 73-81

Progovac L., and Benítez-Burraco A. 2019. From Physical Aggression to Verbal Behavior: Language Evolution and Self-Domestication Feedback Loop. Frontiers in Psychology 10: 471683

Proust- Lima C., Amieva H., Letenneur L., Orgogozo J., Jacqmin-Gadda H., and Dartigues J. 2008. Gender and education impact on brain aging: A general cognitive factor approach. HAL Open Science

Prüfer K., Munch K., Hellmann I., Akagi K., Miller J.R., Walenz B., Koren S., Sutton G., Kodira C., Winer R., and Knight, J.R. 2012. The Bonobo Genome Compared with The Chimpanzee and Human Genomes. Nature 486(7404): 527-531

Prüfer K., Racimo F., Patterson N., Jay, F., Sankararaman S., Sawyer S., Heinze A., Renaud G., Sudmant P.H., De Filippo C., and Li H. 2014. The Complete Genome Sequence of a Neanderthal from the Altai Mountains. Nature 505(7481): 43-49

Quintero-Rivera F., Sharifi-Hannauer P., and Martinez-Agosto J.A. 2010. Autistic And Psychiatric Findings Associated with the 3q29 Microdeletion Syndrome: Case Report and Review. American Journal of Medical Genetics Part A 152(10): 2459-2467

Quran. Sura 96. Oxford World's Classics edition

Ra A. 2016. The Foundational Falsehoods of Creationism. Publisher. Pitchstone Publishing

Randolph-Seng B., and Nielsen M.E., 2007. Honesty: one Effect of Primed Religious Representations. The International Journal for The Psychology of Religion 17(4): 303-315

Rappaport R.A. 1999. Ritual and Religion in the Making of Humanity (Vol. 110). Cambridge University Press.

Reich D., Green R.E., Kircher M., Krause J., Patterson N., Durand E.Y., Viola B., Briggs A.W., Stenzel U., Johnson P.L., and Maricic T. 2010. Genetic History of an Archaic Hominin Group from Denisova Cave in Siberia. Nature 468(7327): 1053-1060

Richards G., Baron-Cohen S., Stokes H., Warrier V., Mellor B., Winspear E., Davies J., Gee L., and Galvin J. 2020. Assortative Mating, Autistic Traits, Empathizing, and Systemizing. BioRxiv: 2020-10

Richards G., Kelly S., Johnson D., and Galvin J. 2023. Autistic Traits and Borderline Personality Disorder Traits are Positively Correlated in UK and US Adult Men and Women. Personality and Individual Differences 213: 112287

Richards G., Kelly S., Johnson D., and Galvin J., 2023. Autistic Traits and Borderline Personality Disorder Traits are Positively Correlated in UK and US Adult Men and Women. Personality and Individual Differences 213: 112287

Riekki T., and Lindeman M., and Raij T. 2014. Supernatural believers attribute more intentions to random movement than skeptics: An fMRI study. Social Neuroscience 9: 400-411

Rinehart N.J., Bradshaw J.L., Brereton A.V. and Tonge B.J., 2002. Lateralization in individuals with high-functioning autism and Asperger's disorder: a frontostriatal model. Journal of Autism and Developmental Disorders 32: 321-332

Ritskes R., Ritskes-Hoitinga A., Stødkilde-Jørgensen A., Bærentsen K.B. and Hartmann T. 2004. MRI Scanning During Zen Meditation: The Picture of Enlightenment. The Relevance of

The Wisdom Traditions in Contemporary Society: the Challenge to Psychology 195: 85-89

Rizzolatti G., Fogassi L., and Gallese V. 2001. Neurophysiological mechanisms underlying the understanding and imitation of action. Nature Review Neuroscience 2(9): 661-670

Roelfsema M.T., Hoekstra R.A., Allison C., Wheelwright S., Brayne C., Matthews F.E., and Baron-Cohen S., 2012. Are Autism Spectrum Conditions More Prevalent in an Information-Technology Region? A School-Based Study of Three Regions in The Netherlands. Journal of Autism and Developmental Disorders 42: 734-739

Rogers L. 1995. Evolution and Development of Brain Asymmetry, and its Relevance to Language, Tool, and Consciousness. International Journal of Comparative Psychology 8(1): 1-16

Rogers L.J., and Bolden S.W. 1991. Light-dependent development and asymmetry of visual projections. Neuroscience Letters 121(1-2): 63-67

Rogers S. J., and Pennington B. F. 1991. A theoretical approach to the deficits in infantile autism. Development and Psychopathology 3(2): 137-162

Rosenkranz P., and Charlton B.G. 2013. Individual differences in existential orientation: Empathizing and systemizing explain the sex difference in religious orientation and science acceptance. Archive for the Psychology of Religion 35(1): 119-146

Rossler J. and Perner J. 2013. Teleology: Belief as Perspective. In: Baron-Cohen S., Lombardo M., and Tager-Flusberg H (Eds.). Understanding Other Minds: Perspectives from developmental social neuroscience.

Ruby P., and Decety J. 2004. How would you feel versus how do you think she would feel? A neuroimaging study of perspective-taking with social emotions. Journal of Cognitive Neuroscience 16(6): 988-99

Ruby P., and Decety J. 2004. How would you feel versus how do you think she would feel? A neuroimaging study of perspective-taking with social emotions. Journal of Cognitive Neuroscience 16(6): 988-999

Rudie J.D., Brown J.A., Beck-Pancer D., Hernandez L.M., Dennis E.L., Thompson P.M., Bookheimer S.Y., and Dapretto M. 2013. Altered functional and structural brain network organization in autism. Neuroimage Clinical 2: 79-94

Ruffman T., Garnham W., Import A., and Connolly D. 2001. Does Eye Gaze Indicate Implicit Knowledge of False Belief? Charting Transitions in Knowledge. Journal of Experimental Child Psychology 80(3): 201-224

Russell, D. W. 1996. UCLA Loneliness Scale (Version 3): Reliability, validity, and factor structure. Journal of Personality Assessment 66(1): 20–40

Sabbagh M.A., Xu F., Carlson S.M., Moses L.J., and Lee K. 2006. The development of executive functioning and Theory of Mind. A comparison of Chinese and U.S. preschoolers. Psychological Science 17(1): 74-81.

Sakai K., Rowe J.B., and Passingham R.E. 2002. Active maintenance in prefrontal area 46 creates distractor-resistant memory. Nature Neuroscience 5: 479–484

Saler B. 1987. Religion and the Definition of Religion. Cultural Anthropology 2(3): 395-399

Samson A.C., Phillips J.M., Parker K.J., Shah S., Gross J.J., and Hardan A.Y. 2014. Emotion Dysregulation and the Core Features of Autism Spectrum Disorder. Journal of Autism and Developmental Disorders 44: 1766-1772

Saravanan B., Jacob K.S., Johnson S., Prince M., Bhugra D., and David A.S. 2007. Belief Models in First Episode Schizophrenia in South India. Social Psychiatry and Psychiatric Epidemiology 42: 446-451

Saxe R., and Kanwisher N. 2003. People thinking about thinking people. The role of the temporo-Parietal junction in "Theory of Mind". Neuroimage 19(4): 1835-1842

Saxe R., and Wexler A. 2005. Making sense of another mind: the role of the right temporo-Parietal junction. Neuropsychologia 43(10): 1391-1399

Scandurra V. 2012. Developmental dispraxia correlated with autism spectrum disorders core symptoms. Neuropsychiatrie de l'enfance et de l'adolescence 5(60): 203

Schatz H.B. 2022. The God Table: A New Origins Theory of Religion and Civilization. Archaeological Discovery 10(4): 215-261

Schiele M.A., and Domschke K. 2018. Epigenetics at the Crossroads Between Genes, Environment and Resilience in Anxiety Disorders. Genes, Brain, and Behavior 17(3): e12423

Schjoedt U. 2009. The Religious Brain: A General Introduction to the Experimental Neuroscience of Religion. Method and Theory in the Study of Religion 21(3): 310-339

Schmahmann J.D., Weilburg J.B., and Sherman J.C. 2007. The neuropsychiatry of the cerebellum - insights from the clinic. Cerebellum 6(3): 254-267

Schmidt K. 2010. Göbekli Tepe–the Stone Age Sanctuaries. New Results of Ongoing Excavations with a Special Focus on Sculptures and High Reliefs. Documenta Praehistorica 37: 239-256

Scoville W. B., and Milner, B. 1957. Loss of recent memory after bilateral hippocampal lesions. Journal of Neurology, Neurosurgery and Psychiatry 20: 11–21

Senju. A., Southgate V., White S., and Frith U. 2009 Mindblind Eyes: An Absence of Spontaneous Theory of Mind in Asperger Syndrome. Science 325 (5942): 883-885

Shadmehr R., and Holcomb H.H. 1997. Neural correlates of motor memory consolidation. Science 277(5327): 821-825

Shah A., and Frith U., 1993. Why do autistic individuals show superior performance on the block design task? Journal of Child Psychology and Psychiatry 34(8): 1351-1364

Shah R., Kulhara P., Grover S., Kumar S., Malhotra R., and Tyagi S. 2011. Contribution of Spirituality to Quality of Life in Patients with Residual Schizophrenia. Psychiatry Research 190(2-3): 200-205

Shariff A. F., and Norenzayan A. 2007. God is Watching You: Priming God Concepts Increases Prosocial Behavior in an Anonymous Economic Game. Psychological Science 18(9): 803–809

Shenhav A., Rand D., and Greene J. 2011. Divine Intuition: Cognitive Style Influences Belief in God. Journal of Experimental Psychology 141: 423-428

Shepard R., and Cooper L. 1982. Mental Images and Their Transformations. The MIT Press

Shilton D., Breski M., Dor D., and Jablonka E. 2020. Human Social Evolution: Self-Domestication or Self-Control? Frontiers of Psychology 14(11): 134

Siddle R., Haddock G., Tarrier N., and Faragher E.B. 2002. Religious Delusions in Patients Admitted to Hospital with Schizophrenia. Social Psychiatry and Psychiatric Epidemiology 37: 130-138

Silberman S. 2015. NeuroTribes: The Legacy of Autism and the Future of Neurodiversity . Avery: Penguin Books RandomHouse

Simons J.S., Spiers H.J. 2003. Prefrontal and medial Temporal lobe interactions in long-term memory. Nature Review Neuroscience 4(8): 637-648

Singer T., Seymour B., O'doherty J., Kaube H., Dolan R.J., and Frith C.D. 2004. Empathy for Pain Involves The Affective but not Sensory Components of Pain. Science 303(5661): 1157-1162

Slyke Van, J.A. and Szocik, K., 2020. Sexual selection and religion: Can the evolution of religion be explained in terms of mating strategies? *Archive for the Psychology of Religion 42(1)*: 123-141.

Smith B.P., Lucas T.A., Norris R.M., and Henneberg M. 2018. Brain Size/Body Weight in The Dingo (Canis Dingo): Comparisons with Domestic and Wild Canids. *Australian Journal of Zoology 65(5)*: 292-301

Smith C. 1955. Religious Education: Conveying the Truth of the Bible. The Expository Times 67(3): 67-69

Smith S.S., Waterhouse B.D., and Woodward D.J. 1987b. Locally applied progesterone metabolites alter neuronal responsiveness in the cerebellum. Brain Research Bulletin 18(6): 739-747

Smith S.S., Waterhouse B.D., Chapin J.K., and Woodward D.J. 1987a. Progesterone alters GABA and glutamate responsiveness: a possible mechanism for its anxiolytic action. Brain Research 400(2): 353-359

Solomon M., Ozonoff S.J., Ursu S., Ravizza S., Cummings N., Stanford L., and Carter C. 2009. The neural substrates of cognitive control deficits in autism spectrum disorders. Neuropsychologia 47(12): 2515-2526

Sosis R. 2004. The Adaptive Value of Religious Ritual: Rituals Promote Group Cohesion by Requiring Members to Engage in

Behavior That is too Costly to Fake. American Scientist 92(2): 166-172

Sosis R., and Alcorta C. 2003. Signaling, Solidarity, and the Sacred: The Evolution of Religious Behavior. Evolutionary Anthropology: Issues, News, and Reviews: Issues, News, and Reviews 12(6): 264-274

Sosis R., Kress H.C., and Boster J.S. 2007. Scars for War: Evaluating Alternative Signaling Explanations for Cross-Cultural Variance in Ritual Costs. Evolution and Human Behavior 28(4): 234-247.

Sosis R.H. 1997. The Collective Action Problem of Male Cooperative Labor on Ifaluk Atoll. The University of New Mexico

Sosis R.H. 2000. Religion and Intragroup Cooperation: Preliminary Results of a Comparative Analysis of Utopian Communities. Cross-cultural Research 34(1): 70-87

Southgate V., Senju A., and Csibra G. 2007. Action anticipation through attribution of false belief by 2-year-olds. Psychological Sciences 18(7): 587-92

Sperry R., Gazzaniga M., Bogen J. 1969. "Interhemispheric relationships: the neocortical commissures; syndromes of hemisphere disconnection" in Handbook of clinical neurology. eds. Vinken P. J., Bruyn G. W. North Holland: 273–290

Spikins P. 2009. Autism, The Integrations of 'Difference' and The Origins of Modern Human Behaviour. Cambridge Archaeological Journal 19(2): 179-201

Spratt E.G., Nicholas J.S., Brady K.T., Carpenter L.A., Hatcher C.R., Meekins K.A., Furlanetto R.W., and Charles J.M., 2012. Enhanced Cortisol Response to Stress in Children in Autism. Journal of Autism and Developmental Disorders 42: 75-81

Sroufe L. A., Carlson E. A., Levy A. K., and Egeland, B. 1999. Implications of attachment theory for developmental psychopathology. Development and Psychopathology 11(1): 1–13

Staddon. J. 2017. Scientific Method: How Science Works, Fails to Work, and Pretends to Work 1st Ed. Rutledge. New York

Staes N., Smaers J.B., Kunkle A.E., Hopkins W.D., Bradley B.J., and Sherwood C.C. 2019. Evolutionary Divergence of Neuroanatomical Organization and Related Genes in Chimpanzees and Bonobos. Cortex 118: 154-164

Stanford C.B. 1998. The Social Behavior of Chimpanzees and Bonobos: Empirical Evidence and Shifting Assumptions. Current Anthropology 39(4): 399-420

Stark R. 2002. Physiology and faith: Addressing the "universal" gender difference in religious commitment. Journal for the Scientific Study of Religion 41(3): 495-507

Statistics Canada. 2012. Canadian Survey on Disability, 2012: Developmental disabilities among Canadians aged 15 years and older. Statistics Canada: https://www150.statcan.gc.ca/n1/pub/89-654-x/89-654-x2015003-eng.htm

Steel J.G., Gorman R., and Flexman J. E. 1984. Neuropsychiatric testing in an autistic mathematical idiot-savant: evidence for nonverbal abstract capacity. Journal of the American Academy of Child Psychiatry 23: 704-707

Sterling L., Dawson G., Estes A., and Greenson, J. 2008. Characteristics Associated with Presence of Depressive Symptoms in Adults with Autism Spectrum Disorder. Journal of Autism and Developmental Disorders 38: 1011-1018

Stojanovik V., Perkins M., and Howard S. 2001. Language and conversational abilities in Williams syndrome: How good is good? International Journal of Language and Communication Disorders: 36(S1): 234-239

Stojanovik V., Perkins M., and Howard S. 2006. Linguistic heterogeneity in Williams syndrome. Clinical Linguistics & Phonetics 20(7-8): 547-552

Stompe T., Ritter K., Ortwein-Swoboda G., Schmid-Siegel B., Zitterl W., Strobl R., and Schanda, H. 2003. Anxiety and Hostility in the Manifest Dreams of Schizophrenic Patients. The Journal of Nervous and Mental Disease 191(12): 806-812

Striedter G.F., and Northcutt R. G. 2019. Brains Through Time: A Natural History of Vertebrates. Oxford University Press

Suchan J. and Karnath, H.O. 2011. Spatial orienting by left hemisphere language areas: a relict from the past? Brain 134(10): 3059-3070

Suzuki N. and Hirai M. 2023. Autistic Traits Associated with Dichotomic Thinking Mediated by Intolerance of Uncertainty. Scientific Reports 13(1): 14049

Swain D., Scarpa A., White S. and Laugeson E. 2015. Emotion Dysregulation and Anxiety in Adults with ASD: Does Social Motivation Play a Role? Journal of Autism and Developmental Disorders 45: 3971-3977

Swettenham J., Baron-Cohen S., Charman T., Cox A., Baird G., Drew A., Rees L., and Wheelwright S. 1998. The frequency and distribution of spontaneous attention shifts between social and nonsocial stimuli in autistic, typically developing, and nonautistic developmentally delayed infants. Journal of Child Psychology and Psychiatry 39(5): 747-753

Tager-Flusberg H. and Sullivan K. 2000. A componential view of Theory of Mind: evidence from Williams syndrome. Cognition 76(1): 59-90

Tamminga C.A., van Os J. M.D., and Ivleva E. M.D. (eds). 2020. Psychotic Disorders: Comprehensive Conceptualization And Treatments. Oxford University Press

Tepper L., Rogers S.A., Coleman E.M., and Malony H.N. 2001. The Prevalence of Religious Coping among Persons with Persistent Mental Illness. Psychiatric Services 52(5): 660-665

Theofanopoulou C., Gastaldon S., O'Rourke T., Samuels B.D., Messner A., Martins P.T., Delogu F., Alamri S., and Boeckx C. 2017. Self-Domestication in Homo Sapiens: Insights from Comparative Genomics. PloS One 12(10): e0185306

Thomas J., and Kirby S. 2018. Self Domestication and the Evolution of Language. Biology and Philosophy 33: 1-30

Thomson J.A., Aukofer C., and Dawkins R. 2011. Why We Believe in God(s): A Concise Guide to the Science of Faith. Pitchstone Publishing

Tomasi D., Volkow N. 2012. Laterality Patterns of Brain Functional Connectivity: Gender Effects. Cerebral Cortex 22(6): 1455–1462

Toth K., Dawson G., Meltzoff A.N., Greenson J., and Fein D., 2007. Early Social, Imitation, Play, And Language Abilities of Young Non-Autistic Siblings of Children with Autism. Journal of Autism and Developmental Disorders 37: 145-157

Travers R.M.W. 1941. A Study in Judging the Opinions of Groups. Archives of Psychology 266. Woodworth RS (Eds). Columbia University, New York, NY.: 1–73

Trut L. N. 1999. Early Canid Domestication: The Farm-Fox Experiment: Foxes bred for Tamability in A 40-Year Experiment Exhibit Remarkable Transformations that Suggest an Interplay Between Behavioral Genetics and Development. American Scientist 87(2): 160-169

Trut L., Oskina I., and Kharlamova A. 2009. Animal Evolution During Domestication: The Domesticated Fox as A Model. Bioessays 31(3): 349-360

Trut L.N., Kharlamova A.V., Kukekova A.V., Acland G.M., Carrier D.R. Chase K., and Lark, K.G. 2006. Morphology and Behavior: are they Coupled at The Genome Level? Cold Spring Harbor Monograph Series 44: 81

Trut L.N., Markel A.L., Borodin P.M., Argutinskaya S.V., and Zakharov I.K. 2007. To the 90th anniversary of Academician Dmitry Konstantinovich Belyaev (1917–1985). Russian Journal of Genetics 43: 717–720

Unal S., Kaya B., and Yalvaç H.D. 2007. Patients' Explanation Models for Their Illness and Help-Seeking Behavior. Turkish Journal of Psychiatry 18(1): 38-47

Underwood L., McCarthy J.B., and Tsakanikos E. 2010. Mental Health of Adults with Autism Spectrum Disorders and Intellectual Disability. Current Opinion in Psychiatry 23(5): 421-426

Usman H., Tjiptoherijanto P., Balqiah T.E., and Agung I.G.N. 2017. The role of religious norms, trust, importance of attributes and information sources in the relationship between religiosity and selection of the Islamic bank. Journal of Islamic Marketing 8(2): 158-186

Vallortigara G., and Rogers L.J. 2005. Survival With an Asymmetrical Brain: Advantages and Disadvantages of Cerebral Lateralization. Behavioral And Brain Sciences 28: 575-589

Vallortigara G., Regolin L., and Pagni P. 1999. Detour behaviour, imprinting and visual lateralization in the domestic chick. Cognitive Brain Research 7(3): 307-320

Van Goozen S.H., Matthys W., Cohen-Kettenis P.T., Buitelaar J.K., and Van Engeland H., 2000. Hypothalamic-Pituitary-Adrenal Axis and Autonomic Nervous System Activity in Disruptive

Children and Matched Controls. Journal of the American Academy of Child and Adolescent Psychiatry 39(11): 1438-1445

Van Heijst B.F., Deserno M.K., Rhebergen D., and Geurts H.M. 2020. Autism and Depression are Connected: A Report of Two Complimentary Network Studies. Autism 24(3): 680-692

van Zomeren, A. H., and Brouwer, W. H. 1994. Clinical neuropsychology of attention. Oxford University Press

Von Hippel W., and Trivers, R. 2011. The Evolution and Psychology of Self-Deception. Behavioral and Brain Sciences 34(1): 1-16

Wager T.D., Rilling J.K., Smith E.E., Sokolik A., Casey K.L., Davidson R.J., Kosslyn S.M., Rose R.M., and Cohen J.D. 2004. Placebo-Induced Changes in FMRI in the Anticipation and Experience of Pain. Science 303(5661): 1162-1167

Wang L., Li J., Shuang M., Lu T., Wang Z., Zhang T., Yue W., Jia M., Ruan Y., Liu J., and Wu Z. 2018. Association Study and Mutation Sequencing of Genes on Chromosome 15q11-Q13 Identified GABRG3 as a Susceptibility Gene for Autism in Chinese Han Population. Translational Psychiatry 8(1): 152.

Waxman S.G., and Geschwind N. 1975. The Interictal Behavior Syndrome of Temporal Lobe Epilepsy. Archives of General Psychiatry 32(12): 1580-1586

Weingard R. 1977. Space, Time and Spacetime.

Welsh M., Pennington B. F., and Groisser D.B. 1991. A normative-developmental study of executive function: A window on prefrontal function in children. Development Neuropsychology 7(2): 131-149

Wheelwright S., Baron-Cohen S., Goldenfeld N., Delaney J., Fine D., Smith R., Weil L., and Wakabayashi A. 2006. Predicting Autism Spectrum Quotient (AQ) from the Systemizing

Quotient-Revised (SQ-R) and Empathy Quotient (EQ). Brain Research: 1079(1): 47-56

White S.W., Smith I., and Brewe A.M. 2021. Brief Report: The Influence of Autism Severity and Depression on Self-Determination Among Young Adults with Autism Spectrum Disorder. Journal of Autism and Developmental Disorders 52(6): 2825-2830

White S.W., Smith I., and Brewe A.M. 2022. Brief Report: The Influence of Autism Severity and Depression on Self-Determination Among Young Adults with Autism Spectrum Disorder. Journal of Autism and Developmental Disorders 52(6): 2825-2830

White S.W., Smith I., Miyazaki Y., Conner C., Elias R., and Capriola-Hall N. 2019. Improving Transition to Adulthood for Students with Autism: A Randomized Controlled Trial Of STEPS. Journal of Clinical Child and Adolescent Psychology 50(2): 187–201

White. S. 1970. Some General Outlines of the Matrix of Developmental Changes Between Five and Seven Years. Bulletin of the Orton Society 20: 41-57

Whiteley P., Todd L., Carr K., and Shattock P. 2010. Gender Ratios in Autism, Asperger Syndrome and Autism Spectrum Disorder. Autism Insights 2

Wilkins A.S., Wrangham R.W., and Fitch W.T. 2014. The "Domestication Syndrome" in Mammals: a Unified Explanation Based on Neural Crest Cell Behavior and Genetics. Genetics 197(3): 795-808.

Wilkins A.S., Wrangham R.W., and Fitch W.T. 2014. The "Domestication Syndrome" in Mammals: A Unified Explanation Based on Neural Crest Cell Behavior and Genetics. Genetics 197(3): 795–808

Willard A.K., and Norenzayan A. 2013. Cognitive biases explain religious belief, paranormal belief, and belief in life's purpose. Cognition 129(2): 379-391

Williams D., and Happé F. 2010. Representing Intentions in Self and Other: Studies of Autism and Typical Development. Developmental Science 13(2): 307-319

Wilson M.L., Boesch C., Fruth B., Furuichi T., Gilby I.C., Hashimoto C., Hobaiter C.L., Hohmann G., Itoh N., Koops, K., and Lloyd J.N. 2014. Lethal Aggression in Pan is Better Explained by Adaptive Strategies than Human Impacts. Nature 513(7518): 414-417

Wimmer H., and Perner J. 1983. Beliefs about beliefs: Representation and constraining function of wrong beliefs in young children's understanding of deception. Cognition 13(1)

Wing L. 1981. Language, Social, and Cognitive Impairments in Autism and Severe Mental Retardation. Journal of Autism and Developmental Disorders 11(1): 31-44

Witelson S., and Pallee W. 1973. Left Hemisphere Specialization for Language in The Newborn Neuroanatomical Evidence Of Asymmetry. Brain 96: 641-646

Wobber V. and Hare B., 2009. Testing the Social Dog Hypothesis: are Dogs also More Skilled Than Chimpanzees in Non-Communicative Social Tasks. Behavioural Processes 81(3): 423-428

Won Y.J., and Hey J. 2005. Divergence Population Genetics of Chimpanzees. Molecular Biology and Evolution 22(2): 297-307

Woods R. 2017. Exploring How the Social Model of Disability can be Re-Invigorated for Autism: In Response to Jonathan Levitt. Disability & Society 32(7): 1090-1095

Wrangham R.W. 1986. 16. Ecology and Social Relationships in two Species of Chimpanzee. Ecological Aspects of Social Evolution: 352-378

Wrangham R.W. 1993. The Evolution of Sexuality in Chimpanzees and Bonobos. Human Nature 4: 47-79

Wrangham R.W. 2019. Hypotheses for the Evolution of Reduced Reactive Aggression in the Context of Human Self-Domestication. Frontiers of Psychology 20(10): 1914

Xu G., Jing J., Bowers K., Liu B., and Bao W. 2014. Maternal Diabetes and The Risk of Autism Spectrum Disorders in The Offspring: A Systematic Review and Meta-Analysis. Journal of Autism and Developmental Disorders 44: 766-775

Yamakoshi G. 1998. Dietary Responses to Fruit Scarcity of Wild Chimpanzees at Bossou, Guinea: Possible Implications for Ecological Importance of Tool Use. American Journal of Physical Anthropology: The Official Publication of The American Association of Physical Anthropologists 106(3): 283-295

Yates L., and Hobson H. 2020. Continuing to Look in the Mirror: A Review of Neuroscientific Evidence for the Broken Mirror Hypothesis, EP-M Model and STORM Model of Autism Spectrum Conditions. Autism 24(8): 1945-1959

Yonelinas A., Kroll, N., Quamme J., Lazzara M., Sauve M., Widaman K., and Knight R. 2002. Effects of extensive Temporal lobe damage or mild hypoxia on recollection and familiarity. Nature Neuroscience 5: 1236–1241

Zacks J.M. 2008. Neuroimaging studies of mental rotation: a meta-analysis and review. Journal of Cognitive Neurosciences 20(1): 1-19

Zalla T., and Sperduti M. 2015. The Sense of Agency in Autism Spectrum Disorders: A Dissociation Between Prospective and Retrospective Mechanisms? Frontiers In Psychology 6: 140359

Ziaullah M. 1984. Islamic Concept of God. Kegan Paul International

Zuccala M., Modini M., and Abbott M.J. 2021. The Role of Death Fears and Attachment Processes in Social Anxiety: A Novel Hypothesis Explored. Australian Journal of Psychology 73(3): 381-391

About the Author

Diagnosed with Autism Spectrum Disorder at age 24, I grew up feeling like I did not fit into society. From a young age I have had a passion for science and how it works. I have also been curious regarding why people believe what they believe. Religion and creator concepts have always intrigued me. This book is my attempt to understand the world of religion and that aspect of the human mind.